Hitler's Great Panzer Heist

Hitler's Great Panzer Heist

Germany's Foreign Armor in Action
1939–45

Anthony Tucker-Jones

STACKPOLE BOOKS

Copyright © 2007 by Anthony Tucker-Jones

Published by
STACKPOLE BOOKS
5067 Ritter Road
Mechanicsburg, PA 17055
www.stackpolebooks.com

Printed in the United States of America

10 9 8 7 6 5 4 3 2 1

Library of Congress Cataloging-in-Publication Data

Tucker-Jones, Anthony.
  Hitler's great Panzer heist : Germany's foreign armor in action, 1939–45 / Anthony
Tucker-Jones.
    p. cm.
  Originally published: Barnsley, South Yorkshire : Pen & Sword Military, 2007.
  Includes bibliographical references and index.
  ISBN 978-0-8117-0363-5
  1. World War, 1939–1945—Tank warfare. 2. World War, 1939–1945—Germany.
3. World War, 1939–1945—Equipment and supplies. 4. World War, 1939–1945—
Confiscations and contributions—Germany. I. Title.
  D793.T73 2008
  940.54'1343—dc22
                              2008009130

Contents

Introduction and acknowledgements

Adolf Hitler's audacious panzer blitzkrieg across the length and breadth of Europe during 1939-41 has joined the lexicon of major military achievements. In the space of just over a year and a half the *Wehrmacht* defeated the armies of eight different countries before turning on the Soviet Union. Since the end of the Second World War a fascination has developed for Hitler's near legendary panzer forces, but what is not generally appreciated is that so many of his divisions were obliged to use vast quantities of often inferior captured equipment. In fact he supplemented his panzers through a combination of conquest and alliance with a conservative estimate of at least 22,300 foreign armoured fighting vehicles, and well over 70,000 motor vehicles.

Whilst Hitler's dismemberment of Czechoslovakia and his theft of its Skoda tanks and weapons factories is well documented, the Nazis' systematic recycling and manufacture of military equipment across the occupied territories, especially in France and Italy, is much less well known. Nor is it understood that French tanks, under the control of Vichy, resisted the Allies, inflicting in some instances considerable casualties, in a series of campaigns. This book is designed to examine not only how and why Hitler and his generals went about appropriating Europe's weapons stocks, but also what impact this had on his war effort and his ability to maintain control in the occupied territories. In some theatres of operation particularly at the start of the war the impact of 'Hitler's Great Panzer Heist' was to be quite profound, whilst in others it was to prove a positive hindrance.

No book is ever conceived in isolation so, in the first instance, I would like to offer my gratitude to Tim Newark, editor of *Military Illustrated* and Pat Ware, former editor of *Classic Military Vehicle*. In particular I must thank Tim for commissioning the original article that formed the framework of this book, similarly my appreciation to Pat for allowing me to draw on research conducted for his publication over the last five years. Preston and Tim Isaac of the excellent Cobatton Combat Collection provided hands-on insight into the problems faced in assimilating foreign equipment, and post-war Czech armoured vehicle production. Eastern Front expert Nik Cornish was similarly kind enough to offer his wisdom regarding Lend-Lease to the Soviet Union and access to his considerable photo library. David Fletcher of Bovington Tank Museum provided sterling assistance with the photographic research and advice.

Finally a word of caution with the figures and totals in this book; unit commanders and factory managers always tended to be optimistic with their returns, so numbers should be treated as representative of the trends rather than final.

Anthony Tucker-Jones

Barnstaple, Devon
2006

Chapter One

Guderian's Czech Connection

German General Heinz Guderian stepped from his staff car pulling his favourite leather trench coat tightly around his shoulders. Several German and Czech officers hurried toward him. The grinning Germans clicked smartly at the heel and saluted, the subdued Czechs, in startk contrast, had nothing to feel respectful about, as the Nazis had just occupied their country. Guderian was led to a large storage shed; when the doors were flung back a flicker of a smile spread across his face. Inside were rows and rows of tanks.

Guderian arrived in occupied Prague in mid–March 1939, setting off a chain of events that was to have far reaching consequences for Adolf Hitler's delusional aspirations for Europe. Two things were foremost in the General's mind - much needed tanks and armaments factories. After an inspection tour of German panzer units he had driven south-east across Czechoslovakia to the university city of Brno on the Svratka River to view Hitler's latest spoils. The Czech connection represented both the beginning and endgame of Hitler's great panzer heist, which enabled him wage a brutal war across Europe for six long years.

Hitler, Guderian, Walther Model, Walther Nehring, Erwin Rommel, Wilhelm Ritter von Thoma and his other emerging panzer leaders looking at the map of Europe in the late 1930s knew that the Czechoslovakian arms industry was one of the best on the continent; in fact at the time it was the second largest in the world. Hitler hated Czechoslovakia and viewed the country as an aberration that had been carved from the dismembered Austro-Hungarian Empire at the end of the First World War. Not only did he want to bring the thousands of Germans living within its borders back into the fold of the Reich, he wanted to smash the young nation.

Heinz Guderian was to prove a key player in the evaluation, seizure and assimilation of foreign armour into Germany's armed forces and was one of the founders of Germany's *Panzerwaffe* or tank arm. Guderian's military career began in the Goslar Jager Regiment with which he served during the First World War. In the 1920s Guderian served as a captain under Major Oswald Lutz with the 7th (Bavarian) Motor Transport Battalion, where he quickly gained a reputation as an expert in the employment of motorised units. The pair served together again in 1931 when Lutz, now a Major General and Inspector of Motor Transport Troops, appointed Lieutenant Colonel Guderian as his Chief of Staff. Guderian chose Major Walther Nehring, another tank advocate, as his assistant. Just two years later Adolf Hitler became Chancellor.

Under the terms of the 1919 Treaty of Versailles the German Army was officially forbidden to possess tanks, and had to train with dummy 'paper panzers'. Secretly it also tested equipment in the Soviet Union in order to circumvent the treaty. Guderian went to Sweden in 1929 as an observer and gained first hand experience with Swedish tanks, ironically based on a First World War vintage German design.

Hitler soon found a way round the ban and ordered the production of a dozen *Land-Schlepper* or 'agricultural tractor' for training purposes, which was, in reality, the Panzer I chassis without the turret. When Hitler saw the experimental Panzer Mk I being put through its paces at the Army Weapons Office's Kummersdorf training ground, he turned to Guderian and said: 'That's what I need! That's what I want to have!'[1] The 1st Tank Regiment came into existence and soon grew into the 1st, 2nd and 3rd Panzer Divisions, with Guderian taking command of 2nd Panzer.

Hitler's greed for conquest was always about resources; he started small until he had embroiled the whole of Europe. In a very short time, based largely on sheer opportunism, he began to expand the Third Reich. It started quietly in 1935 with the coal rich Saarland; this region had been under a League of Nations mandate since the end of the First World War. The Saarland voted in January with a resounding 'yes' to be reunited with Germany. The day before this was due to officially take place, on 28 February, Hitler sent his personal bodyguard regiment the *Leibstandarte SS* Adolf Hitler, in a display of Nazi party power. The unit formed part of the *SS-Verfugungstruppe* (SS-VT) the forerunner of the elite *Waffen-SS*.

The following year Hitler surprised everyone by re-occupying the Rhineland, which had been demilitarised since 1918. Guderian's tanks were not deployed to avoid antagonising the French, although his division was placed on alert. This event proved a turning point for it convinced Hitler that Britain and France would not meddle in his domestic affairs. In the meantime General Guderian became Chief of

Fast Troops in 1938 in charge of all armoured, anti-tank, motorised and cavalry units. The number of panzer divisions was expanded with the creation of the 4th and 5th as well as four additional panzer brigades. Hitler's panzer arm needed tanks that combined the right balance of armament, armour and speed, but deliveries of the newly designed Panzer III and IV were slow, which meant relying on the poorly armed Panzer I and II.

When the storm clouds began to gather across Europe in the late 1930s, Adolf Hitler knew only too well that German rearmament was far from complete. Despite his grandiose plans Germany was not geared up for total war. On the eve of the Second World War his armed forces or *Wehrmacht* had a just over 3,300 tanks, of which only 629 were *Panzerkampfwagen* (PzKpfw) Mk III and IV. These forces were out-classed by France's tanks and vastly outnumbered by Russia's. If Hitler were to accelerate the timetable for his attack on the Soviet Union he desperately needed to supplement his meagre tank force. Skoda would provide him with the means to achieve this. The Czechs were first class tank builders and German intelligence indicated they had up to 500.

Two German officers in particular were closely interested in Skoda's tank designs, firstly Major General Walther Model who, in the mid-1930s, had been appointed Head of Section 8 of the German Army General Staff. His job was to assess foreign weapons and he had travelled to Spain during the civil war to evaluate amongst other things Italian and Soviet armour. Also Major Ferdinand Schorner, later field marshal, in the Foreign Armies Branch of the German General Staff would have taken an interest in such things. Taking the Czechs' tanks from their well equipped and sizeable army would not be easy and first there was the matter of *Anschluss* or political union with Austria. Hitler's supporters helped orchestrate a political crisis that forced annexation upon the Austrians.

German intelligence sources showed that the meagre Austrian mechanised forces consisted of a single tank battalion, equipped with M35 small tanks and M35 heavy armoured cars, and a Motorised Jäger Battalion. Guderian was instructed to resume his command of 2nd Panzer Division and on 12 March 1938 along with the *Leibstandarte* was ordered to move into Austria. He met Hitler at Linz, the Führer's Austrian birthplace, where 60,000 people and the Austrian Army enthusiastically greeted them with open arms.

General Guderian rolled into Vienna at the head of 2nd Panzer in the early hours of 13 March. He was warmly welcomed into the city centre by an Austrian military band and General Stumpfl, commander of the Vienna Division of the Austrian Army. A parade was held for Hitler including the 2nd Panzer and 27th Infantry Divisions and the *Leibstandarte*. A few days later Guderian dinned with some of Austria's generals and then travelled to Neusiedel-am-See to visit the Jäger Battalion followed by a visit to Bruck an der Leitha home of the Austrian Tank Battalion. What he found there were seventy-four M35 light tanks which, it transpired, were imported Italian L3/35 tankettes, and twenty-seven M35 ADGZ Austrian built armoured cars.[2]

Guderian was impressed by what he saw of the tank battalion remarking:

> This latter was commanded by Lieutenant Colonel Theiss, a particularly fine officer who had suffered considerable physical injury as a result of a severe tank accident. His troops made a first-class impression and I soon struck up an easy relationship with his young officers and men. Both morale and discipline in these two units were so excellent that their incorporation into the Reich Army could be anticipated as both profitable and pleasant.[3]

The M35 light tanks were quickly issued to Panzer Regiment 33 as its first tanks until they were replaced by Panzer I and IIs. The vehicles were then sent to Wunsdorf for training purposes with the School for Army Motorisation. The ADGZ armoured cars were issued to the German Police and served in Danzig in September 1939. The Germans were so unimpressed that they only ever manufactured a further twenty-five for the SS in 1942, which were used to fight partisans on the Eastern Front. In the meantime they also set about confiscating the Austrian Army's motor transport, which amounted to about 1,000 vehicles.

Remaining in the Vienna area, Guderian's 2nd Panzer Division began to receive eager Austrian recruits by the autumn. A young German officer named Erwin Rommel was appointed Commandant of the Austrian War Academy at Wiener Neustadt thirty miles south of Vienna in November 1938. He was one of Hitler's acolytes and they had first met in the mid-1930s when Rommel was commanding the 3rd Battalion, Goslar Jägers, Guderian's old regiment. Rommel later recalled wistfully that this posting was the happiest period in his life.

Colonel Ritter von Thoma, who had commanded Hitler's first tank battalion, on returning from advising the Nationalists' armoured forces in Spain in June 1939, was given command of a tank regiment in Austria to put into practice his recent experiences. By midsummer 1939 five

Austrian divisions had been added to the German Army order of battle.[4] Lieutenant Colonel Theiss was later placed in charge of panzer service manuals, a post he held until the end of the war, and served under Guderian.

Despite Austria's lack of armour and motor vehicles her industries were soon to serve the Nazi war effort. From 1938 until the end of the Second World War the Austrian motor industry produced vast quantities of motor vehicles for the Axis armed forces, initially from their own designs and later from German ones. In total the Austrian firms Austro-Daimler and Steyr produced about 25,000 cars and trucks.[5] Austria's huge gunpowder plant, Skodawerke Wetzler A.G., was taken over by I.G Farben and placed under German control.[6] Similarly Baron Rothschild was forced to sell his Austrian steel mills to the Hermann Goering Reichswerke.

Just a month after the bloodless takeover of Austria, Hitler cast an eye over Czechoslovakia. Once secured it would provide a southern springboard into Poland, the gateway to the Soviet Union. On 9 June he called on the intelligence gathered by Major General Model's Section 8, the Foreign Armies Branch of the German General Staff and others when he requested additional information on the Czechs' armament. Hitler was not disappointed when he immediately received a thorough report on every Czech weapon available. He also wanted to know if Czechoslovakia's defences were still manned at reduced strength. Model and his staff were given the secret mission of spying on the Czech's defensive fortifications along the Sudeten border to assess their capabilities.

Ultimately the 'liberation' of the ethnic Germans in Czechoslovakia's Sudetenland provided Hitler with all the pretext he needed to get his hands on the Czech tanks and more importantly the factories producing them. On the pretence of manoeuvres, Hitler moved his 1st Light Division and 11th Panzer Regiment to Saxony and then to the Czech border in September 1938. That same month he convened a conference in Munich with representatives from Britain, France and Italy. No one wanted war. Hitler was granted 11,000 square miles of territory along with almost 3 million Sudeten Germans and 800,000 Czechs.

Once Britain and France had weakly acquiesced to Hitler's demands, the 1st Light Division, supported by the 13th and 20th Motorised Infantry Divisions, crossed the frontier on 4 October unhindered. German forces passed through the first lines of defences and were greeted by thousands of ethnic German soldiers heading home and still wearing their Czech uniforms. Hitler painlessly occupied the Sudetenland, once again meeting no resistance. Rommel commanded Hitler's personal escort for the triumphal march into the region. Admiral Miklós Horthy the Hungarian regent also regained southern Slovakia as a result of the Munich settlement.

When they annexed the Sudetenland the next motor vehicle manufacturer to be taken over by the Germans was the Czech firm of Tatra. It also was to produce large numbers of motor vehicles for the German armed forces and its Axis allies. Tatra military cars built under the auspices of the Germans were to end up serving as far afield as Libya with Rommel's *Afrika Korps*. Czechoslovakia lost the bulk of its industry with Hitler acquiring 70 per cent of its iron and steel, 86 per cent of its chemicals and 70 per cent of its electrical power. The state went bankrupt overnight.

Within days of marching into the Sudetenland Hitler wanted to know how quickly he could act against the rest of the country. General Keitel, Chief of the German High Command, informed him that there were twenty-four divisions, including three panzer and four motorised divisions already in the Sudeten area that, given the order, could move quickly and without the need for significant reinforcement. In November the 5th Panzer Division was formed at Opplen in Upper Silesia; recruits were drawn not only from the Silesians but also from Sudeten Germans. The German Army was instructed by Hitler on 17 December 1938 to prepare for occupation of the rest of the country based on the assumption there would be no serious opposition from the Czech armed forces. He also gambled that Britain and France would let him have his way with the rest of Czechoslovakia in order to avoid a general war in Europe. The Czech Army, numbering some 800,000 men, was first class as were the Czechoslovak defences and armament industries, so again Hitler avoided open armed confrontation.

Hitler's plans were cunning and centred on fracturing the Czechoslovak state even further. After the Munich Agreement the Czechs, under the government of President Hacha, granted autonomy to Slovakia, but it received intelligence on 9 March 1939 that Slovak separatists were plotting to overthrow the republic. The Slovak Prime Minister, Dr Tiso was dismissed but promptly flew to Berlin to see Hitler on 13 March. The following day he returned to Slovakia and declared independence, rupturing the union between the two peoples. Hitler's troops occupied Moravska-Ostrava, one of the Czechs' key industrial towns and were poised along the border of Bohemia and

Moravia. The beleaguered Hacha turned to Hitler who announced he would take the Czech people under the protection of the German Reich. Hacha informed his cabinet they must surrender.

On 15 March the British Foreign Secretary, Lord Halifax, and one of the architects of the Munich agreement, solemnly informed the House of Lords:

> The occupation of Bohemia by German military forces began at 6 a.m. this morning. The Czech people have been ordered by their Government not to offer resistance. ... Herr Hitler issued an order to the German armed forces this morning to the effect that German military detachments would cross the frontier of the Czech territory in order to assume impartial control of the safety of the lives and property of all inhabitants of the country.[7]

Behind the scenes Joseph Stalin had drawn up plans for the Soviet Union to intervene. Marshal Zhukov later claimed:

> We were prepared to come to the aid of Czechoslovakia, our aviation and tanks were alerted; up to forty divisions were massed in the regions adjacent to the western border. But the Czechoslovak rulers of that time declined this aid and preferred abject surrender. On March 15, 1939, Germany occupied Prague. This was a natural consequence of the 'appeasement' of Hitler.[8]

Hitler spent the night of the 15th in Prague, his only recorded visit to the Czech capital. Rommel was once again at the Führer's side; his reward was promotion and appointment to Hitler's Headquarters Staff. The very next day Hitler issued a decree proclaiming that the territory occupied by German troops belonged to the German Reich as the 'Protectorate of Bohemia and Moravia'. Constantin von Neurath, former German Foreign Minister, was appointed Reich Protector to give the whole exercise a veneer of respectability. Protectorate security was assigned to a Sudeten German SS-Gruppenführer (Major General) Karl Hermann Frank. Another Sudeten German, Konrad Henlein, was appointed Head of the Civil Administration; it would be one of his jobs, along with Frank, to ensure Czechoslovakia's weapons factories continued to churn out arms for Hitler.

At the same time Hitler undertook to place Slovakia under German protection. Tiso found German troops entering Slovakia and under the Treaty of Protection Germany gained exclusive rights to exploit the Slovak economy. Admiral Horthy, continuing to enjoy the crumbs from

Hitler's table, occupied the Czechoslovak region of Ruthenia placing Hungarian troops up against the Polish border.

While Britain and France were preoccupied with the fate of Czechoslovakia, Hitler also seized Memelland from Lithuania, which had once been part of East Prussia. The Lithuanians were in no position to resist and a week after reviewing his troops in Prague Hitler arrived in the Baltic port of Memel. The dismemberment of Czechoslovakia was complete and Hitler was free to set about seizing the Czech Army's considerable stocks of weapons. The rearmament of Germany was putting a strain on the economy. However, the brazen occupation of Bohemia and Moravia and the seizure of Czech weapons, gold and currency reserves greatly alleviated this. The destruction of the Czechoslovak state also meant the Germans could secure air bases in an independent Slovakia ready for when Hitler's attentions turned east.

Winston Churchill was alert not only to the potential repercussions over appeasement of Germany's claims on Czechoslovakia, but also the significance of the Skoda works. 'We certainly suffered a loss through the fall of Czechoslovakia equivalent to some thirty-five divisions,' he later observed. 'Besides this the Skoda works, the second most important arsenal in central Europe, the production of which between August 1938, and September 1939, was in itself nearly equal to the actual output of British arms factories in that period, was made to change sides adversely.'[9] Churchill appreciated that from now on the Skoda works would be making munitions for Hitler's war machine and warned: 'Czechoslovakia deserted and ruined by the Munich Pact; its fortress line in German hands; its mighty arsenal of Skoda henceforward making munitions for the German armies... .'[10]

Lord Halifax, apart from offering diplomatic platitudes, made no mention of the dangerous weapons windfall that Hitler secured. At the time he seemed more concerned with the £10 million that had been made available to the Czech government, of which £3 million was outstanding.[11] Nevertheless, he saw Hitler's hand behind events, telling the House of Lords on 20 March:

> It is difficult to avoid the conclusion that the bulk of the incidents which occurred before the German invasion were deliberately provoked and that the effects were greatly magnified. ... It is not necessary, I think to say much upon the assertion that the Czechoslovak President really assented to the subjugation of his people. In view of the circumstance in which he came to Berlin, and the occupation of Czech territory which had already taken place, I

think most sensible people must conclude that there was little pretence of negotiation, and that it is more probable that the Czech representatives were presented with an ultimatum under the threat of violence, and that they capitulated in order to save their people from the horrors of a swift and destructive aerial bombardment.[12]

What happened next went largely unnoticed but was key to the subsequent invasions of Poland, France and Russia. The panzers rolled into Brno, the second largest city in the Czech republic, at around 10.00 on 15 March. The German ethnic minority numbering some 50,000 greeted them with enthusiastic cries of 'Heil Hitler,' while the rest of the population simmered with resentment. Located in Brno was Zbrojovka, the largest Czech armament factory, which produced everything from small arms to tanks.

General Guderian recalled:

On the morning of the occupation, the Commander-in-Chief of the Army sent for me. He informed me of the accomplished fact and ordered me to go at once to Prague, where I was to collect data concerning the advance made in wintry weather by our panzer units and to examine the Czech armoured equipment.

In Prague I found my successor as commanding general of XVI Army Corps, General Hoeppner, who informed me of his experiences during the advance. In Brno I examined the Czech armoured equipment and found it serviceable. It was to prove useful to us during the Polish and French campaigns. During the Russian campaign it was finally replaced by heavier German equipment.[13]

He was disappointed to discover the haul for Hitler's first great panzer heist was not as large as had been anticipated. Skoda had built 424 LT-35s, but many had been exported and only half of those taken from the Czech Army were operational.[14] Similarly none of the follow-on LT-38 ordered by the Czechs had been built. Nonetheless, Hitler quietly confiscated 219 LT-35 tanks and more importantly two tank plants, Skoda and CKD (Ceskomoravska Kolben Danek), that were responsible for the LT-35 and TNHP or LT-38 respectively. CKD was re-designated Bohmisch Mahrische Maschinenfabrik (BMM) in 1940. Hitler had already ordered Hermann Goering to organise a huge armaments programme and the Skoda works were absorbed into Goering's Reichswerke.

Hitler instructed the German administrator of the Protectorate to ensure that the Czechs and Slovaks surrendered all tanks in both regions to the *Wehrmacht*. Lieutenant General Ferdinand Catlos, the Slovak Defence Minister, was allowed to raise three infantry divisions from the ruins of the Czechoslovakian Army for border security. The Slovaks got to keep the Czechoslovakian equipment stored within their borders, but ended up with little more than a dozen tanks.

The CKD built LT-38, re-designated the PzKpfw 38(t) was to be an altogether different proposition to that of the LT-35. An order for 150 had just been placed at the time of annexation and Hitler instructed that it should be completed. He and Guderian were impressed by its initial performance and ordered another 1,400. This though was the tip of the iceberg as Hitler demanded a further 5,000 be built as self-propelled and assault gun chassis during the course of the Second World War. In total the Czechs built over 6,500 armoured fighting vehicles including 1,400 tanks, 2,000 self-propelled guns and 2,500 tanks destroyers for the Nazi war effort.

Due to the lack of resistance to the German annexation almost the whole of the Czechoslovak Army's vehicle stocks fell into German hands. The *Wehrmacht* appropriated most of the motor vehicles or passed them on to its Hungarian and Romanian allies. Motor transport yielded thousands of cars and trucks including about 1,865 Praga Av and Tatra 82 heavy cars, as well as Wikov MNO, Tatra 82 and Tatra 85 trucks.[15] In addition to the Czech tank manufacturers, Hitler took over Praga and Skoda motor vehicle factories, which continued to churn out wheeled vehicles for the Germans.

The overall bonanza of military equipment from the Czech Army was vast. In one fell swoop the Germans acquired 469 tanks, 1,500 planes, over 500 anti-aircraft guns, 43,000 machine guns, over 1 million rifles, 1,000 million rifle rounds, 3 million field gun rounds and the Skoda arms works, second only to Krupps in Germany.[16] Czech military supplies were used to equip four panzer divisions and fifteen infantry divisions.[17] However, the booty taken from the Czech Army was only used to outfit the low category German divisions,[18] and the Germans were less impressed with Czech small arms.[19]

A copy of Guderian's report found its way to, amongst others, General Georg Thomas, Head of the War Economy and Armaments Office of the German Armed Forces High Command. He helped oversee the German Army's expansion from its Versailles limits of seven infantry and three cavalry divisions, to fifty-one divisions including to thirty infantry divisions (including four motorised and three mountain divisions), five panzer divisions and four light divisions, in the run up to war.

Unlike the Austrians, Hitler did not want the Czechs conscripted into the *Wehrmacht*; the Czech Army was quietly disbanded and its officers pensioned off. The 10th Panzer Division was formed in Prague just a month after Hitler took over using Panzer Brigade 4. It may have attracted Sudeten Germans and was well placed not only to cow the Czechs but also to take part in the invasion of Poland.

The impact of the acquisition of Czechoslovakia's tank facilities went way beyond the German Army. The Skoda works at Pilsen had been supplying Romania and Yugoslavia; these countries were now obliged to negotiate with Hitler for vital spare parts. Hitler's seizure of Skoda also posed a problem for Russia's Red Army. Moscow had outstanding contracts with Skoda and the Russian ambassador to Berlin called on the German Foreign Minister on 17 April to enquire about them. Germany was concerned about a Three-Power-Alliance between Russia, Britain and France and the Foreign Minister pointed out that the current atmosphere was not favourable for the delivery of war materials to the Soviet Union.

The seizure of CKD also threatened to sour relations that Guderian had helped to forge with Sweden. In 1938-39, just before the German takeover, the company had received an order for ninety tanks from the Swedish government. The Germans demanded they be diverted to the *Wehrmacht* but, due to design problems, these Swedish tanks could not be delivered to the German Army until late 1941. In consolation Sweden was granted a licence to build the tank indigenously.

Czech tanks were also instrumental in arming Hitler's east European allies. The satellite Hungarian, Romanian and Slovakian armies were equipped with the PzKpfw 38(t), while the Hungarians also produced their own version of the LT-35, known as the Turan. Romania started the war with the Skoda LT-35, but most of these were lost at Stalingrad and replaced by ex-German 38(t)s. In 1940 Germany also provided the Bulgarian Army with 35(t)s. Hitler remained short sighted for, although the Czech armour was good in its day, it soon became obsolete in comparison with the Russian T-34. When Hungary requested to build the German Panzer Mk V Panther tank in 1944, the deal fell through because of the exorbitant cost for the production licence.

Following a meeting with Winston Churchill on 1 August 1939, Major General Sir Edward Spears recalled:

Then we spoke of the immense advantage which had accrued to Germany by her seizure of Czechoslovakia. Neither of us doubted that in the year that had since elapsed Germany had armed infinitely faster than had either the French or ourselves.

I knew Czechoslovakia well. There was no doubt that the already vast German arms industry, driven at furious pace, had gained an enormous accession of strength by the possession of the Skoda and Witkowitz [steel] works.[20]

The French were not blind to the danger either. Shortly after, Spears, who became the Prime Minister's personal representative during the Battle of France, and Churchill, were guests of General Alphonse Georges, French Commander-in-Chief, in Paris. 'Georges lamented,' says Spears, 'as a major disaster, the gain by Hitler of Skoda, one of the greatest armament firms in the world.'[21]

Despite the absorption of Czechoslovakia's tank force, when Germany invaded Poland in September 1939, its six panzer divisions were still much weaker than had been intended. Hitler's force of 3,000 tanks included barely 100 medium PzKpfw Mk IIIs and 211 of the more powerful PzKpfw Mk IVs. Significantly, included in the invasion force were the LT-35 re-designated the PzKpfw 35(t); these were armed with a 37mm gun comparable to the Mk IIIs, but they were half the weight and therefore a lot faster.

The 1st Light Division and 11th Panzer Regiment, while stationed at Paderborn in April 1939, received 128 LT-35s. In July the division decided to discard all its light Panzer Is and some of its IIs; this left it fielding 114 LT-35s, sixty-five Panzer IIs and forty-two Panzer IVs, a total of 221 tanks. In a stroke, thanks to this injection of Czech armour, the division became the pre-eminent panzer force within the German Army. The Czechoslovak LT-35 went into action with the 1st Light Division on 1 September 1939, which was the only really combat-ready armoured formation in the entire German Army. Only fifty-nine of the new 38(t)s were ready to serve with the 3rd Light Division in Poland, while just fifteen were sent to fight in Norway in 1940.

During the conquest of Poland, Guderian called on Hitler to hasten delivery of the Panzer Mk III and IV. This was held up by limited production capacity and the Army High Command's habit of hanging on to them. By the spring of 1940 Hitler's tank force had increased to 3,348 vehicles, of which 629 were Mk IIIs and IVs, and 371 were Czech PzKpfw 35(t)/38(t) while the remainder were the light Mk Is and IIs.

Following the successful invasion of Poland, Hitler sought to head off political muttering in the Protectorate of Bohemia and Moravia with a show of force. He despatched the *Leibstandarte SS* Adolf Hitler to

Prague on 4 October. There they were posted prominently as guards on public buildings. The SS-VT had performed poorly in Poland where there were allegations of looting and murder. They did not stay in Prague long, but the message was clear.

In March 1940 the SS-VT became the *Waffen-SS* and due to rivalry with the Army over equipment allocation, initially had to make do with Czech equipment, in particular artillery. It was not until 1942 that Hitler agreed to support Albert Speer's proposal that 5 to 8 per cent of military output be allocated to the *Waffen-SS* on the condition that they provide concentration camp inmates to work in the factories. The elite *Waffen-SS* found themselves having to use the 7.5cm PaK40/3 auf PzKpfw 38(t) Ausf H (which was issued to the 1st SS Panzer Division *Leibstandarte* in December 1942) and the subsequent Marder III self-propelled gun, both of which were based on the Czech tank chassis.

General Guderian, commanding the German 19th Panzer Corps, records 2,574 tanks were available for the attack on France, the Anglo-French force had in excess of 4,000 tanks. Almost 10 per cent of Hitler's tank force attacking France was of Czech origin. According to Guderian, the 1st Light Division, re-designated the 6th Panzer Division on 18 October 1939, deployed 106 Czech PzKpfw 35(t)s, while 228 Czech PzKpfw 38(t)s were fielded mainly with the 7th and 8th Panzer Divisions.

The 7th Panzer Division, commanded by General Erwin Rommel, only had some three dozen German designed vehicles. His division nicknamed the 'Ghost Division' because it was everywhere, was to single-handedly capture 450 enemy tanks. Czech guns also served the *Wehrmacht* during the invasion of the Low Countries and France. A Czech 4.7cm anti-tank gun was mounted on the Panzer I chassis and, between March 1940 and February 1941, over 200 were converted. First seeing action in Belgium and France the conversion stayed in service until 1943.

The 6th Panzer Division and its Skodas proved highly efficient striking across the River Meuse towards the Channel covering 217 miles in nine days. At the beginning of March 1940 it had moved into the Wester Woods, east of the Rhine ready to take part in Operation Sickle Cut, the armoured thrust through the Belgian Ardennes region into France. Skodas belonging to First Lieutenant Dr Franz Bake's 1st Company, 65th Panzer Battalion, were to lead the drive on the Meuse. Unhindered by the French Air Force the 3.7cm guns of Bake's eighteen Skodas, supported by assault guns armed with short 7.5cm guns, poured fire into the French defences across the river. They then forded on 13 May 1940, losing just one tank, which sank up to its turret. Over the next three days Bake's company accounted for seven French tanks, two of which Bake knocked out.[22]

On 16 May 6th Panzer Division's 35(t)s came up against a French armour counter-attack, then four days later encountered the British 36th Brigade. Despite their mechanical shortcomings 6th Panzer Division's Czech tanks gave a good account of themselves when they crossed swords with the formidable French heavy tank, the Char B1 bis, of the 2eme Division Cuirassee (2DCR). By the time of the attack on Guise on 17 May Lieutenant Bake knew that their 3.7cm guns could not penetrate the frontal armour of the French tanks, nor was it powerful enough to knock out an enemy tank with a single round. In one instance after a close engagement with some heavy French tanks, Bake and his crew took three shots to destroy the tank they were fighting.

Only at Arras on 21 May did the panzers suffer any real setback, when a depleted French light mechanised division with some seventy Somua tanks and a British armoured brigade with another seventy-four tanks successfully attacked three German divisions. Unfortunately in the confusion the British found themselves under attack by the French and knocked out four Somuas before the error was realised. The Germans eventually threw back the Anglo–French counter-attack using their 88-mm anti-aircraft guns in a dual anti-tank role.

By 24 May the 6th Panzer Division was poised to attack Cassel, HQ of the British Expeditionary Force (BEF). However Hitler ordered a halt, thereby saving the BEF from total destruction. When the attack did come the British 145th Infantry Brigade was prepared; only when it attempted to retreat was the garrison lost. First Lieutenant Bake and his Czech tanks were involved in stopping the British tanks breaking out from Cassel in the direction of Waten. Circling south he caught them in the flank and his sixteen tanks opened fire at once. The first two British tanks were blown to pieces followed by six others.[23] The Germans then pressed home their attack and soon Bake's tank had accounted for another three British tanks. When the fighting came to a stop fifty tanks had been destroyed several hundred British soldiers killed and 2,000 captured.[24] In total the division had taken sixty tanks, five armoured cars, ten artillery pieces and eleven anti-tank guns, thirty motor cars and 233 trucks.[25] The 6th Panzer Division then pursued the retreating French.

Hitler's triumphant panzers took up strategic positions on the streets of Paris, which had been declared an open city, on 14 June. The Parisians soon discovered, as the Poles had done, that these tanks were very real and not made of cardboard as the French press had implied. A week later the Armistice bought an end to the fighting in France. The German Army Weapons Office directed in October 1940 that two examples of every captured vehicle were to be shipped to them for evaluation at Kummersdorf. They were then forwarded to the Army Vehicle Office's Tank Museum in Stettin-Altdamm.

By the spring of 1941 Czech armour accounted for a staggering 25 per cent of the total German tank force. For the invasion of Russia the 6th Panzer Division was still partly equipped with the 35(t) and the 7th, 8th, 12th, 19th, 20th and 22nd Panzer Divisions with the 38(t). 6th Panzer Division took 103 35(t)s with it to Russia as part of 4th Panzergruppe striking toward Leningrad. They came in for a nasty shock at Rasyeinya when the 2nd Soviet Tank Division, using heavy KV-1 and KV-2 tanks, counter-attacked. The Skodas and German built-armour were no match for these monsters, but the Russians did not know how to use their heavy tanks effectively. The days of using tanks as an infantry support weapon were finished; from now on it would be tank to tank. Despite reaching Leningrad the division was diverted to the attack on Moscow.

The Czechs' factories played another role in the preparations for the invasion of the Soviet Union. In the spring of 1941 the factory at Milowitz near Prague was engaged to make the submersible Tauchpanzer IIIs, which had been converted for the proposed invasion of Britain, suitable for river crossings. Three sections of Tauchpanzer III and IV assigned to the 18th Panzer Division crossed the River Bug at Patulin on 22 June 1941.

The lack of replacement tanks and the attrition rate meant that the panzer divisions soon began to wither on the Eastern Front. On 2 October 1941 6th Division's 35(t)s were combined with 7th Division's 38(t)s in a temporary panzer brigade as no replacements had been received since June. In particular the Skoda tanks did not perform well in the cold weather, which affected the pneumatic clutch, brake and steering controls. When the Soviets' counter-offensive came the Skodas helped cover the retreat of 3rd Panzer Army.

Promoted to captain, in Russia Bake found himself tending to broken down and disabled Skodas while commanding the regimental tank recovery section. He returned to an active role in the fighting when, on 1 December 1941, he took charge of the 11th Panzer Regiment's 1st

Tank Company. Eight days later Bake lost his last tank, which had to be destroyed when they abandoned Elisorowo. The 6th Panzer Division's very last tank broke down on 10 December near Klin. Having lost all its Skodas and German panzers the unit became known as the '6th Panzer Division of Foot' and in April 1942 was sent to France to recuperate.

The 22nd Panzer Division's tank force was still 60 per cent 38(t)s by September 1942. When Oberst, or Colonel, Hermann von Oppeln-Bronikowski, commander of the 204th Panzer Regiment, was ordered to move to assist the Romanian 3rd Army in November only thirty-nine of his 104 tanks would start. Four exploded after mice had chewed through the electrical cables. He reached the Romanians with thirty-one tanks on 11 November 1942, but at Peschanny the Romanian 14th Infantry Division fled in the face of advancing Soviet T-34 tanks.

Oppeln counter-attacked and his 38(t) successfully hit a T-34 between the turret and the hull. Because his Skodas were inferior to the T-34s they had to close to within 600 metres for the 3.7cm gun to be effective and by the end of the battle von Oppeln had just twenty tanks left.[26] The Russians attacked again on 20 November and 22nd Panzer Division accounted for twenty-six Soviet tanks. However, the neighbouring Romanian divisions fled and the Germans had to withdraw.[27] By this stage Czech tank production had been switched over to self-propelled guns, the LT-35 and LT-38 tanks having served their purpose.

Chapter Two

Poland and the Low Countries

Polish General Wladyslaw Anders, commanding a division ninety miles south-east of Danzig and just thirteen miles south of the East Prussian border, recalled seeing hordes of German planes heading south for Warsaw on 1 September 1939. This air armada heralded Hitler's blitzkrieg on Poland. His *Luftwaffe* destroyed most of the Polish Air Force on the ground within hours and blasted Polish troop concentrations, munitions factories, fuel depots, railways, bridges and radio stations. After the dive-bombers came artillery bombardment followed by armoured cars, panzers and motorised infantry smashing through the Poles' battered defences. The German ground element of the blitzkrieg swept over the Polish 1,750 mile long frontier just before 06.00. Anders' boss, Marshal Smigly-Rydz, Commander-in-Chief of the Polish Army would be unable to fend off Hitler's panzers.

In a huge pincer movement Hitler attacked Poland from the north, the west and the south with 1.25 million men organised into sixty divisions, nine of which were armoured. General Guderian, commanding one of 4th Army's Corps stationed in Pomerania was to cut off Polish forces in the strip of land that separated the Reich from East Prussia. He noted:

> Polish forces in the Corridor were estimated at three infantry divisions and the Pomorska Cavalry Brigade. They were reckoned to possess a limited number of [Italian built] Fiat-Ansaldo tanks. The Polish side of the border was fortified. We had good observation of their field works. A secondary line of defensive positions was to be anticipated along the River Brahe.[1]

In fact the Poles' armoured fighting vehicles were mainly of French origin, such as First World War vintage Renault FT light tanks and Peugeot armoured cars as well as French half-tracks. Britain had also supplied some Carden-Loyd tankettes and Vickers six-ton tanks, which the Poles reworked. In terms of armour they were simply outnumbered and outclassed from the start, with about 600-900 7TP light tanks and TK tankettes.

These forces consisted of 169 Polish PZinz built 7TP (an improved version of the Vickers 6-tonner), fifty Vickers 6-tonners, sixty-seven Renault FT-17, fifty-three Renault R-35s, about 700 TK/TKS tankettes and 100 various armoured cars.[2] The 7TP was armed with a 37mm gun and only about twenty TKS had been upgraded from a machine gun to a 20-mm capable of taking on the Panzer I and II.

During the inter-war period the Polish Armed Forces relied on American and French surplus motor transport. The Poles had then begun to licence build a variety of foreign vehicles including cars, trucks and buses for both military and civilian use in the 1930s.

The Polish Army's mechanised forces were organised into a single armoured brigade and two motorised brigades; additionally there were eleven cavalry brigades and thirty infantry divisions. The armoured brigade comprised two battalions of 7TP tanks and one battalion of French R-35s. The bulk of the 7TPs served with the 1st Light Tank Battalion attached to the Prusy Army and the 2nd attached to the Piotrkow Operational Group of the Lodz Army. The remaining 7TPs formed two light companies which assisted in the defence of Warsaw.

The Polish motorised brigades each employed one company of the British Vickers tanks, and two companies of Polish built TK tankettes (which were versions of the British Carden-Loyd Mark VI) and two motorised cavalry regiments. There were eighteen independent companies each equipped with thirteen TK tankettes, attached to the infantry divisions. The cavalry brigades also had a reconnaissance squadron of thirteen tankettes and eight armoured cars.[3]

Geographically western Poland formed a massive salient, caught between German East Prussia to the north and Germany's Slovak allies to the south, that was largely impossible to defend. Hitler's intention was to envelop Poland's armies in two separate encirclements; the first to the west was to close along the River Vistula, while the eastern one was to meet along the River Bug. The Poles should have gathered their forces behind the Vistula and San, but some of the very things Hitler desired, Poland's main industrial areas and the Silesian coalfields lay near the frontier.

For Marshal Smigly-Rydz his lack of mobility was more disastrous than the Polish Army's incomplete mobilisation. The Poles could not conduct a fighting withdrawal from their forward areas because they would be unable to fall back to their rear positions fast enough to avoid being overrun. A third of the Polish Army was concentrated in or near the salient where they were under threat of envelopment. Smigly-Rydz commanded another third in reserve, north of the central axis between Lodz and Warsaw; the rest faced east. The four Polish armies in the salient were supposed to strike west into Germany and drive on Berlin; in reality they were forced eastwards into Hitler's trap.

Polish intelligence was clearly faulty regarding Hitler's panzers. A German witness recalled:

A panzerman told me how his unit was attacked by enemy cavalry. Imagine it, sabres against steel plate. A prisoner taken after one such charge is said to have told the interrogating officer that his regiment had been assured that German tanks were made either of cardboard or of wood and sacking. My panzer informant recalled seeing one officer charge up to one of the vehicles in his squadron, rise up in his stirrups and give a vicious downward stroke with his sabre. This shattered in his hand and the Pole looked dumbfounded. Immediately he pulled out a pistol and fired several rounds at the panzer, finally shooting himself, determined to die rather than surrender.[4]

It appears that the Poles thought the Germans were using their old 'paper panzer' wooden training tanks. 'The Polish Pomorska Cavalry brigade, in ignorance of the nature of our tanks, had charged them with swords and lances and had suffered tremendous losses,' recalled General Guderian grimly.[5] When the surviving cavalrymen were marched off to prison camp, some of them paused at the roadside to rap on parked German tanks still convinced that the armour was made of cardboard. The 7TPs of the 1st and 2nd Light Tank Battalion went into action on 4 September. The 1st managed to hold the Germans up but was eventually driven back across the Vistula. The 2nd battalion commenced battle near the Prudka River, Belchatow.

By the end of the first week of September the 4th Panzer Division, part of 10th Army, had not only fought its way through Polish forces holding the ground between Petrikau and Lodz, but had reached the highway leading directly to Warsaw. What the Germans did not know was that the Polish Commander, General Kutreba, had massed twelve divisions and was planning to strike 10th Army pushing north toward the Polish capital. The advancing 16th Corps soon found itself under threat from the Western Polish Army. However, the bulk of the Polish forces were to be trapped at Kutno.

Poland's tanks proved to be little more than a nuisance to the advancing panzers. At Raszyn, south-west of Warsaw, two Polish light tanks held up elements of the 4th Panzer Division long enough for the Poles to blow the bridges. The tank battle though was short-lived and the Germans forded the river, the bridges were repaired and they pushed into Warsaw's suburbs on 8 September. When the *Wehrmacht* reached the Vistula the following day 60,000 Poles and 130 guns were captured in the Kielce-Radom Pocket.

Marshal Smigly-Rydz ordered a retreat into south-eastern Poland on the 10th, but by now the Germans had already turned the defensive lines of the Vistula, Bug and San. Eight days later the Marshal fled to Romania. In the meantime up to six Polish divisions were rushing to the capital's aid and 4th Panzer fought a defensive battle on two fronts during 10-14 September.

In sheer desperation the Polish Army launched a series of ill-coordinated attacks. On 12 September Polish infantry, supported by two companies of tanks, were thrown against the Germans in Mokotow, in south-eastern Warsaw and 4th Panzer was forced to pull back. The panzers learned the hard way about the dangers of fighting in urban environments. In the Warsaw suburbs 4th Panzer lost fifty-seven of its 120 attacking tanks to Polish gunners. The Polish 26th and 27th Divisions were then thrown into the assault, overrunning German positions. This success was short lived. The Polish 2nd Tank Battalion, withdrawn to Brzesc, took part in the Battle of Wlodawa on the 15th; two days later the crews destroyed their tanks and fled into Romania. The Polish 1st Tank battalion after fighting in the Battle of Tomaszow Lubelski on the 21st destroyed the last of their tanks and surrendered to the Germans.

The outclassed Poles soon found themselves trapped on the western side of the River Bzura and by 17 September their counter-attacks were being conducted in an increasingly piecemeal and half-hearted fashion. That same day the Russians invaded eastern Poland occupying the Ukrainian and Belorussian populated provinces. The Red Army met little resistance and occupied Vilna the following day, linking up with the Germans at Brest-Litovsk on the 19th.

The few TKS armed with the 20mm anti-tank gun proved a potent weapon in the right hands as the 6th Panzer Division discovered. Near Pociecha in central Poland on 18 September officer cadet Roman Orlik of the Volhynian Cavalry Brigade successfully used his tankette to knock out three PzKpfw 35(t)s, including one commanded by Lieutenant Victor Hohenlohe (Prince von Ratibor) from 6th Panzer's 11th Panzer Regiment. By that point all was lost, further resistance was futile and the

Polish Army began to surrender en masse.

The remains of nineteen Polish divisions and three cavalry brigades, about 100,000 men trapped in the Kutno area, surrendered to the German 8th Army on the day of the Soviet linkup. In south-eastern Poland at Lemberg and Przemysl the Poles launched a series of furious counter-attacks using tanks against elements of the German 1st Mountain Division assigned to 14th Army. The arrival of the Russians ended German attempts to capture Lemberg and the city capitulated with honour. The last elements of the Polish Army surrendered on 5 October.

Despite some fierce fighting Hitler's German and Czech built panzers easily overwhelmed Poland's forces. The Germans suffered 40,000 casualties, including 8,000 dead and lost 217 tanks, but had scattered the approximately 800,000 strong Polish Army.[6]

Guderian, arriving at Brest-Litovsk, was only given until 22 September to withdraw east of the line of demarcation and it irked him to have to leave some of his damaged tanks behind. After negotiation with the Russians it was agreed that all German equipment could be removed, but that captured from the Poles would have to be left behind because time did not permit organising transport.[7] One of Stalin's first acts was to set about exterminating the leadership of the Polish Army in his occupied zone culminating in the Katyn massacre.

Although they dismissed the Poles' armour the Germans had still lost several hundred tanks during the invasion. On closer inspection of Poland's captured armour it transpired that the 7TPs/Vickers 6-tonners were better armed than Germany's PzKpfw Is and IIs that formed the bulk of its *Panzerwaffe*.[8] The *Panzertruppen*'s haul in Poland was not large, capturing only about sixty 7TPs in a salvageable condition as well as the factory. Some of these took part in the German victory parade held in Warsaw on 8 October 1939. The Germans soon discovered they needed some of Poland's armour for police duties because the panzers were worn out.

A number of 7TPs were quickly pressed into service with the occupation forces and captured TK/TKS tankettes were gathered at the armoured vehicle workshop in Warsaw for repair. The Warsaw Light Panzer Company was equipped with two platoons of these in July 1940 for security and training duties. That year the company made a show of strength, driving their captured TKS and 7TP through the streets of Warsaw to mark the first anniversary of the fall of the Polish capital. The *Luftwaffe* also supplied a flight of bombers to awe the locals. By March

1941 the armoured vehicle workshop in Warsaw reported that fifty-five TKS were available to serve with the re-titled Light Panzer Company East.[9]

In addition numbers of Polish tankettes were supplied to the *Luftwaffe* based in Poland for airfield security. Some even ended up serving German forces in France and Yugoslavia. Poland's French built R-35s eluded capture as they had not taken part in the action and fled to Romania where they were seized by the Romanian Army.[10] In addition to the *Wehrmacht*, a significant proportion of the Polish war booty went to Romania in exchange for oil.[11]

Hitler discovered the Poles had been working on a medium tank known as the 10TP, based on the American Christie tank. A single prototype was built in 1936-37 and it was intended to create two battalions equipped with these tanks within the motorised brigades. It did not go into production and as it was only armed with a 37mm gun the Germans did not bother resurrecting the project during the occupation.

The Polish Army lost well over 25,000 motor vehicles and the *Wehrmacht* seized those that had not been destroyed in the fighting.[12] The Germans also took over the state-run engineering enterprise Panstwowy Zaklad Inzynierii (Pzinz) in Warsaw which was licence-building Polski Fiat motor vehicles. In preparation for the impending Operation Barbarossa, the invasion of the Soviet Union, 15,000 Polish pattern Panjewagen horse-drawn carts were acquired for the German infantry divisions, in order to increase their mobility.[13] The Germans also made use of Polish small arms such as the 9mm Radom wz 35 pistol, which entered *Wehrmacht* service as the P 35(p).

Other Polish factories were also put to work for the *Luftwaffe*, for example a factory in the Zoliborz district of Warsaw was manufacturing airscrews until the Polish Home Army burned it to the ground on 30 September 1942. The following month the Polish resistance blew up every railway line leading out of the Polish capital. This cut vital links with the Eastern Front and stopped a crucial ammunition and supply train destined for German troops at Stalingrad.[14] Poland's role in Hitler's war on Russia was to thwart Guderian's career.

One Polish company known as the 'Firm,' with offices in Warsaw and Minsk, the Belorussian capital, was employed to supply the *Wehrmacht* on the Eastern Front. In reality it indulged in several sidelines which included gun running to Soviet partisans; supplied with official passes the 'Firm's' trucks were able to pass through both German and partisan lines unmolested.[15] However, the Germans saw the Poles as little better than slaves and the best workers were sent to work in German armament factories.

Deliberate obstruction of Warsaw's rail network first began to make itself felt during the winter of 1941. The results had a major impact on German troops slowly freezing to death on the Eastern Front. When General Guderian visited the 112th and 167th Infantry Divisions in Russia on 14 November 1941 he was alarmed to discover a complete lack of adequate winter clothing. Many men were suffering frostbite and the vehicles were immobilised. Guderian was furious, as he had requested warm clothing in September and October, and took steps to find out what was going on. The Army's Quartermaster-General insisted winter clothing had been issued. After making some telephone calls Guderian discovered it had been stranded for weeks at Warsaw railway station due to a lack of trains and disruption to the lines.

When Guderian saw Hitler in late December a heated argument took place over the issue. Guderian pointed out that the cold was causing twice as many casualties as the Russians. Hitler accused him of not seeing the bigger picture and that winter clothing had been issued. When the Quartermaster-General was summoned he had to admit the kit remained in Warsaw. The damage had been done, Hitler's troops froze and a week later Guderian was relieved of his command for ordering an unauthorised withdrawal.

The Poles fared far worse than the Western Europeans under Nazi rule and their fate bore little similarity with that of Denmark or the Netherlands or even Vichy France. The Germans not only carved up Poland with the Soviet Union but also split it up further. Parts were annexed, while others were incorporated into the Reichkommissariat of 'Ostland' and 'Ukraine', while the remains were administered as the 'Generalgouvernement'. The Germans kept between 400,000 and 600,00 police and troops in Poland, though the Poles resisted from the start with the Armia Krajowa or Home Army coming into official existence in 1942, with a maximum strength of 400,000.

Many German rear area security forces were soon desperate for military equipment and made use of whatever was available locally. Policing the occupied territories tended to end in a muddle of jurisdictions between the police, SS and the German Army. In 1942 Reichsführer-SS Heinrich Himmler became responsible for anti-partisan operations within the protectorates and the Chief of the Army's General Staff for those within the operational zones. Things were further simplified with the appointment of an SS General as

Coordinator of Anti-Partisan Operations in the East, but confusion and duplication of effort continued right up until the end of the war.[16]

In particular captured Polish equipment was used to assist in crushing Operation Big Scheme. This was the Polish resistance movement's plan for a national uprising to coincide with the arrival of Soviet forces from the east in the summer of 1944. The result was 'Burza' the rising in Warsaw, which started in anticipation of the Red Army crossing the River Vistula after the spectacular success of Stalin's Operation Bagration. Unfortunately Soviet help did not come and the Warsaw rising was brutally dealt with by the *Waffen-SS*.

The revolt, codenamed Tempest, commenced in eastern Poland where the Home Army's 3rd, 9th and 27th Divisions attempted to wrest control from the Germans ahead of the advancing Red Army. By 4 August 1944 the Polish Home Army had secured most of Warsaw. However, lacking heavy weapons and ammunition, it was unable to consolidate its three main defensive enclaves within the city. The Germans counter-attacked on 10 August and four days later the Home Army had been divided into six enclaves.[17] The Poles held out for two months before surrendering on 5 October.

After conquering Poland in September 1939 Hitler wanted to attack France as quickly as possible to secure his western borders before turning east again, but was informed that it would take months to refit the tanks used in the campaign. Nearly every single vehicle needed an overhaul. General Thomas, Head of the War Economy and Armaments Office, pointed out that Germany had a monthly steel deficit of over 0.5 million tons and General von Stülpnagel, Quartermaster-General, reported that ammunition stocks were insufficient to ensure victory over the French.

After six months' recuperation Hitler's forces invaded Norway and Denmark on 9 April 1940. The outnumbered Danes offered virtually no resistance but the Norwegians, with belated British and French military assistance, lasted until early June. A German troop ship landed men in Copenhagen, while a motorised brigade followed by an infantry division sped over the Danish-German border as paratroops landed on the Aalborg airfield. Within four hours it was all over for the Danish Army.

Norway's heaviest armour consisted of some old Swedish Landsverk armoured cars, while the Danes' few armoured vehicles also included Landsverks and Lynx armoured cars, which fell into German hands. More importantly the Germans captured the Danish Ford and General Motors assembly plants. Initially, unlike Poland, the Germans treated

Denmark with leniency and strangely the Danish armed forces were not disbanded until early 1943, with the Danish police following suit in September 1944.

Hitler next timed his attack on the Low Countries – Belgium and the Netherlands – to coincide with his invasion of France on 10 May 1940. The Germans easily brushed aside the Belgian Army's pitifully few light tanks. The Belgians had relied on British and French equipment for their mechanised forces. These included a number of British built T13B2 (based on the Carden-Loyd Mark VI light tank) tracked anti-tank gun carrier, armed with a 47mm, and just forty-two T15 tankettes (based on the British Vickers-Carden-Loyd designs)[18] and some Minerva armoured cars. The Belgian Army also had twenty-five French built AMC Renault 35 ACG 1 light cavalry tanks.[19] None of these vehicles did them any good.

The defence of neutral Belgium was hampered by a complete lack of cooperation with the British and French armies. Just as the Germans were attacking Belgium, General Bernard Montgomery, leading elements of the British 3rd Division, was not allowed to enter the country. Nonetheless they endeavoured to take up positions to help defend Brussels, only to have their way blocked by Belgian troops objecting to their presence. The Belgians even fired on the British thinking they were German paratroops. The speed of the German blitzkrieg meant the defence of the River Dyle and Brussels became impossible and the bickering became academic.

Once the Germans were slicing through the Ardennes British forces in Belgium were in danger of being cut off and on 16-17 May were forced to start withdrawing. This was done in an orderly manner and at this stage no equipment was abandoned. Lieutenant Colonel Brian Horrocks, leading his carrier platoon, anti-tank battery and two machine-gun battalions, claimed to be the last British soldier out of Belgium before the remaining bridge over the Escaut Canal was blown.[20] His next stop was Dunkirk where everything the British Army possessed was abandoned to the Germans. Ten days after the withdrawal, the Belgians sued for peace.

The Netherlands' armoured forces were also pitifully small. The Dutch had imported two dozen Swedish built M36/38 Landsverk armoured cars in the late 1930s and built a single Wilton-Fijenoord armoured car. They were to have received at least two batches of T15 tankettes; the first went to the Dutch East Indies Army, but subsequent deliveries to the Dutch Home Army were interrupted by the war. The

Dutch Army also had forty British Vickers light tanks on order, but on completion in 1939 the British War Office took them over for training purposes.

The French 7th Army moved to Breda to help the Dutch fend off a German panzer division and German airborne troops intent on capturing the Dutch government at The Hague. Although the airborne attack on The Hague went horribly wrong, once the panzers had seized the bridges over the River Maas (Meuse) the Dutch were cut off. The French advancing without tanks bumped into the panzers and under air attack were forced to fall back. In Rotterdam Dutch marines and the Dutch Navy bravely tried to fend off the Germans. The *Wehrmacht* called for their surrender on 14 May as the *Luftwaffe* bombed the city into submission. The Dutch Army surrendered within six hours still virtually intact. Although colonial Dutch troops remained in the Netherlands East Indies, they were disarmed when the Japanese landed in Java in March 1942.

The German exploitation teams found little they liked amongst the Belgium armed forces inventory, though they did press into service perhaps 1,000 Belgian built motorcycles and sidecar, some trucks as well as a few tracked light artillery tractors and wheeled armoured tractors. The Ford and General Motors' plants in Belgium, as well as local firms, were forced to work for the Germans. In particular the Belgians had a good reputation for motorcycle manufacture and the Germans kept the Gillet 750 motorcycle with sidecar in production during the war.[21] Most, if not all, of this equipment though remained in the Low Countries for police work.

The only armoured vehicles the Germans seemed to have requisitioned belonging to the Belgium Army were a few Ford/Marmom Herrington artillery tractors [22] and the Familleureux Utility B tracked light artillery tractor.[23] Over 300 utility tractors either supplied by Britain or built by the Belgians under licence fell into the *Wehrmacht*'s hands. The latter were used by the German Army to tow anti-tank guns and in some instances to even deliver the mail.[24] Some may have ended up with German forces in France or Italy and some of those built for the Dutch were used in the German invasion of Crete.

In the Netherlands the *Wehrmacht* seized a dozen brand new Van Doorne M 39 or DAF PT3 armoured cars, which had taken no part in the fighting, and pressed them into service.[25] The Germans took over the factory, but despite its advanced design, apart from completing the initial batch, they did not build any more. The *Wehrmacht* also took back into service a number of 10.5cm artillery pieces which they had sold to the Dutch in 1939. The Dutch had a Ford motor assembly plant in Amsterdam, while DAF at Eindhoven had been converting trucks into artillery prime movers. DAF had also produced the limited numbers of the M39 armoured car.

A few Dutch armoured cars were to see action on the Eastern Front with the *Wehrmacht* and the police. Between 1940-42 the 227th Infantry Division fielded half a dozen M36/38s and the 18th Infantry Division was issued with some of the M39s in 1940.[26] In a bizarre postscript to the seizure of the Netherlands' armour, the single Wilton-Fijenoord ended the war in the grounds of the Reich Chancellery in May 1945.[27]

In Poland, Belgium and the Netherlands the Germans captured further huge stocks of weapons. Czech, Polish and Belgian small arms factories were all put to work manufacturing German small arms for the *Wehrmacht*.[28] In addition Hitler got his hands on much needed steel. In the late 1930s the German High Command had warned that German steel production could not cope with a prolonged conflict and that new foundries and furnaces should be built. Hitler's problem was solved with the occupation of Czechoslovakia and the conquest of France and the Low Countries. Germany was able to increase crude steel output by almost 50 per cent.

Once again most of the captured Belgian, Danish, Dutch and Norwegian military equipment was used for internal security purposes. The levels of resistance in these countries were never a serious problem for Hitler and retribution for acts of sabotage or the killing of German security personnel was invariably swift and harsh. The Germans publicly proclaimed that 100 hostages would be shot for every German killed. In Poland this amounted to 8,000 executions, in the Netherlands 2,000 and in France 29,660.[29]

Initially an SS security regiment was sent to Denmark and two to the Netherlands and Norway. These were disbanded in February 1941 and the personnel sent to join the *Waffen-SS*. Subsequently in Denmark there were only two German police battalions, in the Netherlands one regiment and in Belgium no German police units were deployed at all. The German uniformed regular police in the Netherlands were issued with some of the captured Landsverk armoured cars.

The Dutch instigated the first general strike in a German occupied country in February 1941. At its height Belgian resistance numbered 45,000, but only 7,000 of these were actually armed. Similarly Danish resistance only fielded 45,000 supporters by the time of the German surrender. In Norway by the end of the war the resistance totalled 40,000.[30] Nonetheless, collaboration with the German security forces was widespread and considerable. For example in May 1941 the Belgians raised the Factory Guard to protect installations on the Germans' behalf. While Poland and the Low Countries had not supplemented Hitler's panzer forces, France was to prove to be a second Czechoslovakia.

Chapter Three

Dunkirk and North Africa

In the summer of 1940 throughout England's south-eastern ports, thousands of grimy and exhausted looking British soldiers embarked on trains and trucks. Like some badge of honour many had chalked 'BEF' on their battered helmets. The locals treated them as if they were conquering heroes, handing out hot tea and sandwiches amongst the ragged multitudes. While the soldiers were rightly relieved to be home safe and sound, having escaped total defeat at the hands of Hitler's panzers, they had left behind in northern France many comrades and all of Britain's available tank force. In terms of saving manpower the evacuation of the British Expeditionary Force (BEF) was a miracle; in terms of equipment losses the retreat was disaster of the first magnitude that could have proved fatal.

Many British officers were dismayed at having to abandon their equipment at Dunkirk. 'It was impossible to evacuate our heavy weapons and transport,' recalled Lieutenant Colonel Horrocks, 'so as soon as we got inside the bridgehead we were ordered to immobilise our vehicles and move on foot. The drivers hated doing this because in war each driver develops a feeling of affection for his own lorry or truck. It was a horrible sight – thousands of abandoned vehicles, carriers, guns and pieces of military equipment of all sorts. It was a graveyard of gear.'[1]

In the wake of Dunkirk, Hitler captured almost every tank the British Army possessed and most of its motor transport. The *Wehrmacht*'s haul of abandoned equipment included 600 tanks,[2] some 75,000 motor vehicles, as well as 1,200 field and heavy guns, 1,350 anti-aircraft and anti-tank guns, 6,400 anti-tank rifles, 11,000 machine guns and tens of thousands of rifles.[3] The events in France in May 1940 were a serious blow to Britain's armoured forces.[4]

The Mark VIB, armed with just a machine gun, was the most numerous British light tank by the late 1930s and it provided the majority of the tanks deployed to France. The Germans also captured numbers of the A9, A10 and A13 cruiser tanks all armed with a 2-pounder (40mm) gun as well as the Matilda I, armed with a machine gun, and heavier Matilda II infantry support tanks, equipped with a 2-pounder.[5] When war broke out in September 1939 the British only had two Matilda II in service, but a number were issued to the 7th Royal Tank Regiment in France. The British Army desperately threw fifty-eight Matilda Mk Is and sixteen Mk IIs at the 7th Panzer Division and the SS-Totenkopf Division at Arras. They overran the German gun batteries with ease forcing the panzers to counter-attack. While the Germans easily dealt with the Mk Is, the Mk IIs proved a tougher nut to crack and they lost at least a dozen tanks before the British counter-attack was stopped. This was a foretaste of what the Italian Army was to experience in North Africa.

In total the British lost twenty-nine Matilda IIs in France.[6] The Germans were understandably delighted to have Britain's heaviest tank fall into their hands for full technical exploitation. At Arras one of the Matilda IIs was discovered to have fourteen gouges where anti-tank rounds had failed to penetrate its armour. This meant when the Germans came up against British armour in North Africa and on the Eastern Front they were already thoroughly familiar with its capabilities and how to defeat them. The Germans were also to capture numbers of Matilda IIs in North Africa, Greece, Crete and Russia. Many were redeployed against their former owners.

After the Fall of France and the BEF's escape from Dunkirk, the British Army also found itself bereft of transport. When the war started the British Army had approximately 85,000 motor vehicles.[7] The bulk of these had been shipped to France with the BEF, but just over 5,000 were retrieved during the evacuation and the rest were left behind. More could have been saved but most were often abandoned prematurely, for example the Army had over 10,000 30-cwt light lorries, but over half were discarded. The Germans captured so many British Army 8-cwt trucks that they installed new bodywork and issued them to the German Army as the Kfz.15

In the wake of Dunkirk it has been estimated that Hitler ended up with about 345 operational British tanks that could have been re-used by the *Wehrmacht*.[8] Fortunately, he was unable to greatly profit from the capture of Britain's armour for, without access to spares, there was little the Germans could do to make them serviceable. Even so they were to re-deploy a number of Matilda tanks and universal carriers in different guises. The defeat of the BEF also caused the British Army a serious technological setback. The priority became making good the losses; this resulted in all technological development of new weapons being suspended while industry churned out those designs already available. By 1941 the Germans had begun to create a noticeable qualitative gap that the British were never able to close throughout the Desert War.

By the summer of 1940, despite the low priority placed on tanks, Britain's armoured units possessed about 240 medium and 108 cruiser tanks as well as 514 light tanks.[9] As the fighting with the Italians in North Africa escalated many were despatched to Egypt. By early July 1941, for the defence of the British Isles, the Army could muster 1,141 infantry and cruiser tanks; however, only 391 were considered fit for action. British repair facilities at this stage remained lamentable and a month later 25 per cent of the infantry tanks were still out of action, as were 157 of the 400 cruiser tanks.[10] The British motor industry went to work with gusto and vehicles were also ordered from the USA and Canada. Incredibly four months of increased production made good the losses of wheeled vehicles in France.

Following the defeat of France and the mauling of the British Army, the situation looked extremely grim for British interests in North Africa. When Mussolini declared war on 10 June 1940 it seemed certain that the Italian Army would attack eastward from the port of Bardia and Fort Capuzzo in Libya, with the intent of seizing the strategically important railhead fifty miles away at Mersa Matruh in Egypt. Initially this proved not to be the case. Mussolini had courted Hitler's militaristic embrace through the May 1939 Pact of Steel, which would eventually end in dramatic divorce. Mussolini, though, knew Italy would not be ready for war with the Western powers until 1941-42, but Hitler could not wait.

In the sun baked wastes of North Africa Hitler, under the Rome-Berlin Axis agreement, gained a vast Italian tank force, including three Italian armoured divisions by proxy. The Italians were to contribute in excess of 5,000 tanks to the Axis war effort in Africa and the Balkans. They were also to provide the Germans forces directly with around 1,000 tanks in metropolitan Italy after the relationship soured and Hitler occupied his former ally.

In 1940 there was a very real danger that the Italians would drive the under strength British forces from western Egypt and back across the strategically vital Suez Canal. In reality Mussolini's Italian panzers were to prove a pale shadow of their German cousins wreaking havoc throughout Europe. It was the inadequacies of Italian armour that was to embroil Germany in this secondary theatre of operations.

Mussolini gained an inflated impression of the capabilities of the Italian Army after his invasion of Abyssinia (modern day Ethiopia) and his intervention in the Spanish Civil War in the mid-1930s. Hitler and his pro-mechanised warfare advocates had watched with interest the Italian Army's performance during both wars. Hitler had tried to dissuade Mussolini from his Abyssinian conquest, seeing it as an unnecessary diversion, but in October 1935 Mussolini had thrown three army corps, some 500,000 men supported by Ansaldo light tanks, artillery, aircraft and poison gas against the doomed Abyssinians. The latter had attacked the steel monsters with their bare hands.

An Abyssinian counter-offensive in December drove the Italians back, ironically using German and Japanese weapons. The Italians had responded by bombing the Abyssinians stronghold at Amba Aradam using 170 aircraft and 280 guns. Airpower not tanks had been the deciding factor in Abyssinia. In May 1936 Mussolini annexed the country and then committed himself to General Franco's Nationalist cause in Spain. He had backed Franco with the *Corpo Truppe Volontarie* (CTV) some 50,000 strong, under General Mario Roatta (formerly head of Italian intelligence). The Italians supplied the CTV and Nationalists with a few hundred L.3/33 and L.3/35 tankettes.[11]

The Italians first saw action in the Malaga campaign during January–February 1937 when 10,000 Italian troops joined the Nationalist offensive. Franco was cunning, for he knew he could not lose and anticipated Mussolini's resolve would harden, despite international criticism, once his men had tasted victory. On this occasion nothing could stop the L.3/35s, because 30 per cent of the 12,000 Republican troops did not even have rifles and there was little ammunition for those who did. Roatta's CTV easily reached the coast and Malaga fell.

What is generally regarded as the first armoured clash of modern times took place in February 1937. During the battle at Guadalajara, north-east of Madrid, Italian light tanks proved all but useless in the face of local Republican air superiority and armour.[12] The Italian tanks were scattered by Soviet supplied fighter aircraft. Ironically the Nationalists were irritated by the pompous Italians and were almost as pleased as the Republicans when they suffered a series of military mishaps.

Nonetheless, by 1940 Mussolini considered himself the strongman of Africa having waged a series of brutal colonial wars during the 1930s. Superficially he was in a dominant position in Africa with half a million Italian and colonial troops under arms facing Commander-in-Chief Middle East, General Sir Archibald Wavell's, meagre force of 50,000. Mussolini could invade either British controlled Egypt or Sudan from

Libya or Italian East Africa. In North Africa, Commander-in-Chief, Air Marshal Balbo mustered two armies totalling 250,000 men, against an eventual motley collection of 36,000 British, Indian and New Zealand troops. In East Africa, Abyssinia and Eritrea, the Italians fielded 200,000 men under the Duke of Aosta. They could strike north into Sudan garrisoned by just 9,000 British and colonial troops, south into Kenya defended by 8,500 men or north-east into British Somaliland defended by a mere 537 men.

By no stretch of the imagination were the Italian forces mechanised in the same sense as the victorious German Army. The Italian Army in North Africa, in what is now Libya, consisted primarily of conscripted Italian and Libyan infantry. It was a marching force, short of everything, particularly tanks, transport and artillery, essentially all the modern necessities of war. In addition training was poor and, although the morale of the few tank and artillery units was good, the calibre of their guns was far too light.

Italian armour presented a major shortcoming being consistently too light, under gunned and under armoured. Initially the Italian forces in North Africa had very few tanks and those it did have were inadequate. In the Western Desert even the British Rolls-Royce armoured car, armed with the Boys anti-tank rifle, could easily penetrate the L.3's 12mm armour. Despite its shortcoming the latter was to remain in service until 1943, well past its sell-by-date.

In 1940 the Italian L.6/40 light tank appeared with a turret mounted 20mm Breda automatic cannon and co-axial 8mm machine gun. About 500 were produced, seeing service in North Africa, Yugoslavia and Russia. The first Italian medium tank was developed, just as war was breaking out, in the form of the M11/39, armed with a turret mounted 8mm Breda and a hull mounted 37mm with a limited traverse of thirty degrees. During most of 1940 it was the only medium tank available to the Italian Army.

The Italian 5th Army, equivalent to nine divisions, stationed in Tripolitania, initially guarded the French Tunisian border, but with the defeat of France and the formation of the pro-German Vichy government, Tunisia was no longer a security threat, although the Italians rapidly began to fear the Free French in Equatorial Africa. The 10th Army in Cyrenaica, consisting of five divisions, was bolstered with four from the 5th Army in June 1940, bringing the Italian forces facing Egypt up to some nine infantry divisions numbering about 250,000 men.

Despite the Italian Army's impressive statistics, it was really only adequate for policing duties or for fighting poorly armed locals, not for conducting a major offensive operation. The Italian generals knew this and, despite Mussolini's grandiose plans, the Italian Army was in no position to advance so the initiative passed to the British in Egypt. At the outbreak of hostilities the British had less than 10,000 men available, so a series of aggressive operations was conducted to keep the Italians off balance. Maddalena and Capuzzo were temporarily seized on 14 June. Three days later the Western Desert Force was created out of the HQ of 6th Division under Major General Richard O'Connor. But he only had a single armoured unit, two tank and two artillery regiments, and two infantry battalions in the immediate vicinity of Mersa Matruh.

The Italians suffered the first of many setbacks on 28 June when his own men shot down Marshal Balbo while coming in to land at Tobruk. Marshal Graziani took charge but repeated Balbo's demands to Rome for more supplies before attacking the British. Eventually in July 1940 seventy M11/39s were shipped to North Africa where they formed the Italian 4th Tank Regiment's 1st and 2nd Battalions. Unfortunately for the Italians the M11/39 proved mechanically unreliable.[13]

Earmarked for an advance in August on Sollum, Halfaya Pass and Sidi Barrani was General Berti's (known as the 'Sly Murderer') 10th Army. Under him was the 21st Corps consisting of three divisions supported by the Libyan divisions and the Motorised Maletti Group. The attack never took place and Graziani came under increasing pressure from Mussolini, seeking to emulate Hitler's blitzkrieg across France. Britain's A10 and A13 cruiser tanks were withdrawn from the frontier in anticipation of the attack. Amidst sporadic skirmishing a lone squadron of British tanks was left behind to watch the border, along with some armoured cars.

Fortunately for the British, the Italian Army did not have many tanks deployed in Mussolini's other colonial possessions in East Africa. They had about two dozen M11/39 medium tanks and thirty-five L.3s, and Italian efforts against the British there during 1940 were half-hearted at best. In July 6,500 Italian troops supported by two dozen tanks occupied Kassala just twelve miles inside Sudan. The following month the Italians attacked British Somaliland with a force also supported by tanks and artillery. The vastly outnumbered defenders withdrew to Kenya, where a British build-up was taking place ready for a knockout counter-offensive.

Graziani was finally forced to launch his attack in September 1940. Ironically those Italian divisions with desert mobility experience were in

Albania ready for the invasion of Greece. Graziani massed six divisions with the Libyan troops, spearheading General Bergonzoli's 23rd Corps, supported by the Maletti Group, which was to act as flank guard. The offensive commenced on 13 September with Graziani commanding the operation from way back at Tobruk with inadequate radio communication. Bergonzoli's 'blitzkrieg' advanced sixty-five miles into Egypt before digging in at Sidi Barrani and refusing to go any further for lack of armour and artillery.

Hitler's panzer specialists took a dim view of the Italian Army's capabilities. In the early 1930s Major Nehring, at the behest of Guderian, had been sent on an exchange with the Italian Army and examined their developing tank force. It is doubtful that he was very impressed with the pace of development or their tactical thinking. The L.3 tankette was just going into production and the Italians were six years away from producing their first medium tank. The M11/39 prototype appeared in 1937, whereas the Panzer III and IV went into limited production that year. Major Ferdinand Schorner, who later commanded a German Army Group, also served with the Italian Army during the mid-1930s as an interpreter.

In October 1940 von Thoma flew to North Africa to assess whether German troops should assist Mussolini's forces. Due to the dominance of the Mediterranean by the Royal Navy, Thoma reported back that it would not be possible to maintain two large German and Italian armies in theatre. He recommended sending at least four panzer divisions and conducting the attack toward the Nile with just German troops. Understandably Graziani did not want his men replaced by Germans. According to Thoma, at this stage Hitler was not greatly interested in driving the British from Egypt. Hitler, who had postponed the invasion of Britain and was now focused on Russia, told Thoma he could spare one panzer division to which Thoma responded it would be better not to help at all. Mussolini's inadequate armoured forces were to be left on their own until things reached crisis point.

Graziani had about sixty M11/39s to fend off seventy-five British Cruiser tanks (A9s, A10s and A13s), and 300 L.3s against 200 British light tanks. In October British reinforcements began to arrive, most significant of which were fifty Matilda (the II was dropped after 1940 when the Matilda I was withdrawn) Infantry tanks. This represented the most powerful weapon in the British tank inventory and its 80mm frontal armour could withstand every Italian gun in service. By December 1940 the Italian 4th Tank Regiment only had available twenty-three M11/39s to oppose the inevitable British counter-attack. Within months of the British North African campaign commencing, all the M11/39s were to be either destroyed or captured.

The Western Desert Force (predecessor of the 8th Army), some 36,000 men under General Wavell, launched a counter raid that soon developed into a full offensive. The Italians, outmatched and poorly motivated, did slowly improve their performance but by learning the hard way, and then it was largely too late. Initially they did not know how to conduct armoured warfare against the British. At Alam Nibeiwa on 9 November 1940 General Maletti's artillery continued to fire ineffectually until overrun by British tanks, while at Sidi Barrani and Bardia the British armour caused widespread panic. At Nibeiwa all the M11/39s were taken by surprise and destroyed without a fight by the advancing Matildas. General O'Connor slipped behind the Italians and their defences collapsed.

The British launched Operation Compass, their full-blown counter-stroke, on 9 December 1940, which miraculously rolled the Italians completely out of Egypt. In just three days they captured 38,000 Italian and Libyan prisoners, seventy-three light or medium tanks, 1,000 vehicles and 237 guns.[14] An exact count of the number of vehicles taken was not conducted due to the British Army's habit of keeping hold of anything that might be useful. Bardia fell on 3 January 1941 with the loss of another 40,000 Italian troops, followed on the 22nd, by Tobruk, which gave up 27,000 prisoners, 200 vehicles and 200 guns of various calibres.[15] The defenders also lost about ninety tanks.[16]

The remaining Italian forces were cut off at Beda Fomm on 5–7 February. Their inability to adapt to mechanised warfare had spectacularly dire consequences. General Babini's armoured brigade only had a few days to become familiar with the newly arrived replacement M13/40 tanks that were too lightly armoured and lacked radios. Over 100 were found around Beda Fomm; some were burnt out, but many were undamaged and the majority were recoverable. No count was made of the Italian light tanks taken, but 1,500 lorries were seized and many were pressed into service, along with 200 guns.[17] General Teller, Commander-in-Chief, 10th Army lost 21,000 men.

The Italian armoured forces were now in complete disarray. At Beda Fomm sufficient numbers of functioning M13s were captured to equip for a time the British 6th Royal Tank Regiment. Hitler's blitzkrieg, by proxy in North Africa, had ended as a complete and utter shambles, leaving the British occupying half of Libya. In total 10th Army lost

130,000 prisoners, almost 500 tanks (180 medium tanks and 300 light tanks), 845 pieces of artillery and thousands of wheeled vehicles.[18] The Italian Army was left reeling and Mussolini was furious that his military might had been squandered.

This was a brilliant victory, but unfortunately Wavell missed his opportunity to finish the Italians. Distracted by Mussolini's invasion of Greece on 28 October 1940 the momentum in North Africa was lost. Mussolini launched his attack from Albania, which he had invaded in April 1939 for just such a purpose. His two armoured divisions advanced slowly through the valleys of Epirus and met disaster in the Pindus gorges. The Italians were forced back to the frontier with the Greek Army pressing on their heels. The Greeks then penetrated thirty miles into Albania inflicting 30,000 casualties on the Italians.

When Hitler arrived in Florence on 28 October, for a conference with Mussolini about countering the British in the Mediterranean, he was presented with the invasion of Greece as a fait accompli. Mussolini saw this as sweet revenge for all the previous occasions that Hitler had taken military action without consulting him. Hitler was fuming as this was an unwelcome and ill-conceived distraction and he had already spent time dissuading Mussolini from invading Yugoslavia. To make matters worse Hitler had already been frustrated in his efforts against the British in the Mediterranean by the crafty Spanish dictator, General Franco, and the aging Vichy French leader, Marshal Petain.

Both Greece and Yugoslavia were to become victims of wider strategic interests. British Prime Minister Winston Churchill's ill-fated attempts to help Greece as well as distract Mussolini and Hitler from North Africa, once again saw a large number of British tanks fall into German hands. The 1st Armoured Brigade, New Zealand Division and 6th Australian Division, fully equipped at the expense of those forces in the Middle East, were despatched in early March. 1st Armoured Brigade consisted of the light tanks of the 4th Hussars and Matildas of the 3rd Royal Tank Regiment plus infantry, anti-tank gun and artillery support. Italian armour was no threat to British tanks, but Greek geography and Hitler's panzers were.

After disembarking at Salonika the brigade drove 500 miles to the Yugoslav frontier, wearing out what were already mechanically unreliable tanks. There they joined the Greek 12th and 20th Infantry Divisions as well as the under strength 19th Motorised Division. The latter had about a dozen F-17 light tanks, constituting Greece's sole armoured force. About fourteen Greek divisions were tied down in

Albania, leaving just seven and a half to cover the entire Yugoslav and Bulgarian frontiers, of which only three were defending vulnerable Macedonia. The neighbouring Yugoslavs had twenty-eight infantry divisions and three cavalry divisions, but they failed to mobilise in time and also had few tanks or anti-tank guns.[19]

Although the *Wehrmacht* was preparing for the invasion of Russia, Italian military incompetence in Albania and western Greece, coupled with a coup in Yugoslavia, forced Hitler's hand on 6 April 1941. He was alarmed by the prospect of the British presence in Greece; not only would this be a threat to his southern flank, it also meant British bombers would be in range of the vital Romanian oilfields at Ploesti, which were supplying Germany's industries and the *Wehrmacht*.

Threatened by German, Italian, Hungarian and Bulgarian forces the outcome for the ill-equipped Yugoslav and Greek armies was inevitable. The German 2nd Army struck from Austria, 46th Panzer Corps from Hungary and the 12th Army from Bulgaria. Yugoslav resistance lasted for twelve days. Two Yugoslav divisions east of Nis, lacking anti-tank guns, attempted to hold up three armoured brigades from General von Kleist's 14th Corps. The town fell on 8 April. After humiliating Mussolini in six months' of fighting the Greeks could not withstand Hitler's panzers either.

Salonika fell to the 2nd Panzer Division striking from Bulgaria on 9 April, destroying the 19th Motorised Division, and the Greek 2nd Army east of the River Varadar surrendered. The collapse of Yugoslavia also exposed the Greek troops fighting in Albania. 1st Armoured went into action alongside the Australians on 11 April south of Vevi, but was soon forced to withdraw. Tracks intended for the desert kept coming off and the lack of spares meant mechanical casualties had to be set ablaze and abandoned at the roadside by their crews.

In Albania the Greeks, lacking transport, were unable to withdraw fast enough and were soon cut off by the Germans and surrendered on the 20th. The Greek Central Macedonian Army suffered a similar fate. Yugoslavia surrendered on 17 April and Athens fell ten days later. The Germans seized the Yugoslavs' few French built FT-17 and Czech built T-32 tanks along with a handful of Greek light tanks.[20]

After Operation Demon, the evacuation of Greece, Churchill signalled General Wavell: 'We have paid our debt of honour with far less loss than I have feared.' The loss of troops was lower than might have been expected: some 2,000 killed or wounded and 14,000 captured out of a force of 58,000. Half the British forces were evacuated to Crete.

Once again, like Dunkirk, the loss of materiel was dire, 104 tanks, 8,000 transport vehicles, 296 guns and 209 aircraft.[21] The following month a major German airborne operation attacked Crete and the Allies lost another 1,751 dead, 1,738 wounded and 12,254 prisoners, along with eight Matilda tanks and thirteen light tanks.[20] The Matildas were handed over to Panzer Unit 212 for airfield defence and police duties.

Many questioned the wisdom of compensating for failing to help Poland, by sacrificing so much over Greece, especially when it was ruled by a military dictatorship. Valuable resources that could have been used to completely defeat Mussolini in North Africa were simply thrown away. In addition the German armed forces in the Balkans gained useful weapon stocks that could be used for police duties and to counter local partisans.

Yugoslavia was dismembered in the same manner as Poland; Mussolini annexed Dalmatia and western Slovenia, added Serbian Kosovo to his Albanian possession and set up a puppet state in Montenegro. Hitler wanted Serbian coal and copper so Serbia along with Croatia become independent pro-Nazi states, while he annexed central Slovenia; Hungary took the Backa and some frontier areas while Bulgaria occupied eastern Macedonia. Much of the burden for the occupation fell to the ill-equipped Italian 2nd and 9th Armies consisting of sixteen divisions and fifteen Blackshirt Legions based in western Yugoslavia.

Hitler also decided to come to Mussolini's rescue in North Africa. On 12 February Rommel arrived in Tripoli to command the *Deutsche Afrika Korps* and the emphasis switched from the Italian armed forces to the German *Wehrmacht*. From this point on the fighting was to be of a very different nature. In Cyrenaica the Italians assembled their remaining armoured forces, nominally independent of Rommel. This was the 20th Corps of Manoeuvre or *Corpo d'Armata di Manovra XX* (known as CAM), under General Gastone Gamara consisting of the Ariete Armoured and Trieste Motorised Divisions.

It is worth noting that much of the Axis armoured striking force during most of the desert war was Italian; both the Ariete and Littorio Divisions played an important part at Alamein. The Italian Army eventually had three armoured divisions in North Africa; the 131st Centauro, 132nd Ariete and 133rd Littorio as well as two motorised divisions, the 101st Trieste and 102nd Trente. All these forces were subordinate to German command and served Hitler's cause with mixed results. The armoured divisions were below strength; the tank regiments were supposed to consist of four battalions, but in reality were usually only one light and one medium battalion strong. This was largely due to Italy's inability to produce tanks fast enough.

The Ariete, the first Italian armoured division deployed to North Africa, did not arrive in Tripoli until January 1941 and was eventually destroyed at the second Battle of El Alamein. The Italians made their only attempt to create a true mechanised corps, with the CAM in the summer of 1941. The Littorio Armoured Division, after serving in Yugoslavia, arrived in North Africa in January 1942 and was also destroyed at El Alamein. The Centauro served in Greece and Yugoslavia, being sent to Tripoli in November 1942 and finally surrendered in Tunisia in 1943.

Once bolstered by the *Afrika Korps* the Italian armour showed a marked improvement in confidence and performance. For example, during the Axis re-conquest of Cyrenaica on 7 April 1941, units of the Ariete captured 2,000 men from an Indian Brigade, while at Halfaya Pass the Italian gunners gave a good account of themselves by knocking out seven of the ten attacking Matilda tanks. Italian potential briefly flared at Bir el Gobi on 19 November 1941 when, using German tactics, 137 M13/40s from the Ariete, with artillery support, threw back 159 British Crusader Mk VIs, claiming fifty kills. This British rebuff was due to their contempt of Italian capabilities based on previous experience at Beda Fomm.

The Italian Army, though, never really had a chance to prove itself; poorly motivated, badly led and inadequately equipped, it was outclassed, which led to an inferiority complex. Nor was this something the Germans helped to dispel. With the loss of ten divisions and 130,000 men, captured between 1940-41, the Italian Army received a body blow from which it could never recover, leaving the its armed forces in North Africa subservient to the *Deutsche Afrika Korps*.

Having co-opted Mussolini's armour, Rommel also quickly recycled abandoned Italian vehicles and artillery. The British had been unable to take away but a fraction of the equipment they had captured during 1940. In contrast, with German efficiency, they salvaged and repaired anything useful found lying unattended. Italian artillery soon appeared in German positions and reconditioned Italian lorries, cars and motorcycles were soon on the roads, sporting the palm tree and swastika insignia of the *Afrika Korps*. When General Gariboldi, Italian Commander-in-Chief North Africa, complained that the equipment was Italian property and should be promptly returned, Rommel was of a different opinion.[23] In addition he established Artillery Command 104, equipped with heavy siege guns to reduce Tobruk's defences; its inventory included eighty-four Italian 149mms, thirty-six Italian 105mms, forty-six French 150mms and twelve French 100mms.[24]

In the meantime the Italians were swiftly defeated in East Africa in early 1941, when Italian Somaliland was occupied by British troops, who then pushed into Abyssinia, at the end of February. In Eritrea the Italians put up a stiffer fight at Keren through February and March, until British Matilda tanks turned the tables. Lingering Italian resistance in Abyssinia was overcome by the end of November. Rommel meanwhile manoeuvred himself into position to make life very difficult for the British in Egypt.

Chapter Four

Rommel's Matildas

'Detachments of a German expeditionary force under an obscure general, Rommel, have landed in North Africa,' warned a British intelligence summary captured on the Eritrean front in March 1941.[1] Shortly afterwards that 'obscure' general stood, hands on hips, eyeing a captured British command vehicle - he was also to develop a liking for the British Matilda tank. By March 1941 Rommel had almost 160 panzers in place supported by sixty Italian tanks of dubious value in Cyrenaica. He quickly took the battle to the enemy and during the first two weeks of April reached the Egyptian frontier at Halfaya Pass, with just Tobruk holding out in his rear. There the Australian defenders refused to give in and it was the first time that the panzers drove through infantry who did not automatically surrender.

After the German attack on El Agheila on 24 March they began to press British vehicles into service. This was when Rommel gained two of his distinctive British trade marks. Amongst the haul were three Dorchester Armoured Command Vehicles, fifty Bren carriers and about thirty lorries.[2] 'The command trucks of the captured British generals stood on a slight rise,' recalled Lieutenant Heinz Schmidt who was on Rommel's staff. 'They were large, angular vehicles on over-size tyres, equipped inside with wireless and facilities for "paper" work. We christened them "Mammoths" then, but I did not realise that these useful trucks would be used by Rommel and his staff and commanders right through the long struggle that was now beginning in the Desert.'[3]

One of the Mammoths was issued to Major General Johannes Streich, commander of the 5th Light Division, another went to Rommel's Operations Officer, Staff Major Ehlert, while Rommel took the third for himself. Lieutenant Schmidt was allotted an open staff car similar to the one generally used by Rommel.

Schmidt remembered that Rommel himself was not adverse to a bit of personal scavenging:

Rommel inspected the vehicles with absorbed interest, after a brief interview with the captured British generals. He watched them emptied of their British gear. Among the stuff turned out he spotted a pair of large sun-and-sand goggles. He took a fancy to them. He grinned, and said, 'Booty - permissible, I take it, even for a General.' He adjusted the goggles over the gold braided rim of his cap peak. Those goggles for ever after were to be the distinguishing insignia of the 'Desert Fox'.[4]

Following the defeat of the Italians, fatefully the British 7th Armoured Division was withdrawn to Egypt for a refit just as Rommel was arriving. The 2nd Armoured Division comprising the divisional Support Group and the 3rd Armoured Brigade replaced it; the latter had just eighty-six tanks out of its full complement of 156. It did not help that the 6th Royal Tank Regiment was equipped with captured Italian M13s which, although they had been repaired, lacked radios.

When Rommel struck at Agheila 2nd Armoured conducted a fighting withdrawal. Losses were not serious but the mechanical reliability of the tanks was a growing concern and there were many breakdowns. Then on 2 April fifty enemy tanks bounced the Support Group from Agedabia and a large part of the division was overrun. The 3rd Armoured Brigade was sent to Mechili to cover the withdrawal. In the confusion the British Long Range Desert Group was mistaken for German and a Free French Battalion at Msus, 3rd Armoured's main supply depot, took what they needed and burned the petrol stocks. By the time the Germans reached Mechili the 3rd Armoured Brigade had little or no fighting value. The remains of the brigade, short of petrol and with just a dozen tanks, sped north to Derna only to be ambushed and destroyed on 6 April.

Rommel's conspicuous British Dorchester command vehicle almost became his coffin. Late on 19 April 1941 two British Hurricane fighter aircraft spotted Rommel's column just short of Gambut and swooped to attack three times. Rommel's driver was unable to pull down the armoured shutter in time and a bullet passed through him narrowly missing Rommel's head. When the attack was over the wounded driver was placed in the back and Rommel took the wheel of the Mammoth himself.

Winston Churchill was furious at the loss of the 3rd Armoured Brigade as a fighting force and wrote to General Wavell demanding to know what had happened. Wavell responded explaining the units involved were not ready for action and that his cruiser tanks were appallingly unreliable stating: '3rd Armoured Brigade practically melted away from mechanical and administrative breakdowns during the retreat, without much fighting, while the unpractised headquarters of the 2nd Armoured Division seems to have lost control.'⁵ There can be no hiding the fact that 3rd Armoured was an improvised formation with a regiment of inadequate cruiser tanks, a regiment of equally useless light tanks and a regiment armed with captured Italian tanks. All of this equipment ended up in the hands of the Germans.

Quickly recovering from the shock of the loss of 3rd Armoured Brigade and Wavell's expulsion from Libya, Churchill rallied round. He ordered Britain be stripped of every tank and aircraft that could be spared. This was at a time when the country's factories around Coventry were taking a hammering from the *Luftwaffe*. Churchill wrote to General Wavell on 22 April with an air of optimism and excitement: 'I have been working hard for you in the last few days, and you will, I am sure, be glad to know that we are sending you 307 of our best tanks through the Mediterranean, hoping they will reach you around 10 May. Of these 99 are cruisers, Mark IV and Mark VI, with necessary spare parts for the latter, and 180 "I" tanks.'⁶

The five ships of Churchill's 'Tiger' Convoy escorted by the Royal Navy passed Gibraltar on 6 May and he kept close tabs on its progress. One of the ships was lost after striking a mine, but the rest reached Malta three days later and pressed on to Alexandria unscathed, delivering 238 much needed tanks and forty-three Hurricane fighters. Conscious of the threat to Crete Churchill ordered a dozen infantry tanks be diverted there. Wavell responded that he had arranged for six infantry tanks and fifteen light tanks to be sent. Subsequently the Navy, feeling its luck could not hold in the Mediterranean, escorted another fifty cruiser and fifty infantry tanks round the Cape but they did not reach Suez until mid-July.⁷

Rommel's 15th Panzer Division was ready for deployment by the end of May, meaning that the bulk of those armoured forces facing any British threat would now be German rather than Italian. The German 5th Light Division (which became the 21st Panzer Division) was south of Tobruk, while the Ariete Division's tanks were on the perimeter, along with two Italian infantry divisions. All Generals Wavell's and O'Connor's successes had been swept away in a month. For the next two years Rommel was to fight a succession of British commanders and he was to perfect his defensive–offensive method of mechanised warfare: in Rommel's parlance first the shield then the sword.

While the 'Tiger Cubs' were prepared for action, the British attempted to drive the Germans away from the frontier before 15th

Panzer was ready for battle. Operation Brevity commenced on 15 May and saw the British Army lose yet more tanks to Rommel. The 22nd Guards Brigade with twenty-four Matildas was to capture Fort Capuzzo, while to the south 2nd Armoured's Support Group with twenty-nine cruiser tanks was to screen the attack with a push on Sidi Azeiz. The Guards made little headway losing five Matildas and thirteen damaged. Many of the cruiser tanks broke down on the way to Sidi Azeiz and more broke down on the way back. At Halfaya Pass the 15th Panzer Division captured seven Matilda tanks on 27 May 1941, three of which were still operational.

The *Wehrmacht* had quickly put samples of the British equipment captured in France to work, namely target practice, especially the 'I' or Infantry tanks. Such tests undoubtedly greatly assisted Rommel in North Africa. In fact following Dunkirk two of Rommel's captured Matilda Mk Is and two Mk IIs had been despatched to the Army Weapons Office test centre at Kummersdorf. Like the British, the Germans quickly decided that they had no further use for the Matilda I; in contrast they were impressed by the Matilda II as it outmatched the Panzer Mark IIIs and IVs in all but speed.

One Matilda was even pressed into service as a training aid in preparation for Operation Sea Lion, the proposed invasion of Britain in the summer of 1940. It was shipped off to Terneuzen, the German High Seas Instructional Command for loading practice on an engineer landing ferry, consisting of two barges cobbled together. While the Germans intended to dry land the bulk of their panzers at captured British ports, they also experimented with submersible and swimming tanks. At the end of 1942, with Sea Lion cancelled, the Matilda at Terneuzen, nicknamed 'Oswald', had its turret replaced by a 5cm gun and continued to be used for loading drills in landing craft along the Channel coast.

Churchill wrote to his Minister of Supply and the Chief of the Imperial General Staff in a state of irritation in late August 1941 bemoaning:

> We ought to try sometimes to look ahead. The Germans turned up in Libya with 6-pounder guns in their tanks, yet I suppose it would have been reasonable for us to have imagined they would do something to break up the ordinary 'I' tank. This had baffled the Italians at Bardia, etc. The Germans had specimens of it in their possession taken at Dunkirk, also some cruiser tanks, so it was not difficult for them to prepare weapons which would defeat our tanks.[8]

In response to the Matilda the Germans despatched Czech built Marder III self-propelled anti-guns to assist Rommel, but it was the German 88mm anti-aircraft gun that ended its reign as the 'Queen of the Battlefield'. Its days of dominance were numbered and the Matilda was withdrawn from service in North Africa by the end of July 1941, though it continued to serve with the Australians in the Far East. The Valentine, also armed with a 2-pounder gun, first appeared with the tank brigades of the 8th Army in June 1941.

While the Germans respected the Matilda, the new Cruiser Mk VI (A15) Crusader tank that also came with the 'Tiger' Convoy carried the same 2-pounder gun and its superior cross-country handling was nullified by its niggling unreliability. The Crusader was the most significant British tank deployed to North Africa, especially as approximately 5,300 were built, and the Germans captured large numbers intact. However, it was no real match for the panzers and was to be withdrawn by mid-1943. Under Operation Battleaxe, Churchill's ill-prepared 'Tiger Cubs' were thrown recklessly into action in June with the intention of overwhelming the panzers. Rommel was made of sterner stuff and fought a skilled defence followed by a counterstroke.

A large number of Churchill's 'Tiger Cubs' fell intact into Rommel's hands as a result of Battleaxe. The British committed about 100 Matildas to the offensive; sixty-four were lost, along with twenty-seven Cruiser tanks, and the Germans were left in possession of the battlefield.[9] When word reached Churchill, by his own admission he was disconsolate and retreated to his house at Chartwell for a while. 'Although this action may seem small compared with the scale of the Mediterranean in all its various campaigns', he said, 'its failure was to me a most bitter blow. Success in the Desert would have meant the destruction of Rommel's audacious force.'[10] Wavell took the blame and lost his job.

Some of the Matildas were subsequently issued to the panzer divisions; likewise the *Afrika Korps* put a number of Crusader tanks back to work, at least one was photographed sporting a swastika on its turret.[11] Lieutenant Schmidt confirmed the recruitment of Rommel's Matildas:

I accompanied Rommel on a personal inspection of the battlefield along the frontier from Halfaya to Sidi Omar. We counted 180 knocked-out British tanks, mostly Mark IIs [Matildas]. Some of them were later recovered from the battlefield, repaired, marked with the German cross, and in due course sent into battle against the men who had manned them before.[12]

When Panzergruppe Afrika was established, consisting of the 15th and 21st Panzer Divisions, they were equipped with about 170 Panzer Mark II, III and IV, as well as a dozen Matildas and seventeen Valentine Mk III.[13] Had Churchill known he would have been publicly outraged at the misuse of his 'Tiger Cubs,' while privately probably full of admiration for German ingenuity. Rommel's Matildas went into action with 21st Panzer on 14 September 1941, when three columns pushed into Egypt. A force of lorries, intent on looting a large British supply dump that in the event was found to be empty, followed the two main columns.

By November 1941 the 8th Army had come into being, and a second generation of British infantry and cruiser tanks along with American light Stuart tanks had reached North Africa. The production runs for Britain's early cruiser tanks was fairly limited consisting of 125 A9s, 175 A10s and 335 A13s. All were withdrawn from service in late 1941 having been replaced by the A15 Crusader and American Stuart. They enjoyed mixed success during Operation Crusader launched on 20 November. Like many British tanks the A15 remained plagued by mechanical problems, while the Valentine, the Matilda's successor, was not fast enough to match the panzers.[14]

The British massed 756 tanks, mostly Matildas and Valentines for Operation Crusader. Major General von Mellenthin recalled:

To meet this attack the Panzergruppe had 249 German and 146 Italian tanks. The Italian tanks, with their inadequate armour, and low velocity 47mm guns, were decidedly inferior to all categories of tank on the British side, and moreover they were mechanically unreliable.

Of the German tanks, seventy were Mark IIs, which only mounted a heavy machine gun, and could therefore play no part in the tank battle, except as reconnaissance vehicles. The bulk of our strength consisted of thirty-five Mark IVs and 139 Mark IIIs, we also had five British Matildas, of which we thought highly.[15]

Once more the British tanks were lured into a trap sprung by concealed armour and anti-tank guns and the attack quickly came unstuck. Nonetheless, the British held on and Rommel lost by a narrow margin. His two panzer and single Italian armoured division were over extended and he was forced to retreat. Churchill records:

We now know from German records that the enemy losses in the

'Crusader' battle, including the garrisons now cut off at Bardia, Sollum, and Halfaya and later made prisoners, were about 13,000 Germans and 20,000 Italians, a total of 33,000, together with 300 tanks. The comparable British and Imperial Army losses in the same period (18 November to mid-January) were; 2,908 officers and men killed, 7,339 wounded, and 7,457 missing; total, 17,704, together with 278 tanks. Nine-tenths of this loss occurred in the first month of the offensive.[16]

During these engagements Rommel's Matilda tanks caused confusion on both sides. Lieutenant Schmidt, posted to the 15th Panzer Division, was involved in the capture of a British tank recovery vehicle in November 1941 near Sidi Azeiz. Afterward heading southward toward Maddalena he was alarmed to be informed that he had British tanks behind him. Three anti-tank-guns were set up to block twelve advancing Matildas, two were destroyed and the rest fanned out. Schmidt and his gunners were in danger of being surrounded and were considering retreating when two more Matildas came up behind them. Schmidt takes up the story:

> I glanced back with a vague idea of withdrawal if that were possible amid this fire. To my horror I saw two more British Mark IIs moving towards us.
>   Then to my gasping relief I recognised swastika markings on them: they were two of the British tanks that had been captured at Halfaya during 'Battleaxe' months before. The tanks growled right up alongside me. I exchanged a few swift words with the sergeant-major commanding them. 'Get cracking back to the column with your guns, Herr Leutnant,' he shouted. 'I will keep you covered.'[17]

The British, assuming that Schmidt and his men had been captured, broke off their attack long enough for him to flee with Rommel's Matildas covering their retreat.

Following Operation Crusader Rommel's forces enjoyed another major windfall. He signalled the German High Command stating:

> In the continuous heavy fighting between the 18th November and the 1st of December, 814 enemy armoured fighting vehicles and armoured cars have been destroyed, and 127 aircraft shot down. No estimate can yet be given of the booty in arms, ammunition and vehicles. Prisoners exceed 9,000, including three generals [who in fact were brigadiers and colonels].[18]

A captured Crusader tank was sent back to Kummersdorf for closer inspection.

Despite this everything was far from rosy for Rommel, who by early December, had lost 142 panzers, twenty-five armoured cars and 390 lorries not to mention losses in artillery and anti-tank guns.[19] Only his transportation worries were eased by the capture of considerable numbers of British lorries and trucks. However, in the closing months of December, during three days of heavy fighting Rommel destroyed or captured 111 British tanks and twenty-three armoured cars.[20]

British war correspondents touring the battlefields found ample evidence of the Germans re-employing British tanks. At Halfaya Pass the Germans had removed the turrets from captured British 'I' tanks and sunk them into concrete to provide armoured gun positions. Alexander Clifford recalled: 'A whole row of these straddled the main road a little short of Sollum.'[21]

Clifford and Alan Moorehead visited the smashed and derelict Axis airfield at Gambut. Clifford recalled:

Then we turned aside along a track leading to the coast where, we had been told, a big German tank-repair workshop had been captured intact. The track, a river of dust, writhed down among the wadis until, stretched along the shore, we found tents and huts and stone shelters and trucks and dumps, and the uncouth black shapes of tanks. We examined them carefully through glasses first; for there might easily be Germans there still, and there were certainly no British. But all we saw was ragged Bedouins, creeping about with sacks on their shoulders.

There were thirty-eight tanks in all, hulking great Mark IVs, smaller cruisers, even one or two new British A15s with German black-and-white crosses superimposed on their regimental colours. There were big troop-carrying tractors and every sort of lorry and staff car.[22]

Alan Moorehead added:

The tanks workshops eclipsed anything we had in the forward areas. Bedded in concrete and under canvas were big lathes. Cases of tank precision instruments worth thousands of pounds lay about. One was full of periscopes. Several huge boxes contained new 50mm guns which apparently could be fitted to damaged tanks in this place. There were sheets of armour, new tracks and tyres, a mass of woodwork and steel parts. It almost seemed that they could have built a tank here in the desert by the sea.

The richest prize was about thirty tanks of all kinds which the Germans had left lying about. These tanks had been brought in for repair, and when the retreat was ordered they had been set on fire.[23]

Senior British officers came to appreciate the necessity of recycling captured equipment by 1942. 'There was an odd atmosphere about this desert war; noted Major General Horrocks, now commanding 8th Army's 13th Corps after his escape from Dunkirk: 'that is between the Germans and ourselves. Owing to the constant "to-ing and fro-ing" both armies lived alternately on each other's rations and used quite a quantity of each other's captured equipment.'[24]

By mid-January 1942 Rommel's panzer army was exhausted, but his shorter supply routes meant that he soon bounced back to reach Gazala. He received welcome armoured vehicle reinforcements via Tripoli and before the impending battle the British also introduced additional new equipment, which helped offset early deficiencies. The American built M3 General Grant met with approval, it was reasonably fast, reliable and its 75mm gun could take on German armour and anti-tanks crews on a more equal footing. The only problem was that the gun was mounted on the righthand side of the hull, thereby greatly restricting its arc of fire.

Rommel launched his counter-stroke on 20 January 1942 with 111 panzers and eighty-nine Italian tanks. When the British 2nd Armoured Brigade came up against the *Panzerarmee Afrika* between 21-23 January it lost seventy tanks. The 15th Panzer Division then overran Msus airfield capturing ninety-six tanks, thirty-eight guns and 190 lorries on 24 January.[25] The only thing that marred this operation was a dispute with the Italians resulted in the *Corpo d'Armata di Manovra* being held back.

A triumphant Rommel wrote home to his wife on 27 January:

Everything O.K. here. We're clearing up the battlefield, collecting up guns, armoured cars, tanks, rations and ammunition for our own needs. It will take some time. It's chilly again and rainy, though the rain has its advantages, as it prevents the British getting their planes off the ground from their airfields in Cyrenaica.[26]

In February Walther Nehring, promoted to lieutenant general, flew to North Africa to take command of the *Afrika Korps*. He was wounded during the summer and flown home, being succeeded by von Thoma.

During 1942 the British captured a strange looking armoured vehicle that looked like the uneasy marriage of an ancient agricultural tractor with a field gun. What they had stumbled upon was an example of the Germans unique ability to recycle military equipment that fell into their hands. For the British it was one of the first examples of Hitler's great panzer heist. In reality of course he had been conducting a deliberate policy of misappropriation since 1938. The vehicle was actually a French Lorraine Schlepper tracked carrier mounting a German 15cm howitzer belonging to the Panzer Artillery Battalion of the 21st Panzer Division.

Courtesy of the American Lend-Lease Act, by October 1942 600 medium Grant tanks had arrived in Egypt. The Germans in contrast had to make do by adding additional armour to their existing Panzer Mk IIIs. By mid-1942 the *Afrika Korps* began to receive some Panzer Mk III Specials armed with a longer barrel 50mm gun and protected by spaced armour. The Italians were mainly equipped with the M13/40 (only eighty-two M15/42 were built) but also began to receive new armour in the form of the 75/18 Semovente self-propelled gun. The later first saw action with the Ariete Division in early 1942. British tank strength at 849 seemed unstoppable against the German figure of 560, but the German tanks were of a better quality and the Axis still enjoyed air superiority.

Rommel struck in May seizing Tobruk, where he captured about fifty tanks of all classes from the dispirited garrison.[27] Seized British transport greatly assisted this success as war correspondent Alan Moorehead testifies:

There was little or no difference in the colour of the vehicles of both sides - indeed the Germans by now were using many of our trucks. And so the enemy traffic mingled with the British traffic on the roads and tracks leading into town, and westwards towards [General] Klopper's headquarters. Men who were riding back to the dumps for supplies heard horns blowing behind them. They waved the approaching vehicles on, and as they passed the British drivers looked up and saw they were full of Germans. By now the enemy was more desirous of infiltrating right through the fortress, of stabbing it in the heart, than taking prisoners. British and German vehicles rode down the roads together and by-passed one another without opening fire. All over the plain and among the wadis, the British were coming out holding up their hands.[28]

Additionally Moorehead notes the capture of Tobruk was a significant boost for Rommel's war chest:

> In equipment alone the enemy won the richest treasure the desert had ever yielded. Rommel had here enough British vehicles, enough tanks and guns, enough petrol and fuel and enough ammunition to re-equip at once and drive straight on Egypt. The road lay open before him.[29]

By the time Rommel had taken Tobruk his forces had captured or destroyed over 1,000 armoured fighting vehicles and almost 400 guns, as well as seizing 45,000 prisoners.[30] Rommel's reward for capturing Tobruk was elevation to field marshal.

Rommel's forces were extremely good at recovering tanks from the battlefield. After the Battle of Gazala in May 1942 Colonel Desmond Young, commanding officer of the Indian Public Relations unit, complained bitterly:

> I don't understand why we aren't following up. Why aren't the Indians going in after them? We could have occupied the battlefield yesterday and grabbed all those Jerry tanks lying about. The Germans themselves are milling about all over the place.[31]

Alexander Clifford was equally impressed by the Germans salvage abilities noting:

> The Germans showed brilliant skill and much courage in their tank-recovery organisation. Lame tanks were dragged from the battle while the firing was still on, tended in a mobile workshop almost on the spot, and flung back into the fighting next day. Our recovery units worked themselves to exhaustion, but they simply were not organised like that. They were like doctors coping with a sudden epidemic - they had far more patients than they knew how to deal with.[32]

At Bir Hakeim, on the southern tip of the 8th Army's lines, Free French forces destroyed thirty-two Italian tanks in May 1942, while the British fell back to a place called El Alamein and blunted the German advance. In August Rommel launched a strong armoured thrust and was stopped at Alam Halfa. By early July the depleted Germans had just fifty tanks and the Italians fifty-four whereas their actual authorised strength should have been 370 and 430 respectively. Rommel subsequently made use of a few batteries of captured British 25-pounder guns after 1,500 rounds of ammunition was seized at Deir el Shein in July.[33]

The turning point for Rommel finally came in October/November 1942 by which time his forces were completely outnumbered in terms of manpower and equipment. Crucially the 8th Army had amassed 1,029 tanks (170 Grants, 252 Shermans, 294 Crusaders, 119 Stuarts and 194 Valentines) against 491 Axis tanks (175 Mk IIIs, 38 Mk IVs and 278 Italian M13/40s). With the arrival of the Sherman, the Grants were despatched to Burma to replace the British forces' Matildas, Stuarts and Valentines. After much heavy fighting the Germans were thrown back with the loss of over 400 irreplaceable tanks. The 8th Army lost half its tank force but 350 were repairable.

Rommel's fate was sealed with the Allied landings in his rear on 8 November 1942 in French Morocco and Algeria. Nehring flew into Tunisia to organise the German and Italian defences to protect Rommel's rear. Once he had stabilised the situation he handed his command over to General von Arnim and flew back to Europe. In Tunisia the Germans encountered the British Churchill tank, though they had already examined this tank at close quarters following the disastrous Dieppe raid on 19 August 1942. Some twenty-eight Churchills were put ashore and the Germans salvaged twenty-three of them consisting of six Mk Is, seven Mk IIs and ten Mk IIIs. After technical exploitation at Kummersdorf most of these tanks ended up being used for target practice due to the lack of spares and ammunition.[34]

Despite the Germans' efforts, once squeezed into Tunisia, there could be only one outcome for the *Afrika Korps* and at the end of February 1943 Rommel flew out of North Africa for the last time. By April the Germans just had sixty-nine operational tanks and had run out of petrol.[35] When von Arnim surrendered the following month the Axis' remaining 250 tanks, 1,000 guns and thousands of motor vehicles fell into the Allies' hands along with 250,000 prisoners.[36] Rommel's Matilda and Crusader tanks had long since been lost on the vast battlefields of North Africa.

Chapter Five

The French Heist

At 06.00 on 23 June 1940, just one day after the French capitulation, Hitler took a whirlwind three-hour tour of Paris. His cavalcade drove beneath the Arc de Triomphe down the Place de la Concorde and then he stood as the conquering hero in front of the iconic Eiffel Tower. Before him lay not only France's architectural treasures but also her considerable weapons industries. Accompanying Hitler was the architect Albert Speer, the man who was to play the central role in Nazi Germany's wartime weapons production. Hitler's propagandists had a field day; it was all smiles and laughter. Here was the Führer at the height of his power surveying his vanquished foe.

Italian leader Benito Mussolini opportunistically moved to profit from France's plight and his tanks were soon attacking his helpless and distracted neighbour. Belatedly on 11 June 1940, he cynically threw thirty-two divisions at the French frontier, but they made practically no impression against just six French divisions. In retaliation the French Navy bombarded Genoa's factories, oil tanks and refineries, though the dithering French High Command forbade further offensive operations against Italy.

Although Mussolini's bombers ranged as far as the Loire Valley, on the ground the Italian blitzkrieg failed to materialise. Only when the German panzers came sweeping down the Rhone Valley could Mussolini claim victory over the French Army. From this poor performance Hitler and his generals must have known that his ally's tanks were unlikely to make much impression against the British in Egypt. The Franco-German armistice was signed on 22 June 1940, followed by the Franco-Italian Armistice two days later when the war in France officially came to an end. The Italians wanted the Rhone Valley, including the naval bases at Toulon and Marseilles as well as the disarmament of Corsica, Djibouti and Tunisia. Mussolini got nothing but a few hundred battered French tanks for his trouble.

Hitler was determined France would be a repeat of Czechoslovakia. Indeed after the destruction of Czechoslovakia, France was to be the scene of Hitler's next great panzer heist. In total the French had built well over 6,500 tanks by the outbreak of the Second World War; in May 1940 just over 50 per cent of these were operational. Faulty French intelligence indicated they were facing 6,000 German tanks.[1]

Despite popular perceptions, France had some of the finest tanks in the world. French armour was certainly equal in quality and quantity to that of the Germans. France's military collapsed in May 1940 not because of poor tank resources but because of the inability to use them effectively in containing the *Wehrmacht*'s blitzkrieg tactics. During the First World War France had almost been the very first country to produce the tank and was only just beaten by Britain. Its early assault artillery, little more than guns in steel boxes, was at best crude but led to the highly successful Renault FT-17 light tank. A new production programme during the rearmament of the 1930s ensured France had far more sophisticated tanks than Britain or Germany and with better armament.

France even pioneered the first armoured division with the *Division Legere Mecanique* (DLM - light mechanised division) combining tanks, armoured cars, motorised infantry and artillery. In 1939 it formed the *Division Cuirassee* (DCR), its first real tank division, and by the following year had three DLMs and four DCRs. The Char B1 tank, supported by some of the older Char D2, constituted the main striking force of the DCR, while the H-35/39, R-35 and S-35 tanks equipped the DLM and the light battalions of the DCR. After the Second World War General Gamelin, commander of the French Armed Forces, admitted that the French tank force was vastly better equipped to deal with German tanks, than the Germans were to deal with French ones. At the time it did them no good whatsoever.

While the French had some excellent tanks, the myriad of different types compared with Germany, proved a logistical headache. For example, French ordnance officers were faced with tanks ranging from the tiny Renault FT, through the modern Somua S-35 to the heavy Char B. Also the design of French tanks resulted in crews feeling isolated from each other. The French mindset was to treat tanks as armoured cavalry, using them for reconnaissance and screening work. Added to this was a lack of training and, importantly, tank radios. The failure to coordinate effectively with the rest of the French Army was to have one simple outcome. When war came France's armoured divisions were too dispersed in defensive formations, air cover was non-existent (thousands of French aircraft remained at safe airfields) and French anti-tank guns remained in storage.

In the face of crushing defeat the equipment of France's three armed services suffered very different fates. The bulk of the French Army's 3,200 tanks, that had not been destroyed in the fighting, fell almost intact into German hands. Hitler captured 2,400 French tanks that were in a re-useable condition, of which 560 were eventually converted into self-propelled guns. As a result many French tanks were, from mid-1941, modified and issued for use in Finland, France, North Africa, Russia and the Balkans. Perhaps most tragically they were also to be used by Vichy French forces against the Allies and fellow Frenchmen in North Africa and the Middle East.

In contrast most of the French Air Force fled or was destroyed during the Battle for France and Britain made sure the French Fleet was not taken by sinking part of it at Mers-el-Kebir. After the armistice there were 4,200 French military aircraft in the unoccupied zone and 2,648 in France's North African territories. Although safely out of German reach some argued they would have been better employed defending France from attack in May 1940.

Defeated France was divided into three, the northern German Occupied Zone including the coast down to Spain, the unoccupied south or Free Zone and thirdly the industrial north-east. The local authorities under the watchful eye of the German armed forces ran the Occupied Zone, while a 'sovereign' government in the resort town of Vichy controlled the Free Zone. France's industrial region was treated as a separate entity run directly by the German military authorities in Brussels. Special military authorisation was required for Frenchmen to enter this area.

Hitler's decision for this rather strange arrangement was partly motivated by the desire to keep the powerful French fleet out of British hands. By allowing the existence of Vichy it ensured the fleet remained French and ensured a rival government in exile was not set up in French North-west Africa to contest the occupation of metropolitan France. Vichy France was authorised to maintain an 'Armistice Army' of 100,000 men without heavy equipment, and the French Navy. France's armoured forces lay prostrate at the feet of Hitler who began to eye them as a way of supplementing his seemingly invincible panzer divisions.

The Germans did not take long to start looting vehicles in Paris. From late August they began to confiscate private cars, especially black Citroens, on the grounds that they were needed for the planned invasion of Britain. The buses were also requisitioned by the German Army for a variety of military organisations all keen on sightseeing in Paris. Petrol shortages ensured that the only cars on the streets were grey German military vehicles or the black civilian cars pressed into service.

Hitler's occupation of France not only geographically split the nation but also politically, over the issue of collaboration. Millionaire French automobile entrepreneur Louis Renault was to be greatly tainted by his work for the Nazis. Like Marshal Petain, who was to head Vichy, he was a hero of the First World War. Renault along with Colonel J.E. Estienne was the father of the FT-17 light tank which first saw action on 31 May 1918. This tank was very portable and proved a huge export success worldwide during the inter-war years.

In one fell swoop Germany captured France's major defence industries, including Citroen outside Paris, Laffly and Matford (Ford) at Asnieres, Peugeot at Sochaux, Renault at Billancourt and Somua at Saint-Quen. The Germans were soon en route to Billancourt, outside Paris, one of France's main tank manufacturing plants. Just before the final escape of the British Expeditionary Force from Dunkirk, having knocked out the French Air Force base at Le Bourget, 300 German bombers had attacked Billancourt.[2] They struck targets around Paris on 3 June. Their main objectives were the airfields at Le Bourget, Orly and Villacoublay; while the attack on the Renault works missed, the Citroen plant was set on fire and heavily damaged.

A Daimler-Benz executive was appointed German overseer at Renault and pressure was put on Louis Renault to repair Renault built tanks for the *Wehrmacht*. Initially he agreed until a senior colleague pointed out if they started repairing French tanks for the Germans they would soon be expected to build them for the Germans. Most of his foremen and directors supported his refusal to cooperate, threatening to resign if they were forced to work on Renault tanks. Regardless of German threats they continued to refuse and the Germans backed down. France's other tank manufacturers followed suit, forcing the Germans to maintain the tanks themselves. The German invasion also disrupted French tank orders for Poland, Romania and Poland.

This setback did not prevent the *Wehrmacht* from utilising considerable quantities of French armour. Despite Renault's stance, undoubtedly there was a level of complicity by the French military and French industry as the Germans sought spares, technical details, training manuals and production information. German tank crews, mechanics and other workshop staff spent time at the Renault Poissy works learning how to handle and maintain French tanks. The yard there was filled with captured Char Bs and Renault R-35s. Occupied Czechoslovakia had not thwarted them in a similar quest and had provided Germany's desperately under-equipped tank arm with over 400 tanks as well as the all-important factories to build more. The Germans were determined that France's armour would not escape similar assimilation.

The French Chars de Battaille Renault B1 Bis armed with a 47mm turret gun, a powerful 75mm hull gun and two machine guns was, on paper, an impressive piece of kit. The 47mm was the best weapon of its kind at the time and the tank's steering system was ahead of anything the Germans had. The 1st Panzer Division discovered how ineffective its 20mm and 37mm guns were against the thickly armoured Char B around Juniville. A two-hour tank battle resulted in heavy German casualties before they prevailed. Similarly a second French tank attack had to be driven off. The B1s were able to give a good account of themselves, but generally they saw little action against the invading panzers. Approximately 345 were produced in the factories of Renault, Schneider, F.C.K, F.A.M.H (St Charmond) and AMX. Some were even sent to Kassel in Germany where they were converted into flamethrowers.

Considerable numbers of Somua S-35, the best French tank in 1940 and perhaps in Europe, Renault R-35 (the FT-17 replacement) and the Char Lagers Hotchkiss H-35/H-39 fell intact into German hands. The Germans also took into service limited numbers of the FT-17 light tank, of which some 3,000 had been manufactured, and the four-wheeled A.M.D Panhard type 178 armoured car for policing duties. Italy also took into service quantities of captured Renault R-35 and Somua S-35 tanks after the defeat of France. [3]

Having captured such a vast quantity of French tanks, the Germans set about forming enough regiments to establish four panzer divisions equipped with 399 Hotchkiss and 190 Somua tanks. These tanks though were soon deemed unsuitable for frontline service and as units became operational they tended to be re-quipped with Czech or German built tanks. Despite Renault's protestations it seems that 850 R-35 tanks were overhauled at his factories in Paris.[4] However, because they were slow, only about 100 were actually issued for infantry support and security duties, while twenty-five were sent to the Balkans to help fight partisans. About 400 were also used as self-propelled gun chassis or as artillery tractors.[5]

A large number of French tanks of a questionable combat value were converted into much more useful self-propelled guns, by adding anti-tank guns or howitzers, such as the 105mm or 150mm.[6] In 1943 French chassis were converted to tank destroying roles by mounting 37mm, 47mm and 75mm PaK anti-tank guns on them. Small numbers were produced on Hotchkiss and F.C.M chassis, the Marder I being one such example. This was constructed on the chassis of the captured Lorraine carrier and called the *Panzerjäger* für 75mm Pak 40/1 (Sf) Lorraine Schlepper (f) and Becker converted 184 between 1942-43. They also were deployed to France and likewise saw service in the Normandy battles of 1944.

In fact, surprisingly, a significant proportion of German self-propelled guns were mounted on foreign chassis. One of the best was the 150mm SFH 13/1 auf GW Lorraine Schlepper(f), which consisted of an obsolete Krupp 1917 150mm gun converted to fit the Lorraine tracked munitions and personnel carrier by the German firms Becker and Krefeld. The gun, although really too heavy for the chassis, was nonetheless effective. It was first employed by Rommel in 1942 in North Africa and saw service on all fronts until the end of the war. About twenty-four Lorraine Schlepper were also converted with the 150mm Le FH 18, as well as forty-eight on the Hotchkiss H-39 chassis, twenty-four on the F.C.M chassis and a few Char Bs. All of these odd looking hybrids served in France seeing action during the Normandy campaign against the Allies.

The other *Panzerjäger* types using foreign chassis were relatively unimportant and were produced in small numbers compared with the entirely German models. The ex-French Renault R-35, designated the 47mm Pak 36 (t) auf GW Renault R-35(f), and the Hotchkiss H-39 tanks were fitted with 47mm Czech guns and the PaK 40, but only about twenty of the Hotchkiss, mounting the 75mm PaK 40 L/46, were converted. Once again the occupying forces in France mainly used these vehicles.

On top of France's medium and light tanks, the Germans also gained the remnants of a fleet of 6,000 tracked infantry carriers, which they employed as the Infanterie Schlepper UE 630(f). About half were sent to an assembly plant at Paris-Issy les Moulineaux and overhauled under the direction of the German company MAN (Maschinenfabrik Augsburg-Nurnberg). The windfall of other vehicles from the defeated French Army was massive and included trucks as well as half and full track vehicles, some of which were to be converted by the Germans. Hitler narrowly missed out on 10,000 American trucks, worth $15 million, ordered by the French military. The bulk of the order was not delivered and was diverted to Britain where they became known as 'ex-French contract vehicles'.

Although Renault and the other French tank manufacturers refused to fully cooperate in repairing France's tanks, it did not stop them accepting lucrative contracts to build lorries for the *Wehrmacht*. The French motor vehicle industry was vast; after the First World War Andre Citroen and Louis Renault had competed in Paris to supply the second largest car market beyond America.[7] Notably Renault's factories had a record of militancy and in the late 1930s the Billancourt works had been occupied by part of the workforce, striking for better working conditions. In the end the authorities had sent in the police with tear gas to disperse the strikers.

Prior to the war Renault had not been greatly concerned with defence contracts and after the industrial turmoil had been trying to increase car production rather than tanks. In 1940 military output only accounted for 18 per cent of his overall output. To make matters worse French mobilisation had taken 22,000 of his 30,000 strong labour force.

The Germans, using whatever methods were deemed necessary, successfully prevailed upon Renault and the other big French motor manufacturers such as Citroen, Matford the American Ford franchise in France and Peugeot to accept substantial orders for motor vehicles. They produced well in excess of 50,000 trucks for the Germans,[8] tens of thousands of which were to see operational service with the *Wehrmacht*, in particular on the Eastern Front.

France's final ignominy was to have to pay 400 million francs a day as a contribution to her defence against Britain, some of which went toward the Atlantic Wall. French financial support to Hitler's war effort was colossal, 'occupation costs' alone amounted to $7 billion. On top of this the Bank of France was obliged to provide Germany with credit grants worth another $1.1 billion.[9] In the case of the Low Countries these imposed costs amounted to two thirds of their national income.

By the spring of 1941 a number of German units had been equipped with French tanks ready for the assault on the Soviet Union. They were also issued with several hundred French armoured cars. Hitler expanded the number of his panzer divisions by converting some of the infantry divisions; one such unit was the 18th Panzer Division, which was formed from elements of the 4th and 14th Infantry Divisions. When Major General Walther Nehring took command of the 18th Panzer on 25 October 1940, he was displeased to discover that it lacked heavy equipment, weapons and vehicles.

Earmarked for the invasion of the Soviet Union the division deployed to Prague in March 1941 to make its preparations. The division's officers were despatched to Paris to oversee the shipment of French tanks, which were eminently not suited to Russia's terrain or climate. Nor were the crews given sufficient time to familiarise themselves with vehicles that they soon discovered had limited vision, were labour intensive and heavy on fuel consumption.[10]

The first unit to see action using French tanks was the 211th Panzer Battalion equipped with S-35s and H-39s. This battalion attacked Russia from the Finnish front on 22 June 1941 in support of the Finnish Army's attempted push on Leningrad and the German attack toward Murmansk. For the main assault on the Soviet Union Colonel General Guderian commanded the 2nd Panzergruppe part of Army Group Centre attacking Ukraine; one of his three Panzer Corps included the 18th Panzer Division.

At 03.15 on 22 June Guderian's artillery began softening the Russian defences followed by a dive-bomber attack twenty-five minutes later. The advance units of the 17th and 18th Panzer Divisions crossed the River Bug at 04.15. Half an hour later the lead tanks of Nehring's 18th Panzer forded the Bug. Shortly after Guderian joined Nehring for the crossing of the Lesna and stayed with the division until mid-afternoon. The following morning he returned to check on the progress of Major General von Arnim's 17th Panzer and then Nehring's 18th.

Guderian's first divisional operational objective was reached on 16 July when the 29th (Motorised) Infantry Division entered the city of Smolensk. The following day the division crossed the Dnieper and captured the industrial areas on the north bank. In the meantime the Russians massed twenty divisions at Gomel to threaten Guderian's right flank and they began to counter-attack at Elnya. Nehring's division was committed to the heavy fighting to trap Red Army forces defending Kiev, which fell on 20 September with more than 30,000 prisoners. In October the division was despatched to capture Fatesh and relieve the 9th Panzer Division.

By October the weather began to turn and Guderian's panzers found themselves in a sea of mud. Towropes had to be dropped by the *Luftwaffe* to the stranded crews. Up to this point the Germans had enjoyed tank superiority, but now the panzers were coming up against increasing numbers of the well designed and mass produced T-34. The following month 18th Panzer Division found it had just 30 per cent of its tanks left. It soldiered on until the end of 1943 when as a result of its losses it was reorganised into the 18th Artillery Division.

On 20 December 1941 Guderian flew to Hitler's HQ at Rastenburg in East Prussia. Due to the lack of cold weather clothing for the troops and the inability to effectively counter the T-34, Guderian urged Hitler to allow a withdrawal to the prepared Susha-Oka defensive line for the winter. Hitler's answer was an emphatic no. Five days later, with his infantry divisions under growing Soviet pressure, Guderian ordered the withdrawal. Disobeying Hitler's orders could not go unpunished and Guderian was transferred to the officer reserve pool.

Following the invasion of Russia two new panzer divisions came into being, the 22nd and 23rd in France in September 1941. These may have initially been issued with French armour but, by this stage, the short-comings of French tanks was well appreciated and when they deployed to the Eastern Front the following year, it was with German and Czech armour. Limited numbers of French tanks including a few converted to flame throwers were sent to the Crimea in mid-1942 to assist German and Romanian forces fighting there.

When the 6th Panzer Division arrived in France from the Eastern Front in April 1942 for refit it had no tanks left. The 11th Panzer Regiment found itself issued with surplus French stocks in the form of twenty Somua and Hotchkiss tanks.[11] It would be another two months before the division was supplied with Panzer IIIs and it was not brought fully back up to strength until September. When 6th Panzer returned to Russia at the end of the year to take part in the ill-fated attempt to relieve the 6th Army trapped at Stalingrad, the veteran *Panzertruppen* left their unwanted French tanks behind.

French Char Bs were apparently used to some effect against the lighter Soviet tanks, such as the poorly armoured BT-7 and T-26 (based on American and British designs respectively). However, the French panzers were no match for the heavier Soviet T-28, KV-1 or indeed the T-34, and were rapidly expended during the opening stages of the campaign. Others had been used during the invasion of the Balkans, where a number were to remain in a security role. Even so their mechanical unreliability meant that the bulk of French armour, on operational deployment with German units, was eventually withdrawn to France where they were to serve Hitler resisting the Allies' D-Day landings. In the West three German panzer battalions and elements of two divisions were equipped with French armour.

After the humiliation of defeat France had to suffer the further indignity of having its own armour mustered in support of the German occupation. Germany deployed three French equipped security tank battalions in France, the 100, 206 and 213. The *Abteilung* (battalion) 100 was formed in April 1941 as an *Ersatz und Ausbildungs* (training and recruitment unit) at Schwetzingen in the Rhineland. The following year the battalion was stationed at Satory near Versailles and used to guard the railway and Metro. One detachment was also sent to Vercors in south-eastern France near Grenoble to counter the Maquis or French Resistance.

The battalion was sent to Normandy in May 1944 and deployed west of Carentan with its companies spread out in the area of Baupte, Carentan and Ste. Mere-Eglise. Abteilung 100 was tactically responsible to the 91st Infantry Division and helped build anti-invasion defences. From an authorised strength of twenty-seven French tanks its order of battle in early June 1944 only numbered some fifteen operational tanks.[12] On the morning of D-Day the battalion went to battle readiness and was rapidly destroyed fighting the Americans. It was reduced to an anti-tank company armed with *Panzerfausts* mounted on bicycles, and on 7 July the unit was officially disbanded – its French tanks long since scattered around the Normandy countryside like so much scrap.

The 100's sister battalion, the 206, began life as a reserve formation for the 7th Army at Satory, south-west of Versailles in November 1941. In mid-January 1944 Panzer Abteilung 206 was equipped with a motley collection of twenty-five various French tank types plus three anti-tank guns, possibly 75mm PaK. Five months later it still had twenty-four operational French tanks on its strength.[13] During D-Day the battalion was at Cap de la Hague on the northern most tip of the Cotentin Peninsula, based at Beaumont and probably subordinate to the 243rd Infantry Division. Trapped along with the 243rd, 709th and 91st Infantry Divisions, the 206's inadequate French tanks were completely annihilated during the Americans' battle for the peninsula.

In 1941 as a result of Hitler's order to send armour to the occupied Channel Islands, Commander-in-Chief West, Field Marshal von Witzleben, despatched twenty elderly Renault FT-17/18 to Alderney, Guernsey and Jersey.[14] Those on Alderney were probably the closest Hitler's panzers ever got to invading mainland Britain. When Panzer Abteilung 213 arrived they were handed over to the 319th Infantry Division commanded by Brigadier General von Schmettow, who was also Commander-in-Chief Channel Islands, and deployed for airfield defence. By the end of 1944 only two Renaults were still serviceable, the rest had been cannibalised and were used as airfield pillboxes. Also in 1941 a number of 47mm Pak 36(t) auf GW Renault R–35(f) were sent to the Channel Islands and organised into two battalions that served alongside the 213. By the end of 1942 there were twenty French self-propelled guns on Alderney, Guernsey, Jersey and Sark.[15]

Hitler ordered heavier armour to be despatched to the Channel Islands in September 1941 and, rather than tie up vital German tanks, a number of Char Bs were sent. Recruits were selected from 1st Panzer Ersatz Regiment at Erfurt and ended up at Foissy near Paris. There they formed Panzer Abteilung 213, equipped with Char Bs, under Major Lecht and Senior Lieutenant Graf Hoyos. The workshop staff was sent to the Renault factory which shortly afterwards was visited by RAF bombers. The unit thought it was going to North Africa, but instead went to St Malo and on to the Channel Islands. Arriving on Guernsey on 25 March 1942 the tanks were stationed at Tabor Chapel. Initially seventeen Char Bs went to Jersey and nineteen to Guernsey; of each batch twelve were normal PzKpfw Char Bl bis (f), while the other five were flamethrowers. The company HQ on Guernsey accounted for the additional two.[16] Acting as little more than mobile pillboxes none of these lumbering tanks saw action against the Allies.

The Germans not only deployed French armour in France, the Channel Islands and on the Eastern Front. Even Rommel's *Deutsche Afrika Korps* (DAK) in Libya had some armour of French origin. Despite popular misconceptions, the Germans in North Africa did not have numerical superiority in tanks and were forever desperate for more. As mentioned, the DAK ended up fielding French self-propelled guns including the 150mm SFH 13/1 auf GW Lorraine Schlepper(t) which went into service for the very first time with them in 1942. The Allies captured some and they looked more like agricultural vehicles than weapons of war.

Additionally at least two German divisions in the West used French tanks. In October 1942 the 7th SS Freiwilligen Gebirgs (Mountain) Division *Prinz Eugen* became operational and was equipped with Czechoslovakian, French, German and Italian surplus weapon stocks. The division had a battalion of tanks and by June 1943 a tank company was equipped with Hotchkiss H-39s, which were used in Yugoslavia in counterinsurgency operations against Tito's partisans. The Germans lost three H-39s to partisans armed with an anti-tank rifle, crossing the Kailnovik-Foca road in June 1943, as Tito's men escaped from the Germans' Operation *Schwartz* brushing aside units from the Croatian

369th Division. In total ten independent tank platoons armed with H-39s were sent to the Balkans to help fight the partisans.

Perhaps rather surprisingly Rommel's reconstituted veteran 21st Panzer Division was re-equipped with French armour after its demise in North Africa. The bulk of the division and its equipment was lost with the DAK after the German collapse in Tunisia. It was re-formed at Rennes on 15 July 1943 and issued with French tanks; the division was not redeployed to the front nor were its tanks replaced with German ones. Almost a year on, the division's Panzer Regiment 22, now under Oberst (Colonel) Hermann von Oppeln-Bronikowski, was 50 per cent equipped with French armoured fighting vehicles. They consisted of twenty-three Somua tanks, forty-three Hotchkiss assault guns and forty-five Lorraine self-propelled guns, with only 104 tanks of German origin (98 PzKpfw IVs and six PzKpfw IIIs).[17] Von Oppeln-Bronikowski cannot have been very pleased about having gone from commanding inadequate Czech tanks with the 22nd Panzer to commanding inadequate French tanks with the 21st.

In Normandy it was the nearest panzer division to the Allies' intended invasion beaches, being deployed between Caen and Falaise. Field Marshal Rommel, who took command of Army Group B in February 1944, wanted the panzers well forward to deal with the Allies as soon as they came ashore. He had witnessed Allied tactical air strikes in North Africa and knew if they held their tanks back they would struggle to reach the battle unmolested. Field Marshal von Rundstedt, Commander-in-Chief West, on the other hand favoured the 'crust-cushion-hammer' concept, the crust being formed by the static sea defences, the cushion by infantry reserves and the hammer by the armoured divisions held further back. A messy compromise resulted in half the armoured divisions being held as a strategic reserve, with control ultimately resting with Hitler.

A week before the invasion Rommel inspected the 21st Panzer Division and was not pleased with what he found. On 6 June 1944 the division's efforts to launch a counter-attack, first against British para-troops east of the Orne and then toward the coast, were muddled and botched losing sixteen tanks in the process. Fortunately for the para-troops most of the German armour was diverted north of Caen. Major General Feuchtinger, commander of the 21st Panzer, designated one of Hitler's reserve units, had been reduced to ninety operational tanks and did not start moving northwards until 16.00 hours. His counter-attack towards Bieville failed and his troops were driven eastwards. By the end of the day Feuchtinger and von Oppeln-Bronikowski had lost twenty panzers for little or no tactical gain.

The British were finally halted at Lebisey a mere two miles north of Caen. In the meantime by 14.00 hours the other German mobile reserve, the 12th SS Panzer Division and the Panzer Lehr Division had at last been released for action. The 12th SS headed for Caen, but was subjected to continual Allied air strikes and it was not until 7 and 9 June that the two divisions were brought into action. Four weeks after D-Day von Oppeln-Bronikowski had sixty-one PzKpfw IVs and thirty-two assault guns, although mysteriously none of the Lorraines had been lost.[18]

The German position in Normandy became completely untenable on 15 August when the Allies landed in the south of France. Hitler grudgingly agreed to let the German Army withdraw through the Argentan-Falaise Gap the following day. The 2nd SS Panzer Corps (2nd SS, 9th SS, 12th SS and 21st Panzer Divisions) was to hold the northern flank against the British and Canadians and 47th Panzer Corps (2nd and 116th Panzer Divisions) was to hold the south against the Americans, while Seventh Army and Panzer Group Eberbach conducted a fighting retreat. Feuchtinger's division was sucked into the chaos of the Falaise Pocket with von Oppeln-Bronikowski losing all his tanks like most of the other panzer commanders. Paris was liberated on 25 August along with the Citroen and Renault works.

By early September the Germans had barely 100 serviceable tanks in Western Europe, while the Allies could muster 7,700 medium and light tanks. In September 1944 British paratroops came up against French tanks at Arnhem when they encountered the Char B1 converted into a flamethrower. Miraculously some of the French panzers did escape the collapse of the Western Front, a PzKpfw B2 bis (f) flammn was captured by the Allies as far away as Deventer, Holland, in April 1945.

Chapter Six

T-34 v T-34

Marshal Zhukov phoned Joseph Stalin in the early hours of 22 June 1941 to inform him that the Soviet Union was under widespread German air attack. For a while all Zhukov could hear was Stalin's breathing on the other end of the line; the Soviet dictator seemed lost for words. Despite evidence to the contrary, Stalin had continually insisted Hitler would not invade; he had now been proved badly wrong. Zhukov and other senior Soviet leaders were immediately summoned to the Kremlin. Within hours Zhukov was en route to the front to try and retrieve the rapidly deteriorating situation. A decade of Soviet tank development was about to amount to nothing and within six months Hitler had got his hands on practically all of Stalin's tanks.

The scale of the titanic struggle on the Eastern Front between 1941–45 overshadows every other theatre of operations. The successful destruction and seizure of the Red Army's massive tank fleet in the summer of 1941 by the German Army is almost beyond comprehension. Hitler threw 3,200 tanks at an enormous Russian tank force of some 20,000 vehicles. In his favour only about 60 per cent of the Russian fleet was serviceable at any one time and the bulk of it was obsolete and was easily and quickly dealt with.

To defend the Soviet Union's western border Stalin had 2.9 million men, organised into 170 divisions, supported by 1,800 heavy and medium tanks (which included 1,475 of the latest KV and T-34 tanks) and thousands of completely obsolete light tanks.[1] In reality only fifty-six divisions were actually in the first echelon facing the Germans and many of the others were hundreds of miles away. Within just three weeks the Russians lost 2 million men, 3,500 tanks and 6,000 aircraft to Hitler's unrelenting blitzkrieg.

The Russians had known that war was coming with Germany, but were simply not ready. 'The heart of heavy industry and of our defence industry beat quickly,' records Marshal Zhukov. 'In the years and months before the war their development was intense and fast.'[2] Clearly though it did not beat fast enough as Zhukov goes on to admit: 'From

January 1939 to 22 June 1941, the Red Army received over 7,000 tanks; in 1941 industry turned out about 5,500 tanks of all types. As to the KV and T-34 tanks, the plants managed to put out only 1,861 of them before the war, which was clearly insufficient.[3]

Even Stalin's inner circle of sycophantic henchmen had no real idea of the true capabilities of the Red Army. 'We had a terrible shortage of arms of all kinds in the first months of the war, admitted Nikita Khrushchev. 'I was a member of the Politbureau and part of Stalin's ruling circle, but I still had no way of knowing that we were woefully lacking in rifles and machine guns, not to mention tanks and heavy artillery.'[4]

Stalin's Baltic Military Command under Colonel General Kuznetsov was key to the defence of Leningrad and the vital Kirov Tank Plant. The bulk of the 1,045 tanks at Kuznetsov's disposal were old; 75 per cent of the fleet needed repairs and only 105 were newer models. While the 12th Mechanised Corps was able to muster 84 per cent of its tanks, the 3rd Mechanised Corps could only manage 55 per cent. The latter only had half its authorised tanks and most of these were inadequate T-26s; there were a few T-34s and just two new KV-1s. The 7th Mechanised Corps had none of its authorised 420 T-34s and just forty of its 120 KVs. Clearly this was a recipe for disaster.[5]

At the time of the invasion Hitler had extensive intelligence on certain Soviet tank types, including the BT-5, T-26 and T-28. Prior to the invasion the German High Command established a special department to survey Russian industries, especially the weapons plants as well as sources of raw materials, in particular petroleum. In fact his panzer troops already had extensive experience of re-using Soviet tanks, thanks to the Führer's meddling in the Spanish Civil War during the second half of the 1930s.

Both Hitler and Mussolini were not blind to the advantage of having Spain as an ally in France's rear. They had provided General Franco's Nationalist forces with considerable military support. Under the guise of Operation Magic Fire two German holding companies and a tourist group were set up to funnel material and volunteers to Franco. Germany supplied a 'volunteer' experimental tank, anti-tank and aircraft force unit known as the Condor Legion under General von Sperrle, as well as additional advisors and instructors.

Spain proved invaluable for the development of Germany's early panzer forces. Colonel Ritter von Thoma, a veteran of the First World War, commanded the panzer corps in Spain where his advisors trained Franco's tankers and gained invaluable combat experience.

Panzergruppe Drohne under von Thoma helped the Nationalists to operate 122 Panzer Is.[6] Thoma recalls: 'It could be seen that Spain would serve as the "European Aldershot". I was in command of all the German ground troops in Spain during the war. ...They were used to train Franco's tank force – and to get battle experience themselves.'[7]

Officially the instructors handed their tanks over to the Nationalist crews as soon as they were proficient, limiting themselves to an advisory role, especially in the later part of the war. However, von Thoma, like any soldier, could not resist the opportunity and took part in 192 tank actions during his time in Spain. The Germans soon discovered that the Republican forces' Soviet supplied T-26 tank was superior to the Panzer I, while the German 3.7cm PaK 35/36 anti-tank gun was found to penetrate forty millimetres of armour at 400 yards.

Thoma rapidly realised that Soviet tanks were better than those of the Germans and Italians and acted to get his hands on some. He noted:

> Russian tanks began to arrive on the other side even quicker – at the end of July [1936]. They were of a heavier type than ours, which were armed only with machine guns, and I offered a reward of 500 pesetas for every one that was captured, as I was only too glad to convert them to my own use. The Moors [Moroccans] bagged quite a lot.[8]

By 1938 Franco had four companies equipped with sixty Soviet tanks.

Stalin saw much to be gained by supporting the Spanish Communists within the Republican movement. He positively swamped Spain in tanks, supplying the Republicans in total with nearly 1,000 BT-5, T-26 and possibly the T-28 under the direction of General Dimitri Pavlov. The Soviet BT-5 and T-26 were both vastly superior in armament and armour than their German and Italian counterparts, but were never supplied or used in a decisive manner by the Republicans.

In the 1930s the BT light fast tank was one of the principal Soviet armour types. The main model was the BT-5 (in fact a copy of the US Christie M-1931), which was equipped with a larger cylindrical turret, a 45mm gun, a co-axial MG and a larger engine than its predecessors. With a crew of three and a weight of 11.5 tons it could almost manage 70 mph on the road. The successor model, the BT-7, went into production in 1935 so some of these may have also gone to Spain.

The single turret T-26B light tank appeared in 1933 (the earlier T-26 had twin turrets) and was also armed with a 45mm or 37mm. Its weight though rose from about eight tons to nine reducing its road speed by four mph to eighteen. The T-26's low speed and poor mobility compared with the BT-5 resulted in production being abandoned in the mid-1930s. This may account for why they were so numerous in Spain; Stalin simply offloaded them on the Republicans.

The T-28 medium tank that went into production in 1932 was fitted with three turrets, one again mounting a 45mm and two with machine guns. Despite a crew of six and weighing almost thirty tons it could still manage almost 25 mph. While this tank was not used operationally until 1939 there is evidence to suggest that some were sent to Spain for trials. The Soviets are also believed to have supplied some armoured cars.

The use of tanks during the Spanish Civil War was never really decisive. Despite the Nationalists' lack of effective tanks or anti-tank guns, the Republicans were unable to exploit their superior Soviet armour. Air power and artillery emerged as the key to the war. Some experts erroneously concluded that the anti-tank gun was more effective than the tank, and that experiences in Spain refuted the new theories about massed concentrated mechanised warfare. They failed to take into account the unsuitable terrain, the poorly trained crews and the relatively small numbers of tanks employed, or the fact the panzers could not engage the Russian tanks on an equal footing.

Germany and the Soviet Union drew important lessons from their experiences. Colonel von Thoma fully understood the shock value of massed tanks as an offensive rather than supporting weapon:

> General Franco wished to parcel out the tanks among the infantry in the usual way of the generals who belong to the old school. I had to fight this tendency constantly in the endeavour to use the tanks in a concentrated way. The Francoists' successes were largely due to this.[9]

Thus Blitzkrieg was born. Thanks to his Spanish experience Thoma was to become a general and a divisional panzer commander on the Eastern Front during the Second World War.

General Pavlov, one of the innovators of Soviet mechanisation during the early 1930s, noted the increased use and accuracy of anti-tank weapons. Both the BT-5 and T-26 suffered a gradual reduction in armour effectiveness and this led the Red Army to ensure that its tanks were not only splinter and small-arms proof, but could also withstand direct hits by small calibre artillery. Soviet experiences in Spain led indirectly to the T-34's development, which eventually gave them an important technological edge over the German panzers.

Pavlov's experiences in Spain were to ultimately cost him his life as he drew the wrong conclusions about the deployment of armour. He advocated the French doctrine whereby tanks were used in direct support of the infantry, arguing that the doctrine of blitzkrieg by mass armour as advocated by Marshal Tukhachevsky was not sound. On returning to Russia in 1939 he lobbied in favour of disbanding the unwieldy Soviet tank corps. Tukhachevsky's theories of massing armour was dismissed as heresy and the Soviets' motor/mechanised corps were broken up and the armour dispersed just as Hitler was poised to attack.

Crucially for the Soviet conduct of the opening stages of the Second World War the Red Army's tanks were dispersed to the divisions where they could be destroyed piecemeal. This decision may be seen as the greatest blunder in Soviet military history. In June 1941 Hitler's Northern Army Group thrust toward Leningrad, Central Army Group struck toward Moscow and the Southern Army Group cut into Ukraine. Further south combined German, Hungarian and Romanian forces drove into the Caucasus, while to the far north in Finland thrusts were made toward Murmansk and down the Karelian Isthmus. Soviet pre-1939 gains in both Poland and Finland were soon lost.

Northern Army Group got to within fifty miles of Leningrad and although the Red Army escaped wholesale destruction, the Germans still captured 35,000 prisoners, 400 tanks and 1,000 guns. Further south things were even more catastrophic and by 28 June Minsk had fallen to Central Army Group with the loss of 300,000 prisoners, 3,000 tanks and 3,000 guns. The Southern Army Group moving south of the Pripet Marshes fought its way toward Kiev. The German-Hungarian-Romanian Group captured Uman on 12 August capturing another 150,000 Russian troops. By 27 September Southern Army Group had put the Red Army to flight taking 665,000 men, nearly 1,000 tanks and 4,000 guns. Vyazma fell to the Central Army group on 2 October taking another 600,000 prisoners. Only by December did the German forces begin to lose steam. [10]

Within the space of five months the Germans destroyed or captured 17,000 Soviet tanks, for the loss of 2,700, and reached the very gates of Moscow. The Czech and French tanks were used to some effect against the lighter Soviet tanks, such as the poorly armoured BT-7 and T-26; in contrast they were no match for the heavier T-28, KV-1 or indeed the T-34. In total, the Red Army lost about 1.5 million dead and 2.5 million captured. Soviet losses were such that they could only muster 780 tanks for the Battle of Moscow, of which only 140 were heavy and medium tanks.[11]

How did such massive Soviet losses come to pass? The answer is simple, Stalin had already decapitated the Red Army and the discrediting of Tukhachevsky's doctrine meant Soviet tanks were too dispersed to fend off the panzers of the battle hardened *Wehrmacht* and *Waffen-SS*. By the late 1930s the Red Army was at its strongest and most efficient; all this work was undone in one fell swoop. Fearing a reinvigorated Red Army, Stalin's *Ezhovschina* (as the Great Purge became known) fell upon it with a bloody vengeance in 1937. Approximately 30,000 (of a cadre of 75,000) senior and medium grade officers were shot, imprisoned or sent to the Gulag. Hitler's purge in early 1938 dismissed just sixteen generals, none were imprisoned or shot, with forty-four others simply transferred.

There were over 100,000 Red Army officers on active duty in 1937-38; the total number removed may have been as high as half. With war looming the timing of Stalin's purge could not have been worse. In particular the removal of the able General Tukhachevsky and his officers was a disaster. The General Staff was left completely disorganised with its members constantly looking over their shoulders. The Germans could come to only one conclusion - the *Wehrmacht* could defeat the Red Army.

Stalin received a sharp wake up call during the 1939-40 Russo-Finnish Winter War. Although the Soviets prevailed, it took 1.5 million troops to defeat 200,000 Finns and they lost 1 million killed. Despite the Finns having no armour, Russian tanks had struggled to make an impression. The Finns response included the Molotov cocktail and Soviet armour losses amounted to 2,300 tanks and armoured cars. Lieutenant General Nikita Khrushchev lamented the condition of the Soviet Union's armoured formations. Whilst the Red Army had defeated the small Finnish Army, the Winter War had shown up numerous inadequacies, though secrecy continued to hamper a proper appreciation of the capabilities of Russia's Army. Khrushchev noted:

> Part of the problem was that Stalin tried to supervise our manufacturing of munitions and mechanised equipment all by himself with the result that no one really knew what state our arsenal was in. For example, I remember that in 1941 Stalin instructed me to look into the possibility of mounting diesel engines on airplanes. ... He told me that these diesel engines were being manufactured at the Kharkov locomotive factory. ... Even I, the First Secretary of the Ukrainian Central Committee, had known nothing of these

powerful diesel engines which were being built right there in Kharkov. I didn't have time to conclude whether the engines could be mounted on bombers or not, but they did prove very effective when used to power our T-34 tanks. Unfortunately, we didn't have enough of these tanks built by the time the war broke out.[12]

The Red Army's failures in the summer of 1941 unleashed a second round of purges. General Pavlov, in his role as Commander Western Army Group, further contributed to the Red Army's disastrous performance against the *Wehrmacht*. Stalin's reward was to have him shot. Stalin's purges were renewed the following summer, with second line detachments established to shoot anyone fleeing the battlefield. Marshal Zhukov took the step of implementing these instructions using tanks.

The reason for the Germans incredible successes was in part due to Stalin's 1930s purges, but more specifically because of their superior use of armour, speed, and superior equipment. The Germans found themselves in possession of acres and acres of abandoned Soviet tanks. For a while the decimated Red Army suffered an acute shortage of tanks, guns and aircraft; however most of the Russians' defence plants, including its tank production facilities, escaped Hitler's grasp.[13] Zhukov marvelled at what he called the 'Russian miracle'; the swift dismantling and relocation of the Soviet Union's factories out of harm's way. This allowed the regeneration of the Red Army and ultimately the destruction of the *Wehrmacht*.

The T-34/76 first came out of the Komintern factory in Kharkov in January 1940. It went into mass production in June and by the end of the year 115 had been built. By the time of the German invasion 1,125 had been produced. It first went into action at Grondno, Belorussia the day of the invasion, its appearance taking the Germans completely by surprise. Stalin established a People's Commissariat for Tank Production and new tank plants sprang up east of the Ural Mountains, in particular Uralmashzavod the Ural Machine-Building Plant at Nizhny Tagil and the Chelyabinsk Tractor Factory. Before long these factories were churning out a new improved version of the T-34/76 known as the T-34/85. This had thicker frontal armour to withstand German anti-tank guns, and the KV-2 also began to appear in adequate numbers.

Leningrad, as well as being an important port, was also a major industrial hub accounting for 10 per cent of total Soviet industrial production. In particular the Kirov works was producing the new KV heavy tank, which had only gone into production in February 1940.

Other Leningrad factories produced a vast range of equipment for the Soviet war effort. The very day after the German invasion commenced, the Russians began to explore the feasibility of shifting KV production to Chelyabinsk in the Ural Mountains. The assessment was that within two to three months of the move they could produce fifteen KV tanks a day.[14] However, Moscow foolishly directed the Kirov plant to stay put and go into KV serial production, leaving it within grasp of the Germans. A partial evacuation to Chelyabinsk did not take place until August, though tank production continued at Leningrad throughout the 900-day siege. The tank factory at Kharkov was also evacuated to Chelyabinsk and the combined plants became popularly known at 'Tankograd'. According to Marshal Zhukov the first batch of T-34s came off the Chelyabinsk Tractor Plant production line a month after the relocation of the Leningrad factory.[15]

The Sormovo shipyards in Gorky (Nizhniy Novogorod) on the Volga were quickly put to work producing T-34 tanks as well, and these were employed during the Battle of Moscow. Zhukov, charged with defending the capital, noted that they came just in time and played a conspicuous role in the fighting. Another important factory was the Stalingrad Tractor Works (STZ) that produced tracked tractors for civilian and military purposes. This became the scene of heavy fighting in September 1942 between the Red Army and the *Wehrmacht*.

The Germans re-used, in the thousands, at least three types of captured tracked prime mover built by STZ. The Germans also recycled thousands of Soviet small arms such as the Tokarev 7.62mm pistol. Similarly the PPSh 41 was captured in such large numbers that it became the second most common sub-machine gun after the famous MP 38/40 'Schmeisser'. In the winter of 1941 some of those factories not removed by the Russians from the city of Orel, were put back into production to meet some of the needs of the German Army and provide employment and food for the workers. These included factories turning out tinned goods and shoes, the latter made leather and felt boots, which were desperately needed by the German troops suffering from the bitter cold.

Despite capturing thousands of Russian tanks, because the vast majority were obsolete designs, most were simply discarded by the frontline German units and left behind as they pushed forward. As noted, the newer KV and T-34 numbered less than 1,500 in the Soviet Western military districts. Nevertheless, within a few weeks of the invasion special German staff began to gather up tank samples for possible exploitation by the *Wehrmacht*. At this stage the Germans still had had not had a proper look at the T-34 and KV-1. It was estimated that up to 10,000 Russian tanks were dotted about the Soviet landscape.

The exploitation teams soon discovered that the vast majority of the captured tanks were beyond repair due to battle damage, lack of vital parts or, as in the case of the T-28 and T-35, were simply too heavy to move. The end result was extremely disappointing and by late October 1941 only about 100 tanks were available for use by the German Army.[16]

Efforts were made to assimilate Stalin's tanks in a more systematic way. In mid-1942 refurbished T-34s and KV-1s began to come out of the German tank repair facility in Riga, the capital of the Baltic state of Latvia. The following year Daimler-Benz at Marienfelde in Germany and Wumag at Gorlitz, Germany, began to supply T-34s. When the German military authorities conducted a survey of operational captured tanks with the German Army and *Waffen-SS* the results were again very surprising. In May 1943 there were just sixty-three Russian tanks in use of which fifty were T-34s; in December 1944 there were fifty-three of which forty-nine were T-34s. It has been estimated that only about 300 Russian tanks served with German forces on the Eastern Front at any one time.[17]

It is very likely that many hundreds of others were pressed into service with frontline units, but were never declared due to indifference to official accounting or for fear of having them requisitioned. Once they became available in large numbers the Panzer, Panzergrenadier and infantry divisions on the Eastern Front particularly prized the T-34. They also used limited numbers of Soviet assault guns such as the SU-85 and some armoured cars.

To avoid friendly fire large white German crosses were painted on the turrets; in the heat of the battle this was unlikely to have been completely foolproof. The *Waffen-SS* was also known to paint white SS runes on the turrets of captured Russian armoured cars that they re-employed. One German T-34 crewman, SS Hauptscharführer Emil Seibold, became a panzer ace, ending the war with sixty-nine Soviet tanks to his name. He was awarded the Knights Cross of the Iron Cross on 6 May 1945.

Disabled Russian tanks were also used for static defence. During the German defence of Cholm an immobilised T-34 was used as a strong-point.[18] The town lay on the junction of the Lovat and Kunya Rivers and two important roads, making it a useful springboard. The retreating Germans left behind a holding force sure in the knowledge that a major counter-stroke against the Russians would come to their aid in a couple of weeks.

The German garrison, numbering just 3,500 men, was cut off on 21 January 1942 and Russian tanks were soon attacking the western perimeter. The garrison commander, Major General Scherer, rapidly discovered to his horror that he had no anti-tank guns. Slowly the perimeter was squeezed smaller and smaller and airdrops became the defenders only lifeline. The Russians also beat off repeated attempts to relieve them.

The Soviets then began to prepare for another massed armour attack on Cholm. The defenders found a 3.7cm anti-tank gun. An airlift bought in three other anti-tank guns and a mortar and a disabled T-34 was also pressed into service. The Russians launched their major assault on 23 February, Red Army Day, using an entire infantry division supported by tanks. Poor Soviet tactics resulted in eighteen attacks over two days and nights being driven off. The defenders were finally relieved on 5 May having destroyed forty-two Soviet tanks.

As the tide turned in Stalin's favour the Germans found themselves forced to employ Russian tanks following their defeat at Stalingrad and their attempts to retrieve the situation at Kharkov. The Soviets' successful winter offensive of 1942-43 destroyed first the Romanian 3rd and 4th Armies, then the Italian 8th Army followed by the Hungarian 2nd Army, culminating in the defeat of the Germans trapped at Stalingrad. Field Marshal Friedrich Paulus and the German 6th Army surrendered on 31 January 1943, with the loss of 60,000-100,000 dead and 120,000 starving, frost-bitten POWs. According to Soviet figures total German losses in the Volga-Don-Stalingrad area amounted to some 1.5 million men, 3,500 tanks, 12,000 guns and 3,000 aircraft.

By the end of January the Russians had recaptured Kursk, and were over the Donets to the south-east of Kharkov. The following month they were thrusting toward the Dnieper threatening the German position at Kharkov and Rostov. At Kharkov the newly arrived 1st SS Panzer Corps stood in the Soviets' way but was pushed back. General Paul Hausser, fearing Kharkov could become another Stalingrad, disobeyed Hitler's orders to stand firm and evacuated the city on 15 February. Field Marshal Manstein was then able to launch a power counter-offensive and by 14 March was back in control of Kharkov.

The heavy fighting claimed over 50 per cent of the triumphant 1st SS Panzer Corps' tanks. In particular the 2nd SS Panzer Division *Das Reich* lost seventy-seven tanks and assault guns, weakening it further. Its 1st

Tank Battalion was sent west to train on the Panther tank and did not return in time for Operation Citadel, the Kursk offensive. The *Waffen-SS*'s solution was to take over the tractor works in Kharkov. There the Armoured Pursuit Unit of the 2nd SS Panzer began refurbishing captured T-34 tanks. On a small-scale assembly line the tanks were dismantled, overhauled and re-assembled. The 9th Company within the division's 2nd Battalion, 2nd Panzer Regiment was equipped solely with them.[19] By May 1943 *Das Reich* fielded twenty-five T-34 tanks of which eighteen were available on 4 July, along with ten Czech built Marders.[20]

During the Kursk offensive in early July 1943, T-34 fought T-34. The 2nd SS Panzer Division fielded eight T-34s and, in one instance, its captured tanks fought off a Soviet armoured column. The German T-34s were deployed on some high ground and poured a destructive fire into the advancing Russian tanks.[21] By the end of the offensive, 2nd SS Panzer Corps listed twelve T-34s still on its strength fit for combat, only two of which belonged to *Das Reich*.[22] The 6th Panzer Division also used captured T-34s to spearhead an attack on Rzhavets and the vital crossing points on the River Donets on 11 July. Major Franz Bake led the advance, hoping to slip by the Soviets unnoticed at night. Lieutenant Hutchmann was at the head of the column with two captured T-34s which, it was hoped, would fool the enemy into believing that 6th Panzer was a withdrawing Soviet convoy.

Things went well with the German tanks passing within metres of oncoming Soviet truck convoys. Unfortunately one of the German T-34s broke down just as a Soviet T-34 column, with mounted infantry, was coming the other way. The German T-34 pulled off the road but the Soviets were fooled only momentarily and then began shooting. Major Bake takes up the story:

> Leading the way was a captured T-34. I had ordered radio silence and no firing. Silently, we passed the first enemy barricade, moving by the deadly anti-tank guns which remained silent, believing us to be one of their own units.
>
> When the T-34 broke down with engine trouble, a Panzer IV was forced to assume the lead. Rshvets appeared in front of us. At the edge of the town was a row of T-34s. They readily made way for what they obviously believed to be their own tanks returning from the front. Then a column of tanks appeared heading in the opposite direction.
>
> Lieutenant Hutchmann in the lead tank reported twenty-two T-34s. These passed my unit, almost track to track. But then six or

seven pulled out of the column, turned, rolled back and pulled in behind us.

I ordered the rest to continue and placed my command tank, which was equipped only with a dummy gun, across the road in order to force the enemy tanks to a halt. Seven T-34s rolled up and formed a semicircle around me.

I instructed my operations officer to break out the hollow charges. The two of us left the tank. We slid out of the field of view of the T-34 on our right. Reaching the tanks, we placed the hollow charges on two T-34s and jumped into cover.

The detonations rang through the night. Two T-34s were put out of action. We fetched two more hollow charges and put them in place. Two more T-34s were blown up.

The fifth T-34 was destroyed by one of my tanks.[23]

The Soviets were driven back and blew the bridge; however this was repaired and 3rd Panzer Corps rumbled over. Subsequent Russian counter-attacks drove 6th Panzer Division back across the river.

Once the Germans began to lose on the Eastern Front, units became desperate to press into service whatever Soviet armoured vehicles they could lay their hands on. The vast vehicle dumps were raided and some equipment, particularly armoured cars, were put to work countering the growing Soviet partisan menace which threatened the *Wehrmacht*'s rear areas. In preparation for Operation Barbarossa in early 1941 middle-aged reservists were formed into nine and later fourteen Security Divisions. Equipped with only light weapons and under strength they were assigned to guard lines of communication in the east. By October 1941 the 444th Security Division was making use of captured Russian armoured cars to supplement its firepower.

Numerous counter partisan operations were conducted such as Operations Karlsbad and Hamburg, which commenced in October and December 1941 respectively.[24] At this stage the activities of Soviet partisans were relatively small scale compared with what was to come, but even then the Germans were acutely conscious of how exposed their extended lines of communication were. At the end of 1941 German security forces had to contend with about 30,000 partisans; by early 1944 there were an estimated 200,000 hampering the *Wehrmacht*'s every move.[25]

Predictably the Security Divisions could not cope with the growing Russian resistance and the following year they were joined by five Reserve Divisions. Later seven Field Training Divisions were also sent.

In mid-June 1942 German Police Battalions were organised into motorised Police Regiments, each of which included an armoured car company, and fourteen German Police Regiments served in the Soviet Union.

While the Germans were reusing Soviet equipment, Stalin deployed British and American armour on the Eastern Front. Britain provided Churchill and Valentine tanks as well as the Universal carrier, which had fought Rommel in North Africa. Under its Lend-Lease policy America supplied the M3 Lee and M4 Sherman tanks. The Russians did not like the Churchill or Lee as they were slow and poorly armed in comparison with their own tanks. Lend-Lease tanks, other than the Sherman, were pretty unpopular as they were not well armed or robust enough for the extremes of climate or the low level of crew training. Britain and America also assumed a degree of driving proficiency completely lacking in the Soviet Union at the time. By 1943 20 per cent of Soviet tank brigades were using Lend-Lease tanks and over 10 per cent were entirely equipped with them. During 1941-42 Britain and the Commonwealth sent 3,270 tanks and America shipped another 7,000 from then until the end of the war.[26] Many of these fell into German hands and limited numbers were redeployed.

Having failed to capture Stalin's defence industries Hitler set about smashing them from the air. Operation Gertrud saw the *Luftwaffe* wage a bombing campaign against Soviet electricity generating centres during 1942-43. In November 1944 the Germans conducted Operation Eisenhammer (Iron Hammer) an air offensive against Soviet factories and power plants. Both campaigns did little to curtail the massive Russian armaments production.

Hitler grossly underestimated the Soviets' regeneration capabilities and industrial might and this was ultimately to cost him dearly. By February 1943 the Germans had just 495 tanks in eighteen panzer divisions on the Eastern Front; the writing was on the wall. While many see the *Wehrmacht*'s defeat at Stalingrad in January 1943 as the turning point, in fact the catastrophic destruction of Army Group Centre at the hands of Stalin's Operation Bagration in mid-1944 was a blow from which they could never recover.

Bagration opened on 22 June 1944, three years to the day after Hitler had attacked the Soviet Union. The Soviets threw over a million men, more than 4,000 tanks and self-propelled guns, 24,000 guns and over 5,300 aircraft at the Germans. Three days later Moscow announced its war losses to date as 49,000 tanks, 48,000 guns, 30,000 aircraft, and 5.3

million dead, wounded or missing. It is spectacular how a nation could recover from such appalling losses.

Within a week three German armies had been sent reeling and lost 900 panzers. Despite the best efforts of the 5th Panzer Division to the north of Minsk and the 12th Panzer Division to the south, they were unable to stem the Soviet tide. Ironically the 20th Panzer Division, withdrawing from Bobruisk south-east of Minsk, used a forty-five ton Joseph Stalin self-propelled 122mm gun to cover their retreat.[27] By the end of the summer the German Army lost twenty-five divisions totalling upwards of 350,000 men and 2,000 tanks. German tank production could not keep up with such drastic losses and the redeployment of a few hundred Soviet tanks on an ad hoc basis was never going to make any difference.

Somewhere in France in May 1940 triumphant *Panzertruppen* seated on their PzKpfw 38(t); one of them sports a captured British helmet. The Czechs provided Hitler with over 6,300 of these vehicles in one form or another. *(Author's collection)*

The 7.5cm Pak40/3 auf PzKpfw 38(t) Ausf H. Almost 250 of these were built between November 1942-April 1943 as a mobile anti-tank gun stopgap.

(Author's collection)

A column of Marder IIIs. This Czech based self-propelled gun went into production in April 1943 and almost a thousand of these compact vehicles were built.

(Author's collection)

The vehicle that had the greatest impact on Hitler's war effort was the *Jagdpanzer* 38(t) Hetzer tank destroyer, seen here knocked out on the streets of Prague in May 1945. Almost 2,600 were manufactured.

(Author's collection)

The 38(t) Flakpanzer was produced to help defend the *Wehrmacht* from the Allies' ever-growing air power, in early 1944. It saw action on both the Eastern and Western Fronts.

(Nik Cornish at Stavka)

A German crew with their captured British Scout tracked carrier. The Germans redeployed variants of these vehicles in almost every theatre of operation.

(Author's Collection)

Once committed to Hitler's war effort, Mussolini lost the bulk of his M13/40 medium tanks in North Africa. The Italians built over 780 of these and after the occupation of Italy the Germans kept it in limited production. *(Official War Office Photo via Author)*

One of Rommel's British Matildas back with its original owners. Numbers of these tanks served with the 15th and 21st Panzer Divisions in North Africa.

(Bovington Tank Museum)

German troops posing with a French Hotchkiss H-35 in 1941. This light tank was originally used to equip France's cavalry divisions. *(Author's collection)*

A field full of captured H-39s. France built about 1,000 H-35/39 and the Germans redeployed over 50 per cent. A few also went to Hungary and Bulgaria.

(via Author)

A Hotchkiss H-39 being overhauled. This tank type served the Germans on the Eastern and Western Fronts as well as in the Balkans. *(Author's Collection)*

A captured Renault R-35 is given a close inspection by its captors. The Germans confiscated almost 1,000 of these tanks supplying over 100 to the Italians and 40 to the Bulgarians. *(via Author)*

A German officer examines the rear of a knocked out Somua S-35; re-dubbed the PzKpfw 35-S 739(f) they were re-used by the German, Bulgarian, Hungarian and Italian armies. *(via Author)*

This cumbersome looking self-propelled gun is a 15cm sFH13/1 (Sf) auf Geschützwagen Lorraine Schlepper (f) (Sd Kfz 135/1) and was captured by the British in North Africa, in 1942. *(Official War Office Photo via Author)*

A clearer view of the German self-propelled howitzer on the captured French Tracteur Blindé 37L carrier chassis. Just over 100 were converted and over half saw service on the Western Front in 1944. *(Author's collection)*

B-17 bombers of the United States Army Air Force attempted to shut down the French automobile factory at Billancourt on 4 April 1943. This grainy photo, taken by the French resistance, shows the extent of the damage.   (*US Army*)

Following the attack on Billancourt, B-17s bombed the CAM ball-bearing plant and Hispano Suiza aircraft engine repair depot in Paris on 31 December 1943. The CAM plants at Bois Colombes and Ivry-sur-Seine produced 25,000 ball-bearings a day.
    (*US Army*)

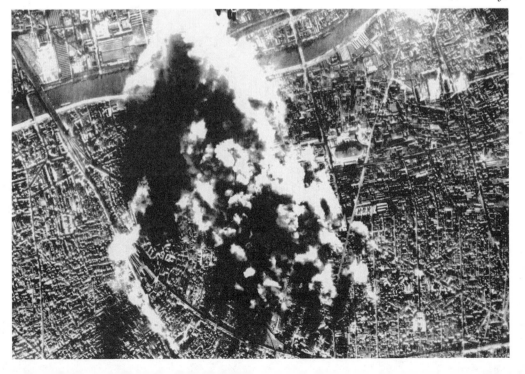

German troops tow away a captured Russian BT-7 Fast Tank. In the summer of 1941 they destroyed or captured some 17,000 Soviet tanks. The BT-7 was produced between 1935-9 during which time about 7,000 were built.
(Author's collection)

Panzertruppen mechanics posing on their captured T-34/76. The 2nd SS Panzer Division *Das Reich* and 6th Panzer Division deployed such tanks during the massive Battle of Kursk. *(Author's collection)*

Refurbished Russian KV-1s began to come out of the German tank repair facility in Riga in mid-1942. These heavy tanks were redeployed by, amongst others, the 1st, 8th and 22nd Panzer Divisions. *(Jochen Vollert Archives - Tankograd Publishing)*

A captured Russian BA-10 armoured car redeployed as the Pz SP Wg BAF 203(r) with the *Wehrmacht*.

(Author's collection)

A Russian ChTZ-S-65 Stalinets tracked artillery tractor being used for road building by the Germans on the Eastern Front in the summer of 1942. *(Author's collection)*

One previous owner. A captured Russian T-37 light amphibious tank redeployed with a German Security Division. They built 1,200 of these. *(via Author)*

Luftwaffe officers examine a captured British Matilda III CS with the 3in howitzer probably belonging to the Red Army. After their experiences in France and North Africa, the Germans were very familiar with the Matilda's capabilities.

(Author's collection)

A captured American M4 Sherman deployed as part of Hitler's Ardennes offensive in December 1944.

(Bovington Tank Museum)

The Hungarian medium Turan tank, based on the Czech LT-35, was obsolete before it even went into production. These examples have been cannibalised after being lost on the Eastern Front.   *(Author's collection)*

The Hungarian Toldi light tank based on the Swedish Landsverk L60 was no match for Soviet armour either.   *(Nik Cornish at Stavka)*

Looking like some sort of medieval battering ram only 60 Hungarian Zrinyi self-propelled howitzers were built. The last few were lost defending Budapest.

(Moscow Central Museum of the Armed Forces via Nik Cornish)

A Russian anti-tank gunner stands proudly by his victim – an Italian L6/40 light tank belonging to the 3rd Mobile Division. Mussolini sent very few tanks to the Eastern Front.

(USSR Ministry of Information via Author)

The Italian 8th Army had just 55 L6/40 to fend off the Soviets' Operation Saturn Offensive in the winter of 1942, with predictable results.

(Krasnogorsk RGAKFD via Nik Cornish)

Chapter Seven

Operation Axis

Deposed Italian leader Benito Mussolini was sitting at an open window of the Hotel Albergo-Rifugo, 100 miles from Rome, on Sunday, 12 September 1943 when he was suddenly roused from his depression by a loud crash. Startled he looked up to see a German glider lying in the grounds of the hotel. Out leapt German paratroops, *Waffen-SS* commandos and an Italian general lead by SS-Sturmbannführer (Major) Otto Skorzeny. The carabinieri guarding Mussolini were unsure what to do; some simply fled while others faced the quandary of whether to open fire on an Italian general or indeed their former leader. At the behest of Skorzeny and Mussolini shouting from his window they decided to lay down their arms.

Skorzeny hurried the former dictator to a small plane, which had just landed, and he was flown to Vienna via Rome. A few days later he arrived at Rastenburg to meet his saviour. While Mussolini was full of gratitude, Hitler was displeased to find his one-time ally was less enthusiastic about his plans to revive Fascism in northern Italy. The disillusioned Mussolini found himself the puppet ruler of his German occupied homeland, the so-called *Repubblica Sociale Italiana* (RSI). He was also allowed to raise a new army largely bereft of heavy equipment. After the occupation of Italy in September 1943 Hitler received his third and final major windfall of armour. In total the German Army and *Waffen-SS* gained almost 1,000 Italian armoured vehicles that were to serve them in Italy and the Balkans against the advancing Allies.

It seems that Mussolini was beginning to tire of his entanglement with Hitler by the spring of 1943. His North African adventure had gone horribly wrong, even with the intervention of Rommel, now the Allies were poised to attack Italian soil. He did not want additional German units in Italy but rather German supplies with which to replenish his exhausted army. When Field Marshal Kesselring told Mussolini he was forming three new German divisions to help defend Italy, Mussolini stated they would make no difference and what he really needed was tanks and aircraft. His initial demands included 300 tanks rising to enough equipment for seventeen tank battalions and thirty self-propelled artillery battalions.[1] He did not get them. The Italian dictator was grasping at straws, between 1940–43 he received less than 200 tanks from Hitler and half of those were second hand French tanks.

Mussolini was in a bad position to defend Italy. He had lost 200,000 men, killed or captured in North Africa. In December 1942 the 225,000 strong Italian 8th Army had collapsed on the Eastern Front contributing to the Germans defeat at Stalingrad. They had regrouped in Ukraine in January 1943, but in disgust Hitler had the survivors shipped home. Mussolini had another 580,000 men tied down in the Balkans fighting Albanian and Yugoslav partisans. Everywhere the Italian Army faced defeat.

To make matters worse the Italians had lost the bulk of their tanks in the fighting in North Africa. Very limited numbers of armoured fighting vehicles remained scattered throughout Albania and Greece, while the few remaining medium tanks and assault guns were gathered for the defence of mainland Italy. The Italians had recognised their tanks' shortcomings from the very start of the war, but were never able to rectify the situation.

They had discovered the L3 tankette was not suitable for modern tank warfare and the M11/39 medium tank was badly designed. At the first opportunity the latter had been replaced with the much better M13/40 and the slightly improved M14/41. Indeed these tanks, despite heavy losses, remained the standard Italian medium tank throughout the war. The improved M15/42 medium tank had an increased calibre to its gun and a more powerful engine, but was only produced in very limited numbers in early 1943. The Italians were mainly equipped with the adequate M13/40 and Semovente self-propelled gun by mid-1943, but it was too little too late.

Mussolini was so short of tanks that when Italian officers inspected the Italian 6th Army on Sicily in June they confirmed that German armour would be needed to help defend the island. Allied Supreme Commander General Dwight Eisenhower was altogether dismissive of the Italian garrison:

> Experience up to that time led us largely to discount the quality of the defence to be put up by the Italian formations; however, in the coming operation they would be defending their own territory, which could easily make a great difference.
>
> Our Intelligence staffs were vitally concerned with the strength of the German garrison.[2]

Having sacrificed the *Afrika Korps* and 5th Panzer Army Hitler was not anxious to strengthen German forces on Sicily. Nevertheless, he decided to reinforce the hastily reconstituted the 15th Panzergrenadier Division, which had capitulated in Tunisia, with an additional division. By July the Hermann Goering Division, with a company of formidable Tiger tanks, originally assigned to the 15th Panzergrenadier, had joined them on the island. German defenders stood at some 75,000 men with about 160 tanks.

'The ultimate size of the German garrison and the strength of the German Air Force in Sicily by the date of the invasion were, of course, unknown, and not very easy to assess. We had therefore to prepare for a considerable reinforcement,' noted Major General Freddie De Guingand, General Montgomery's Chief of Staff.[3] In contrast Mussolini's Sicilian garrison was of a considerable size but of dubious quality. The Italians had four field divisions with about 100 French built light tanks and five coastal divisions totalling 275,000 men to protect the island.[4] The tanks consisted mainly of tankettes and old French Renaults as well as a quantity of the Fiat 3000 light tank, essentially a copy of the Renault FT-17, armed with a 37mm gun.[5] These were supported by a number of Ansaldo 90/53 M-1941 self-propelled guns.

After the surrender of the Axis forces in Tunisia the writing was on the wall for Mussolini. His fate was finally sealed when the Allies' Operation Husky assaulted Italian soil with the invasion of Sicily on 10 July 1943. The British 8th Army, under General Montgomery, landed between Syracuse and the south-eastern tip of Italy. General Patton, with the American 7th Army, landed in the Gulf of Gela between Licata in the west and Scoglitti in the east. The objective of both armies was Messina on the north-eastern tip of the island; in the process it was hoped to trap the German-Italian forces before they could escape over the Messina Straits. It was the first time LSTs (Landing Ships, Tank) and LCTs (Landing Craft, Tank) were employed to put tanks ashore, whereas in Algeria and Morocco the Allies had been obliged to capture the ports first.

The Italians' military performance on Sicily was to be symptomatic of their failing commitment to Hitler's war. When British paratroops captured the Ponte Grande bridge on the day of the invasion they found themselves under attack by Italian troops and four armoured cars. After running out of ammunition they were forced to surrender, but the bridge was recaptured thirty minutes later.

The Hermann Goering Division was informed of the invasion via

Kesselring's headquarters in Rome rather than by the Italians on the ground. The German panzers and the Italian Livorno Mobile Division, the best Italian unit on the island, were ordered to counter-attack the American 1st and 45th Divisions in the vicinity of Gela. The 60-ton Tiger tanks were soon found to be ill suited to the rugged Sicilian countryside and the Italian armour was too light to offer any real resistance against American firepower.

The Italian Mobile Group E, consisting of over fifty light tanks, counter-attacked from Niscemi toward Gela and Piano Lupo, but became tangled with the Goering Division. One column of twenty Italian tanks lost two of its number to American troops with naval gunfire support before turning back.[6] Similarly a battalion from the Livorno was cut to pieces. The following day Italian and German tank forces launched parallel attacks along the Ponte Olivo road, but the rest of the Livorno Division was destroyed while attacking toward Gela.[7] Elements of the Hermann Goering Division with sixty tanks almost reached the beach but were repelled by the American 1st Division and elements of the American 2nd Armored Division. The German tanks and the Italian infantry retreated, having lost half their number.[8]

Within the first two days of the invasion the Allies landed over a beach line about 100 miles long, 80,000 men, 7,000 vehicles, 300 trucks and 900 guns. On 13 July Freddie De Guingand arrived at the British Tactical Headquarters near Pachino. He recalls:

> After dinner we went over to 30th Corps Mess for a drink, and found them entertaining the Italian General commanding the coastal division who had surrendered that day. I had a talk with him. He was obviously very tired of the war, and thought that the Italian field divisions had let him down. He was not fond of the Germans.[9]

Clearly there was bad blood between the Italians and Germans.

The fighting in Sicily triggered a political crisis in metropolitan Italy. Fifteen days after the invasion Mussolini was arrested in Rome and the new government under General Badoglio began to secretly negotiate with the Allies. Hitler was furious and did not trust Badoglio's claims that Italy would remain loyal to the German cause; he knew they were being duplicitous. General Jodl, Hitler's Chief of Operations urged caution, but the Führer knew the situation called for decisive action before Germany's southern flank became unhinged. Hitler declared:

> We'll play the same game while preparing everything to take over the

whole crew with one stroke, to capture all that riffraff. Tomorrow I'll send a man down there with orders for the commander of the 3rd Panzergrenadier Division to the effect that he must drive into Rome with a special detail and arrest the whole government, the King and the whole bunch right away. First of all, arrest the Crown Prince and take over the whole gang, especially Badoglio, and that entire crew. Then watch them cave in, and in two or three days there'll be another coup.[10]

Had the Italians acted quickly they could have sealed the Alpine bridges and tunnels and cut off the *Wehrmacht* already in Italy. The Italians had prepared the Brenner Pass for demolition and if they had blown the vital rail link it would have be out of action for at least six months. Unfortunately, changing sides took time and Badoglio had to establish contact with the Allies and agree terms for an armistice before he could act against the Germans. Six weeks were to be wasted leaving Italy vulnerable to a German counter-stroke. Although Hitler was dissuaded from putting the 3rd Panzergrenadiers into Rome, he swiftly secured the Alpine passes between Germany and Italy and between Italy and France. Eight divisions were assembled from France and southern Germany as Army Group B, ready to rescue those German forces in Italy, some of which were still fighting in Sicily.

In the meantime Hitler convened a conference on 27 July 1943 and presented four options for dealing with Italy if it should abandon the Axis. The first, Operation Eiche (Oak), envisaged a maritime or airborne rescue mission to secure Mussolini's release; the second, Operation Student, was more ambitious and called for the seizure of Rome in order to reinstate Mussolini; the third Operation Schwarz (Black) proposed the total occupation of Italy and the fourth Operation Achse (Axis) planned for the capture or destruction of the Italian Fleet. The last two were to be combined under the codename Axis. By late July Hitler fearing the worst began to draft War Directive 49 outlining the occupation of Italy and all her possessions. The directive was never issued but, on 31 July, a series of separate orders were sent out, informing German commanders of what they should do if Italy dropped out of the war.

The Allies failure to invade Calabria, the toe of Italy and to cut the Messina Straits to prevent the Germans and Italian troops escaping from Sicily, sealed mainland Italy's fate. The Germans successfully evacuated almost 55,000 personnel, fifty-one tanks, 9,789 vehicles and 163 guns during 1-7 August from the island. Despite this achievement they lost vital equipment including seventy-eight tanks and armoured cars, 287 guns and 3,500 vehicles.

The Italian garrison left to their own devices evacuated 7,000 men the week before Rome finally authorised a full-scale evacuation on 11 August. By the time the evacuation had ended five days later, they had managed to save 62,000 men, 227 vehicles and forty-one artillery pieces.[11] The American and British armies reached Messina on 17 August. The Italians lost an estimated 2,000 dead, 5,000 wounded and 137,000 captured and all their tanks on Sicily. This final military disaster was a blow from which the Italian Army would not recover.

Hitler knew that once the Axis forces had been defeated in North Africa the Allies would attempt a major seaborne operation against Italy or the Balkans. In early 1943 Hitler decided he would defend the entire region and a skeleton army headquarters was established in Munich to coordinate the planning for the defence of Italy. However, the growing drain on resources on the Eastern Front and the question over the reliability of the Italian Army, made the prospect of occupying and defending the whole of Italy fairly slim.

Instead plans were drawn up for a defensive line in the Apennines well north of Rome. In August contingency plans were drawn up to deal with an Italian defection. That month five infantry and two panzer divisions crossed the frontier. In central Italy the German 10th Army was activated, able to call on five divisions and another two near Rome.

In August the 1st SS Panzer Division transferred from the Eastern Front to northern Italy leaving behind its heavy equipment and armour. It had to make do with whatever was to hand. The unit's former commander, Sepp Dietrich, was annoyed to be assigned the task of escorting Mussolini's mistress to the rescued Italian dictator.

Up until the end of the Sicilian campaign and the successful escape of four German divisions, Hitler only had two divisions covering the whole of southern Italy. After securing Sicily in August, the Allies invaded mainland Italy at Reggio, Salerno and Taranto at the beginning of the following month.

By September 1943 the Italian Army had twenty-one divisions in mainland Italy - although half of these were of poor quality - four in Sardinia and another thirty-six overseas. To fend off a German takeover of northern and central Italy, the Italian Army had eight infantry divisions and two motorised/armoured divisions, supported by another eight weak infantry divisions. Against these forces the Germans could field about sixteen divisions.[12]

According to the German Intelligence Bureau, established to monitor

Italian troop movements into northern Italy, the Italian Army was suffering a severe ammunition shortage. Field Marshal Rommel, placed in command of securing Italy, was not surprised, he already had a low opinion of Italian defence industries after his experience with the ill-resourced Italian Army in North Africa.

Following the Italian armistice with the Allies on 9 September, Hitler issued the code word Achse (Axis). When the Germans learned of the armistice through a BBC broadcast, Field Marshal Kesselring at Frascati, near Rome, was alerted. For a day or two the fate of those German forces in central and southern Italy hung in the balance. A tense stand off took place between the two German divisions and five Italian divisions equipped with tanks, near the Italian capital. The Italian Army had received an updated version of their medium tank designated the M15/42 and by September just over eighty had been delivered to units deployed around Rome, thereby threatening Kesselring's plans.

If the Allied invasion fleet, gathered off Naples on 8 September, had sailed north and put its forces ashore near the Italian capital, the Italian Army would probably have used these tanks against the Germans and Hitler would have abandoned Kesselring and his eight divisions. Instead fate took a cruel hand and the American 5th Army landed, not near Rome, but at Salerno south of Naples. Field Marshal Kesselring's Chief of Staff threatened to dive bomb the Italian Army if it attempted to resist the *Wehrmacht*'s moves to take over their country. The cowed Italians did nothing.

German forces moved to occupy key points and installations through-out Italy, as well as Italian positions in southern France, the Balkans and the Aegean. The Italian Army handed over all its equipment to the *Wehrmacht*, except in Albania where an Italian division joined the partisans. The Germans had also planned to seize the Italian fleet, but most of the major surface vessels were already on their way from La Spezia and other Italian naval bases to British held Malta. Demoralised Italian troops were disarmed almost without firing a shot and the Germans confiscated all their weapon stocks. The *Wehrmacht* took pos-session of two thirds of Italy, including the industrial north, whose factories were soon put to work churning out arms for the German war effort.

The 1st SS Panzer took part in disarming the Italian Army and returned to the Eastern Front at the end of October, after committing a number of atrocities. Not only were the Germans highly successful in taking over most of Italy, but also the Italian-occupied zones in Albania, the Balkans, Greece and Yugoslavia. Considering the German defeat at El Alamein, the subsequent Torch landings and expulsion from North Africa and Sicily, Hitler must have been quietly pleased with himself for retrieving such a disastrous situation.

The German occupation of Italy was swift and efficient as Winston Churchill records:

> The Germans clamped down their military occupation upon the regions lying north of Rome; a skeleton Administration of uncertain allegiance sat in Rome, now open to the movements of the German Army; at Brindisi the King and Badoglio set up a rump Government under the eyes of an Allied Commission and with no effective authority beyond the boundaries of the administrative building of the town. As our armies advanced from the toe of the peninsula Allied military government took over the task of controlling the liberated regions.
>
> Italy was now to pass through the most tragic time in her history and to become the battle-ground of some of the fiercest fighting in the war.[13]

Rommel, who had fought so long beside the Italians in Libya and Tunisia, felt a pang of regret. Writing to his wife on 10 September 1943 he said:

> The events in Italy have, of course, long been expected and the very situation has now arisen which we have done all we could to avoid. In the south, Italian troops are already fighting alongside the British against us. Up north, Italian troops are being disarmed for the present and sent as prisoners to Germany. What a shameful end for an army! ...[14]

Following Operation Axis Hitler held a conference to decide the fate of Italy's remaining armoured forces. During the meeting it was pointed out that the Italian P26/40 had the best armour of any captured tank. Hitler authorised the construction of 150 to equip four regiments, however problems with the engines meant only sixty were ever supplied. Not only did they confiscate the Italian Army's armour, the Germans continued to build Italian M15/42 and P40 tanks as well as 75/18, 105/25 and 75/46 self-propelled guns for their own use. In total, through seizing armoured fighting vehicles from the Italian Army and continuing limited production, the *Wehrmacht* gained over 1,500 much needed tanks, assault guns and armoured cars.[15]

Some of Italy's best armoured fighting vehicles were the series of assault guns, based on medium tank chassis, that appeared from 1941 onwards. In particular the Semovente assault guns were to prove ideal for the *Wehrmacht*'s defensive battles as they sought to prevent the Allies progressing up the Italian peninsula. The Germans seized almost 200 Semovente assault guns, a number that was to double with continued production. Some of these were issued to the 26th Panzer and 336th Infantry Divisions in Italy. Italian assault guns were used to equip two Panzer, three Panzergrenadier, six Infantry and one mountain division fighting in Italy and the Balkans. The Germans also confiscated a small number of M13/40 and M14/41 medium tanks and about 120 M15/42, some of which were issued to two SS *Sturmgeschütze* detachments, Panzer Battalion Adria and RSI armoured units.[16]

Fiat-Ansaldo was the main tracked and wheeled armoured vehicle manufacturer in Italy. The Germans quickly took over the Fiat works in Turin and its subsidiary, OM, along with Alfa Romeo, Bianchi, Breda, Isotta-Fraschini and Pavesi, all in Milan. Once Italy's industries were firmly under German control they were forced to produce vehicles for the *Wehrmacht*. The Germans not only kept up a limited production of Italian tanks but also motor vehicles such as Alfa Romeo, Fiat and Spa trucks. Alfa Romeo, Bianchi, Isotta-Fraschini, Lancia and OM had manufactured trucks for the Italian Army, and both the German and British forces in North Africa made considerable use of them.

The Germans also put into production the Breda 61 semi-track artillery tractor, essentially an Italian copy of the German SdKfz 7. Several hundred were built in 1943-44 mainly for the *Wehrmacht*. Lancia also built 250 Lince scout cars, based on the British Daimler scout car, in 1944 for Italian paramilitary and police forces.

Despite this continued armoured fighting vehicle production, Fiat was not greatly cooperative and in Turin the Germans were met with strikes, sabotage and other forms of collective resistance. By the beginning of 1944 the Germans response to this was to order all Fiat production equipment be shipped to Germany; the resulting general strike right across northern Italy ensured that Fiat stayed put. Everything ground to a halt and during the first three months of 1945 Fiat only produced ten trucks a day.

The armistice did not have a happy outcome for the Italian people, resulting in a bloody civil war. Winston Churchill noted:

> Mussolini's bid for a Fascist revival plunged Italy into the horrors of civil war. In the weeks following the September armistice officers

and men of the Italian Army stationed in German-occupied Northern Italy and Patriots from the towns and countryside began to form Partisan units and to operate against the Germans and their compatriots who still adhered to the Duce.[17]

The Germans were not foolish enough to allow the RSI's armed forces to have significant numbers of tanks. The 150,000 strong *Guardia Nazionale Repubblicana* (GNR) was established in early December 1943 to retain order in the rear areas. The GNR Combattente had a single armoured battalion. Similarly only two armoured groups 'Leoncello' and 'San Giusto' equipped with some M13/40 and M14/41 medium tanks supported the four divisions of the RSI Army. The Republican Army totalled 400,000 and along with the GNR was only used to fight Italian resistance groups.[18]

By early October Hitler had reinforced his forces in Italy with 27,000 men, following his decision to abandon first Corsica and then Sardinia to the Allies. Field Marshal Kesselring managed to keep the Allies at bay and disarm the Italian Army, he then brought the invaders to a halt 100 miles from Rome. Eight months were to pass before the Allies reached the Italian capital and it would take another eight months before they managed to break out into the plains of northern Italy. During 1944 the Germans relied largely on Panzergrenadier and infantry divisions, which had their own armoured units. The only true panzer formations available in Italy were the 26th Panzer Division, Hermann Goering Panzer Division and the 504 and 508 heavy tank battalions.

The valuable confiscated Italian armour was to be employed resisting the Allies' spring offensive, known as Operation Diadem launched on 11 May 1944. This was intended to ensure the capture of Rome, following a breakthrough of the Gustav Line at Monte Cassino by the US 15th Army, while the British 8th Army pushed up the Liri Valley and US 5th Army advanced up the coast to link up with the Anzio bridgehead. The Allies had landed at Anzio, on the Italian west coast in striking distance of Rome, on 22 January only to find themselves hemmed in by elements of the 26th and Hermann Goering Panzer Divisions as well as the 3rd and 16th SS Panzergrenadier Divisions equipped with about 220 tanks.

The 90th Panzergrenadiers at Ceprano and the 1st Parachute Division at Acre managed to hold the British at bay and kept the road to Rome closed until the end of May. The Italian capital was not secured until 4 June and even then the Allies failed to encircle Kesselring's withdrawing forces. The Hermann Goering Division, though badly mauled, escaped being trapped by the Americans. Unfortunately for Kesselring the division was sent to Russia the following month.

Fending off Operation Diadem, the Germans lost 150 tanks and 300 self-propelled guns - half the available armour in Italy - as well as 720 various calibre guns.[19] These losses show just what a valuable contribution the Italian armour played in the German war effort in Italy. Four of Kesselring's battered infantry divisions had to be withdrawn for refit and another seven were badly weakened. Fortunately for him, four fresh divisions and a regiment of heavy tanks were on the way to help hold up the Allied advance.

The British 8th Army, struggling up the Adriatic coast, was being resisted by elements of ten German divisions by mid-September. This did not greatly deter its advance on the Senio River and by the end of the year the key armoured formations of the German 10th Army, the 26th Panzer and 90th Panzergrenadier Divisions, had suffered heavy casualties. Only the arrival of the 29th Panzergrenadier Division alleviated the pressure on the exhausted 26th Panzer.

Once the Breda and Innocenti factories in Rome, as well as the Ansaldo and Caproni works had been liberated, under British direction they were soon manufacturing spare parts and conducting vehicle overhauls for the Allies. Caproni turned out 450 vehicles a month and Saronno overhauled 1,000 engines a month. When British forces were withdrawn ready for D-Day many of their battered vehicles, which had faithfully motored all the way from Egypt to the Sangro, were left behind for ungrateful relieving units.

Mussolini made one last grand gesture at the end of 1944 when he sought to emulate Hitler's counter-offensive in the Ardennes. Carried out largely by Italians the counter-attack was launched in the Senio Valley on 26 December. Some of the RSI's remaining tanks may have taken part. The 8th Army, although exhausted and short of ammunition, easily stopped this attack.

On the west coast the Germans launched an attack in the Serchio Valley north of Lucca. They broke through to threaten the US 5th Army's lines of communication with its base at Leghorn. The Germans were blocked with the assistance of a division detached from the British 8th Army. This delayed the 5th Army's planned attack toward Bologna and in turn brought the British 8th Army to a halt, because it had to conserve ammunition until the Americans were ready. By the end of December there were still 161 Italian tanks and assault guns serving German units in Italy.[20]

The requirements of the crumbling Eastern Front saw the departure of the 16th SS Panzergrenadier Division from Italy in the New Year. Kesselring was appointed Supreme Commander West in March 1945 and replaced in Italy by General von Vietinghoff. German forces on the Italian front amounted to twenty-three divisions, with two others partly formed and six Italian divisions. The 10th and 14th Armies, holding the left and right flanks respectively, each had a panzer corps.

By the spring of 1945 neither of the German Armies had any reserves of their own, although the battered 29th and 90th Panzergrenadier Divisions remained in von Vietinghoff's Army Group Reserve. These units, plus the 26th Panzer Division, continued to fight tenaciously as they were slowly pushed north. They finally sustained a death blow trying to escape across the River Po on 23 April, losing eighty tanks, 1,000 motor vehicles and 300 pieces of artillery. By this stage it was pointless to continue the fight in Italy. Two days later the last of the *Panzertruppen* laid down their arms and the official unconditional surrender in Italy was signed on 2 May 1945. The remaining panzers and Italian tanks were turned over to the Allies. Mussolini received his last message from Hitler on 24 April informing him that Soviet forces had entered Berlin, four days later he was shot dead by Italian partisans.

Chapter Eight

Recycling Uncle Sam

SS-Obersturmbannführer (Lieutenant Colonel) Otto Skorzeny watched from a hill overlooking the battlefield as his ten tanks, disguised as American vehicles, attacked along the Warche Valley on 21 December 1944. Skorzeny was anxious about this special mission from the very start, although he had been reassured, from a legal standpoint, that it was fine for his men to wear American uniforms as long as they removed them before opening fire. Skorzeny had also been alarmed about the operational security of Operation Grief (Griffon). This had been compromised when American troops had captured German orders in late November 1944. These had been widely distributed on 30 October calling for men with knowledge of the English language and American dialect, as well as captured US clothing, equipment, weapons and vehicles.[1] The Americans had to be aware that some kind of subterfuge was at hand and would have been alert to such deception.

Below Skorzeny one of his Panther tanks, painted in olive drab and supported by German infantry in an unconvincing assortment of American uniforms, advanced on Malmedy. It was driven off by an American anti-tank gun. The other nine tanks attempted to capture a bridge over the Warch in order to reach Stavlot. The first tank was lost to a mine and began to burn. American infantry, manning a roadblock, were forced back but when the Germans attempted to cross the bridge Americans armed with bazookas knocked out two more tanks. Two American tank destroyers then accounted for two further German tanks. Skorzeny, seeing how things were progressing, ordered his men to fall back but none of his remaining tanks made it. So ended the 150th Panzer Brigade's feeble attempt to pass itself off as American. This incident marked one of the stranger aspects of Hitler's Ardennes offensive.

The sheer volume of American tank production meant it was inevitable that the German Army would recycle captured American armoured fighting vehicles. Surprisingly, this was in far fewer numbers than might have been expected. The Germans reused some American

M5 light tanks, M4 medium tanks, M8 armoured cars and M3 half-tracks, but on a completely ad hoc basis. In France the Germans even reused a British Sherman Firefly armed with a 17-pounder gun, captured during the Normandy battle, but again this was on an individual basis.

The Germans under Rommel first came up against American built armour, fighting with the British Army in Egypt and Libya and subsequently with the US Army in Tunisia. America supplied Britain with three main types of tank, the M3 Light Tank or Stuart, the Lee/Grant and Sherman medium tanks. The Sherman became the most important tank in the British Army simply because it eventually outnumbered all other tank types in service. The first Stuarts were delivered in July 1941 and used to replace British built light tanks.[2] These were followed by the M3 medium tank; ordered in 1940, they first went into action in North Africa in May 1942 at Gazala. Dubbed the Grant by the British, their hull-mounted 75mm guns gave the Germans a nasty shock. The introduction of the American Lend-Lease Act in March 1941 enabled the British to receive numbers of the differently armed M3 Lee.

'Up to May of 1942 our tanks had in general been superior in quality to corresponding British types,' noted Rommel in his dairy. 'This was now no longer true, at least not to the same extent.'[3] He went on to add: 'The advent of the new American tank had torn great holes in our ranks. Our entire force now stood in heavy and destructive combat with a superior enemy.'[4] Samples of the M3 medium tank captured in North Africa and in Russia were soon whisked back to Kummersdorf for technical evaluation.

Both the Grant/Lee tank types were replaced as the M4 Sherman became available. This first made its appearance in North Africa in October 1942.[5] While the concept of the M3 was good, it was only really an interim fix. Initial Sherman casualties, lost to German mines and anti-tank guns, occurred with the British 9th Armoured Brigade during the opening stages of the Battle of El Alamein on 23 October. The first tank-to-tank engagement took place the following day between Shermans of the 2nd Armoured Brigade and tanks of the 15th Panzer Division. Rommel was equally impressed by the Sherman: 'Their new tank, the General Sherman, which came into action for the first time during this battle [El Alamein], showed itself to be far superior to ours.'[6] He was not happy about this development.

The M3 light and medium tanks, as well as the Sherman, first went into action with the American Army against the Vichy French in North

Africa. When American units were deployed overseas they normally exchanged their medium M3s for M4s. The only unit not to do this was the US 1st Armored Division. This unit formed part of the Centre Task Force of Operation Torch during the landing in Algeria's Oran area on 7-8 November 1942.

From Oran they were rushed to Tunisia and came under the command of the British 1st Army for the drive on Tunis. The division's 2nd Battalion, 13th Armored Regiment, lost forty-two tanks to the Germans in fighting around Djedeiba and Tebourba. Despite receiving Sherman replacements, by the time of the Axis surrender, the 1st Armored still had fifty-one M3s on its strength.[7] These were handed over to the Free French Forces for driver training. The M3 was then withdrawn from service in the Mediterranean and European theatres of operation.

The British and Germans were soon aware of the Americans' seemingly limitless resources. In Tunisia war correspondent Alan Moorehead observed:

> Most of the American stuff was first-class, and even as good or better than the German... The diesel Sherman was certainly the best tank of its class. The jeeps, at the other end of the scale, were unmatched, and the Germans loved to capture them for their own use, just as we loved to get hold of a Volkswagen.[8]

Senior Lieutenant Heinz Schmidt, after encountering American troops in Tunisia, was amazed at the quality and quantity of their equipment:

> As I drove on everywhere I came on detached groups of American infantry, who had hidden in the rocks and bush of the mountain slopes. Their transport was tucked away in the valleys. A considerable number of jeeps and trucks fell into our hands - all new, and, to us, astonishingly well equipped.[9]

His men also captured six American halftracks, which were used as replacements but they were subsequently lost in the fighting at Kasserine Pass.

Only at Kasserine Pass did the exhausted Germans enjoy any real success against the inexperienced Americans pressing on their western flank. The veteran 21st Panzer Division attacked the US 2nd Armored Division on 14 February 1943 at Sidi Bouzid and large numbers of Grant, Lee and Sherman tanks were destroyed. In total 2nd Armored lost 150 tanks and 1,600 men captured in the heavy fighting.[10] A week later the Germans captured another twenty tanks, thirty armoured personnel carriers and a similar number of 75mm anti-tank guns. Rommel noted:

> The Americans were fantastically well equipped and we had a lot to learn from them organisationally. One particularly striking feature was the standardisation of their vehicles and spare parts. British experience had been put to good use in the American equipment.[11]

In Tunisia the *Panzertruppen* made use of limited numbers of the M4 Sherman and M3 Lee medium tanks captured from the 1st and 2nd Armored Divisions. A German photographer caught a sample of each tank undergoing trials with panzer crews. Additionally an M4 was quickly despatched back to Germany for exploitation. One was captured near Sbetla on 22 February 1943 and driven the 350 kilometres to Tunis in four and a half days. It was then shipped to the Army Weapons Office test centre at Kummersdorf where everyone was suitably impressed; this was the American T-34.

The Germans were also adept at redeploying captured American artillery. In February 1943 Lieutenant Colonel Fritz Fullreide was flown to Tunisia and tasked with defending the Fondouk passes. His German-Italian battle group was equipped with armoured cars, anti-tank guns and some artillery. Two American tank companies captured their forward positions at El Ala on 5 March. In response German commandos drove the Americans out during the hours of darkness and brought two captured light howitzers to bear on a pair of advancing Grant tanks.[12] Three rounds and the tanks were immobilised. Kampfgruppe Fullreide followed this up with an attack on American troops holding the El Zhagales Pass. The Americans were again driven back and the Germans captured a lorry park with a number of re-useable vehicles.

American losses were swiftly replaced following Kasserine and 5,400 trucks were shipped in. It took less than three weeks to deliver them after General Eisenhower's initial request for extra transport for the Tunisian campaign. 'The later move of the entire US 2nd Corps from the Tebessa region to northern Tunisia,' Eisenhower recalled, 'would have been completely impossible without the presence of these additional trucks.'[13]

In terms of the American Army being bloodied at Kasserine, Eisenhower tried to put a brave face on things:

> Eventually the cost was reduced, since most of our personnel were

losses in prisoners, whom we largely recovered at the end of the war. We suffered casualties in personnel and equipment, but by the time the enemy had succeeded in retiring to his former positions his losses in both categories were equal to ours. American losses from 14-23 February were 192 killed, 2,624 wounded, 2,459 prisoners and missing.[14]

On the Eastern Front the Germans encountered thousands of American and British tanks sent to assist the Red Army. Following Operation Overlord and the D-Day landings in Normandy, considerable numbers of American and British Shermans fell into German hands and the *Panzertruppen*, desperately short of replacements, pressed them into service whenever they could. At Villers-Bocage the British 7th Armoured Division lost at least twenty Cromwells, four Sherman Fireflys, three Honeys, three scout cars and a half-track on 13 June 1944, to elements of the 101 SS Heavy Tank Battalion and the Panzer Lehr Division. Some of these were subsequently turned on their previous owners.

This was nothing compared with Montgomery's attempt to secure Caen during June and July which saw the British and Canadian Armies lose well over 500 tanks, numbers of which the Germans were able to salvage. Between them the 21st Panzer Division, 25th Panzergrenadier Division, 10th SS Panzer Division, 5th Parachute Jäger Division, Panzer Brigade 150 and Captured Tank Company 281 mustered thirty-nine Shermans in the summer of 1944.[15] Many other panzer units also employed individual tanks and armoured fighting vehicles. The Germans found it much harder to salvage tanks in Normandy than in North Africa. By this stage of the war the *Wehrmacht* was under constant air attack by Allied fighter-bombers.

In Normandy the Germans even used captured American transport to help facilitate their escape. In mid-June 1944, as the German defence in the Cotentin peninsula collapsed in the face of the American advance toward the port of Cherbourg, the German 77th Infantry Division staged a dramatic breakout. Things initially did not get off to a good start when, in the early morning of 18 June, General Stegmann led his division south only to have his horse drawn transport caught by Allied fighter-bombers. In the chaos Stegmann's car was hit and he was killed. Colonel Bacherer took command of the remaining 2,000 men and pressed on. The German 243rd Infantry Division launched an attack northward with a few self-propelled guns to try a clear a way for the 77th. Bacherer's men successfully burst through the American lines with twelve captured jeeps and 250 American prisoners.[16]

At 05.30 on Saturday 16 December 1944, 2,000 German guns heralded a surprise German offensive through the Ardennes on the Western Front. For the next five weeks the panzers fought a desperate struggle to reach Brussels and Antwerp in what became known as the Battle of the Bulge. It represented the panzers' last gasp before the Allies pushed across the Rhine and, for a time, it was the Americans and British, not the Russians, who faced the bulk of Germany's remaining tank strength.

Hitler tried to reuse American armour to support an audacious piece of subterfuge under the guise of Operation Grief to spearhead the offensive and cause confusion in the Allies' rear areas. SS-Sturmbanführer Otto Skorzeny was appointed to command Panzer Brigade 150, tasked to capture the Meuse bridges before they could be demolished. Skorzeny was a Hitler trustee. It was he who had 'rescued' the deposed Mussolini in September 1943, helped contain the plot against the Führer in July 1944 and kidnapped Admiral Horthy, the Hungarian regent, to stop the country defecting in mid-October. He had first met Hitler the day after Mussolini had been deposed and must have made an impression.

Skorzeny was summoned to Hitler's Rastenburg HQ on 22 October 1944, where he was congratulated on his mission to Hungary and promoted from major to lieutenant colonel. Skorzeny's coup in Budapest had hardly been very subtle as Tiger tanks had backed his seizure of Admiral Horthy. Hitler then outlined Operation Herbstnebel (Autumn Mist) or Wacht am Rhein (Watch on the Rhine) as the forthcoming Ardennes counter-offensive was known. Skorzeny was instructed that he would lead a panzer brigade of 2,500 men under Operation Greif or Griffon. This was to be no ordinary unit for they were to pass themselves off as withdrawing Americans, fully kitted out with American uniforms, weapons and vehicles. The Germans had masqueraded in foreign uniforms before, particularly in Poland and the Low Countries, but nothing had been tried on this scale.

Skorzeny was given less than five weeks to prepare, and to equip his brigade he wanted fifteen American tanks, twenty self-propelled guns, twenty armoured cars, 120 trucks, 100 jeeps and forty motorcycles.[17] Despite the vast numbers of American tanks, self-propelled guns, armoured cars, half-tracks lorries and jeeps captured by the Germans in the preceding months, Skorzeny soon found that the hard pressed frontline commands were reluctant to give up their precious booty.

Under Operation Rabenhugel, Oberkommando West divided the requisition between the three Heeresgruppe or Army Groups in the West. Heeresgruppe G was ordered to provide eight tanks and twenty trucks; Heeresgruppe H was to provide two tanks and fifty jeeps and Heeresgruppe B, five tanks and thirty jeeps, which were to be delivered to Skorzeny's training ground at Grafenwohr.[18]

Despite his repeated complaints, he found himself being supplied with spare German equipment rather than American. During late November 1944 his unit was equipped with five Panther tanks, five StuG assault guns, six German armoured cars and six armoured personnel carriers. Only seventy-four trucks and fifty-seven cars arrived, along with two Sherman tanks and two American armoured cars.[19] Skorzeny discovered he was the recipient of worn out rubbish, as 30 per cent of the vehicles needed repairs and both the Shermans were inoperable.[20] To make matters worse the Brigade found itself flooded with Polish and Russian equipment, provided by units who had little idea of the role to be played by Panzer Brigade 150.

The Brigade also lacked 1,500 American steel helmets and the uniforms that had been gathered were summer issue. American speakers were also found to be in short supply. Skorzeny had little choice but to scale back the Brigade from three to two battalions and gather 150 of the best English speakers into a commando unit called Enheit Stielau.

By late November the Brigade had twenty-two Panthers and fourteen StuGs, with crews provided by the 2nd and 6th Panzer Divisions. When it finally went into battle it only seems to have deployed ten Panthers and five StuGs.[21] The Panthers were disguised with sheet metal to resemble American M10 tank destroyers. These, Skorzeny cynically noted, were only sufficient to: 'deceive very young American troops seeing them at night from very far away'.[22]

His American vehicles were very thin on the ground, comprising four American Scout Cars, fifteen trucks and thirty jeeps, plus a single Sherman, up and running on the eve of the attack. All the vehicles were painted olive drab and given Allied white five pointed recognition stars. The under strength Brigade had little choice but to become three Kampfgruppe, or battle groups, dubbed X, Y and Z.

Rumours began to circulate that this odd assortment of armoured fighting vehicles and motor vehicles had been assembled to dash across France to relieve the German garrisons still holding out in some of the French ports. Another circulated to the effect that they were headed for Paris to seize General Eisenhower, the Supreme Allied Commander. It was only on 10 December 1944 that they found out their true mission.

The Germans massed twenty-eight divisions, eight of which were panzer, totalling some 275,000 men, 950 armoured fighting vehicles and 1,900 pieces of artillery. The main attacking forces were the 6th SS Panzer Army with 450 tanks and self-propelled guns, 5th Panzer Army with about 350 AFVs and 7th Army with no armour. Lying in their path were just 75,000 American troops. Crucially the *Luftwaffe* was not up to the job of securing local air superiority and fuel was critically short. Each German tank had just 150 gallons, enough for two to three days of combat and for them to cover about 150 miles. After that they were on their own. It would be a race against time and the weather. Hitler's generals wanted to restrict their goal to Liege, but Hitler ruled that the panzers must reach Antwerp.

The attack commenced on 16 December 1944 under the cover of heavy cloud. The 1st and 12th SS Panzer Divisions launched the 6th Panzer Army's main thrusts. Panzer Brigade 150's three Kampfgruppen were assigned to the 1st SS and 12th SS Panzer Division and the 12th Volks Grenadier Division. Kampfgruppe Peiper, drawn from 1st SS, consisted of 100 Panzer Mk IV and V, forty-two formidable King Tigers (some estimates put the figures as low as twenty and as high as seventy) and twenty-five assault guns.

Kampfgruppe Peiper placed two captured Shermans at the head of the column to fool the Americans when they rolled into Bucholtz Station.[23] These tanks may have belonged to Skorzeny's Kampfgruppe X commanded by SS-Obersturmbannführer Willi Hardieck, who attended Peiper's operational briefing on 15 December. Finding Bucholtz empty the battle group drove on to Honsfeld and joined a stream of American traffic. The town's defenders were taken completely by surprise and Peiper captured fifty reconnaissance vehicles, eighty trucks and fifteen anti-tank guns, some of which were hurriedly pressed into service.[24]

The following day the column was caught in an air strike and a flak tank was lost and several other vehicles damaged. On 17 December Peiper's troops attacked an American convoy near Baugnez, which surrendered after a brief fight. Some of the thirty captured vehicles joined the German convoy, their American drivers having 'volunteered' to drive to Ligneuville. Some of the American POWs were subsequently shot in what became known as the 'Malmedy Massacre'. Desperately short of fuel Colonel Peiper, instead of pushing west, turned north to seize 50,000 gallons of American gasoline at Bullingen. His force was eventually surrounded and destroyed leaving forty-five tanks and sixty self-propelled guns abandoned north of the Ambleve River.

The American 9th and 10th Armored Divisions were slow to react in the first few days as a sense of chaos spread. Just seven German self-propelled guns prevented 102 Shermans of the 10th from making much effort around Echternach. In the first five days of fighting the Germans destroyed 300 American tanks but it was not enough. General Eisenhower, Allied Supreme Commander, countered by moving the 7th Armored Division to St Vith and elements of the 10th Armored and US 101st Airborne Divisions to Bastogne. The Panzer Lehr Division was not quick enough and the Americans beat them to Bastogne. In the meantime the 116th Panzer Division slipped between Bastogne and St Vith, but Bastogne's defenders held up 2nd Panzer. St Vith fell on 21 December though American artillery fire forced the two Panzer Armies to become entangled with the Fifth.

Once Hohes Venn was reached, Skorzeny's three Kampfgruppen were to pass round their assigned units, but things did not run smoothly and they got tangled up at Losheim. Skorzeny realised by the evening of the second day of the offensive that the 150th Panzer Brigade would not manage to seize the Meuse bridges, so he suggested that his unit serve as a regular combat force. Under the direction of Colonel Wilhelm Mohnke he was ordered to help take Malemdy in order to open up the roads to reach Kampfgruppe Peiper.

All three of his battle groups joined 1st SS Panzer and were thrown into the attack on Malmedy on 21 December. The Americans were tipped off by a prisoner and for three days Skorzeny's fake American tanks battled to capture Malmedy until they were all knocked out. Skorzeny's American dressed infantry attacking Malmedy came under fire by American artillery using the proximity fuse for the first time. The Americans successfully cut the bridges west of Malmedy.

General von Rundstedt counselled Hitler to withdraw the two panzer armies east of Bastogne ready for the inevitable Allied counter-attack. Hitler realised even if the capture of Antwerp could not be realised, retention of the bulge would slow the Allies' attack on the Ruhr. To secure the bulge, Bastogne had to be taken. Two days after the fall of St Vith the weather cleared and allied fighter-bombers began to attack the strung out German armies. Tanks from 2nd Panzer ground to a halt at Celles, just four miles from the River Meuse, their fuel tanks exhausted. The American 2nd Armored finished off the rest of the division. Similarly the 3rd checked the 2nd SS Panzer, while the 116th and

Panzer Lehr also came to a halt. German tanks also failed to capture the encircled town of Bastogne. The siege was lifted by the arrival of the US 4th Armored. Kampfgruppe Peiper's remaining Tiger II was set on fire on Christmas Day.

Early in the New Year under appalling weather conditions the Allies counter-attacked and, on 8 January 1945, Hitler at last authorised a partial withdrawal. A massive Russian offensive on the Eastern Front made it imperative that the 6th SS Panzer Army be re-deployed. Under cover of the weather the Germans began to give up their gains. By 28 January the bulge had been eliminated completely and the Germans had suffered 100,000 casualties as well as losing most of their armour. Both sides are thought to have lost as many as 800 tanks apiece.

Elsewhere to ease the pressure on the Ardennes offensive, the Germans launched a major offensive in Alsace, involving ten divisions. While this attack caused a crisis, Reichsführer-SS Heinrich Himmler squandered Nazi Germany's dwindling reserves. He directed the German 19th Army to launch a diversionary counter-offensive in Alsace once Autumn Mist bogged down, including the 6th, 10th and 17th SS Divisions. The Germans committed their last small reserve in the west, to a battle not directly supporting the Ardennes operation. It was to be the final German attack on the Western Allies and Operation Nordwind (North Wind) got within nine miles of Strasbourg for the loss of 25,000 casualties.

The survivors of Panzer Brigade 150 were withdrawn from the line on 28 December and returned to Grafenwohr where the brigade was disbanded. The only parts of Skorzeny's command that achieved any notable results were the Enheit Stielau commandos. They caused panic and paranoia behind the lines; one captured group spread the false rumour that they were out to capture General Eisenhower and his staff. Lieutenant General Brian Horrocks had a grudging respect for the activities of Skorzeny's men:

> Although, when the time came, only a relatively small number were able to operate behind our lines - certainly no more than fifty jeep loads - their presence had a disproportionate effect, and the atmosphere of suspicion they created greatly hampered the movements of our own personnel. I was once asked by an American sentry to establish my credentials by naming 'the second largest town in Texas'. As I did not know the answer, I had some difficulty in avoiding arrest.[25]

Skorzeny's concerns proved well founded, as a total of eighteen commandoes were captured, court-martialled and shot for masquerading as Americans. Perhaps appropriately a knocked out snow bound PzKpfw M4 748(a) Sherman, belonging to the 5th Parachute Jäger Division, was photographed outside the Hotel des Ardennes. It aptly summed up the failure of Hitler's Operation Herbstnebel; recycling Uncle Sam had got him nowhere.

Chapter Nine

Unreliable Allies

The crews sat with their tank engines idling; they had just moved up to their fighting positions east of the Romanian town of Arad. One of the commanders raised his binoculars and scanned the horizon for Russian T-34s. The brown uniforms of the crews showed them not to be *Panzertruppen* but Hungarians. In fact there were no panzers in the vicinity; they were on their own. The Hungarian Army's 4th Corps, supporting a German offensive, attacked the Romanian town of Arad in September 1944, spearheaded by the Hungarian 1st Armoured Division, the 1st Field Cavalry Replacement Brigade and the 7th Assault Gun Battalion. This was the last independent action by the Hungarian Army during the Second World War and one of the very few successes achieved by the limited armoured forces of Eastern Europe.

Although Arad fell on 13 September the Hungarians were soon engaged in a violent six-day battle with the turncoat Romanians, who, enjoying significant air support, succeeded in destroying twenty-three Hungarian tanks. After the arrival of the Red Army a joint Soviet-Romanian counter-attack was launched to drive out the invaders. The Hungarian 7th Assault Gun Battalion claimed to have destroyed sixty-seven Soviet T-34/85 tanks, at the cost of eight German-supplied StuG III assault guns destroyed and a further twenty-two damaged. The Hungarian troops, lacking air support and completely outclassed by the Soviets, were forced to evacuate Arad just a week after capturing it.

Hitler's efforts to supplement his *Panzerwaffe* by employing the armies of Eastern Europe were his undoing. The Bulgarian, Finnish, Hungarian and Romanian armies were far from mechanised and only had the most rudimentary tank forces. Nonetheless, the German 13th Motorised Infantry Division crossed Hungary into Romania in October 1940 followed by the 16th Panzer Division two months later to 'safeguard' Romanian security. This time there was to be no panzer heist; instead Hitler ended up grudgingly supplying tanks to them. By the end of February 1941 Hitler had massed 680,000 troops in Romania, which had a 300-mile long border with Ukraine stretching from Poland to the

Black Sea, poised to strike the Soviet Union. To his annoyance, thanks to Mussolini they were distracted by the prospect of the British landing at the Greek port of Salonika and thereby threatening his southern flank.

Hitler felt he had little choice but to secure southern Thrace before attacking the Soviet Union. Once this was done the region would be handed over to the Bulgarians. Hitler lent on his Tripartite Pact Allies, Bulgaria and Hungary, offering them territorial concessions if they would assist his panzers.[1] Admiral Horthy, Hungary's ruler, was hardly in a position to refuse, having greatly benefited from Hitler's destruction of Czechoslovakia.

Hitler's troops in Romania crossed the Danube on 28 February and took up position in Bulgaria ready to attack Greece. The Yugoslavs were not so accommodating and, concerned that they might side with the Allies, Hitler incorporated them into his invasion plans. Horthy committed two Hungarian motorised brigades and a cavalry brigade equipped with about 150 Toldi light tanks, Italian supplied L.35 tankettes and Csaba armoured cars for the assault on Yugoslavia. King Boris of Bulgaria provided the Bulgarian 5th Army, equipped with less than sixty tankettes and light tanks.

Horthy's armoured forces proved an embarrassment; his troops reached Novi Sad on the Danube, but one armoured unit, after driving thirty miles south of the border, ran out of petrol. On 13 April German and Hungarian troops entered Belgrade. King Boris's infantry divisions followed the panzers across the Macedonian frontier, occupying most of Yugoslav Macedonia and moved to administer the Greek regions of eastern Macedonia and western Thrace, much to the irritation of Mussolini.

The East European and Italian armoured formations supporting Operation Barbarossa, Hitler's invasion of the Soviet Union, proved more of a liability than an asset. Admiral Horthy and Romanian ruler, General Ion Antonescu, were to regret being so intoxicated by the panzers' triumph in Western Europe and in the Balkans. In total the Finnish, Hungarian, Italian and Romanian satellite armies provided in excess of 1 million men, including the Hungarian 1st and 2nd, Italian 3rd Mobile, Romanian 1st and Slovak Fast armoured divisions. Ultimately Hitler was to pay a terrible price for relying on them.

Hitler's East European Allies were able to commit barely 300 armoured vehicles to the invasion of Russia. In return for German assistance in Libya, Mussolini's contribution initially consisted of the 60,000 strong *Corpo Spedizione Italiane* in Russia (CSIR) consisting of the Pasubio and Torino Infantry Divisions and the 3rd Mobile Division, Principe Amedeo Duca d'Aosta. However, Mussolini could spare no medium tanks after his losses to the British. The armour of the 3rd Mobile was totally inadequate for the campaign against the Red Army, consisting of a light tank group equipped with the obsolete L.3 tankette.[2]

In 1941 Hungary had just 189 armoured vehicles and Horthy's total contribution to Hitler's *Panzerwaffe* amounted to about 1,200-1,500 tanks, assault guns and armoured cars throughout the war. These were used to equip Hungary's armoured divisions and assault artillery battalions. Leading Hungarian manufacturers were Ganz, Manfred Weiss at Csepel and MÁVAG (Magyar Királyi Államvasutak Gépgyára – Hungarian Royal State Railroads Machine Factory), Budapest and MVG (Magyar Vagonés Gépgyar –Hungarian Railway Carriages Factory) at Raba. Armoured vehicle production was painfully slow and amounted to about 1,000 vehicles for the whole of the war. They built just 120 38M Toldi light tank, 500 40M Turan medium tanks, sixty 43M Zrinyi assault howitzers, around 100 40M Nimrod self-propelled guns and 171 39M Csaba armoured cars.[3]

The Turan I was patterned on the Czech LT-35 and armed with a 40mm gun, while the subsequent Turan II had a 75mm. The 43M Zrinyi II, armed with a 105mm assault howitzer mounted on a widened Hungarian Turan tank chassis, was designed in 1942. The earlier Zrinyi I was only developed as a prototype armed with a 75mm gun. The Hungarian Army was also supplied with a few hundred German LT-35/38, PzKpfw IV and StuG III as the Turan and Zrinyi were late going into production.

Horthy committed large numbers of troops to Barbarossa including the Carpathian Group and the Mobile Corps.[4] The latter had to requisition cars and tractors to supplement its obsolete armour.[5] Forming part of the German 17th Army the Mobile Corps fought well in the Ukraine, but was prevented from entering Nikolayev because of the presence of Romanian troops. After reaching the Donets the Corps was withdrawn and returned home in November 1941.

General Antonescu willingly provided the largest number of the satellite forces.[6] However, his armoured forces were very weak; in June 1941 the Romanians had just over 180 tankettes and light tanks, including 126 Czech LT-35s and seventy-three French R-35s. Many of the French tanks had come from the fleeing Polish Army and, lacking spares, were not committed to the invasion. Unlike Hungary, neighbouring Romania had no indigenous tank capability. General von Rundstedt's Army Group South included the equivalent of fourteen Romanian divisions. Six months before Operation Barbarossa Hitler secretly allocated Romania a key role. He directed:

> It will be the task of Romania to support the attack of the German southern flank, at least at the outset, with its best troops; to hold down the enemy where German forces are not engaged; and to provide auxiliary services in the rear areas.[7]

Romania fielded its 3rd Army, consisting of the Mountain Corps and Cavalry Corps, as well as the 4th Army. These forces totalled about 150,000 men, but later with reinforcements swelled to over 300,000. At the time of the invasion the Romanian Army only had a single tank brigade. On 22 June 1941 the Romanians pushed into southern Russia but the 4th Army, after suffering 98,000 casualties, was withdrawn in October 1941 for refit. The Mountain Corps fought with the German 11th Army in the Crimea and the Cavalry Corps with 1st Panzer Army. Romanian forces were involved in the attack on Sevastopol and fought across the Kerch Straits, while others were in the Caucasus with the 3rd Panzer Army.

Premier Tiso's rump Slovak State provided Army Group South with a Slovak Army Corps of two infantry divisions. Lacking transport they were mainly restricted to a security role and were sent home in August 1941. In contrast the Slovak Mobile Division, under Major General Agust Malar, fought with some distinction during the winter of 1941-42 and helped cover the German withdrawal from the Caucasus after Stalingrad. The division had a single tank company with just twelve Skoda tanks.[8] The Slovaks also provided a Security Division that served in Ukraine.

The Finns, who had found themselves at war with Stalin over a boundary dispute in 1939, also threw their lot in with Hitler. The Finnish Army, with just three battalions of captured Soviet tanks, got to within thirty miles of Leningrad, while other Finnish forces, supported by a German division, struck north of Lake Lagoda. The Bulgarians formed their 1st Armoured Brigade in June 1941. Trained by German officers it fought against Bulgarian and Yugoslav partisans. While Bulgaria had taken part in the invasion of Yugoslavia and Greece, and declared war on Britain and America in December 1941, King Boris was less keen to entangle himself with Russia. Arguing that his Army lacked mechanisation, Boris wisely avoided taking part in Barbarossa.

Needing additional manpower for his 1942 offensive, Hitler despatched Field Marshal Keitel to persuade Antonescu, Horthy and Mussolini to provide additional troops, and reinforcements began to arrive during the summer. The Hungarians sent the 2nd Army, consisting of 3rd, 4th and 7th Corps, bringing their contribution up to 200,000 men. A single Hungarian armoured division equipped with PzKpfw 38(t), Panzer Mk III/IV, Toldi light tanks, Csaba armoured cars and Nimrod self-propelled guns supported these forces.[9]

Similarly Antonescu formed his 1st Tank Division, later re-designated 'Greater Romania' and organised along German lines, by expanding his existing armoured brigade.[10] A complete lack of tanks prevented him from completing any other armoured divisions, although the 5th and 8th Cavalry Divisions were being converted in 1944 when Romania defected. The 1st Tank Division was mainly equipped with the inadequate LT-35 and some CKD light tanks.

Mussolini despatched reinforcements in the shape of the 2nd Corps and the Alpine Corps. These formations along with the CSIR, re-designated the 35th Corps, created the 227,000 strong Italian 8th Army. The heaviest armour sent to Russia by Mussolini was the L6/40 light tank and this represented an appalling capability gap. The Italians also fielded the L40 47/32 light assault gun and AB41 armoured car in Russia. The Finns bolstered their armoured forces by creating an armoured division in August 1943 totalling 150 tanks. These were organised into two brigades equipped with outdated Soviet T-26 light tanks and an assault gun brigade with German supplied StuG IIIs.

Although Bulgaria resisted calls to join the war against Russia it provided reinforcements to alleviate pressure on German security forces in the Balkans. In January 1942 the Bulgarian 1st Army occupied most of Serbia and from mid-1943 was fighting Yugoslav partisans. Toward the end of 1942 the Bulgarians became alarmed by German weapons deliveries to neutral Turkey, Bulgaria's traditional foe, so as a counterweight Hitler agreed to equip two armoured brigades, one cavalry division and ten infantry divisions. The Germans shipped Panzer III and IV tanks as well as StuG III assault guns to the Bulgarian 1st Armoured Brigade in July 1943.

The Hungarian 2nd Army under General Jany reached the front at Kursk in June 1942 and moved to hold the line along the Don, south of Voronezh. By the end of August General Italo Gariboldi's Italian 8th Army had become a cause for concern to the Germans. Deputy Chief of

Staff, General Blumentritt, was appalled by what he found:

General Halder had sent me on a flying visit to the Italian sector, as an alarming report had come in that the Russians had penetrated it. However, I found the attack had been made by only one Russian battalion, but an entire Italian division had bolted.[11]

Fatefully the Romanian 3rd Army under Colonel General Dumitrescu came back into the line in October to the north-west of Stalingrad. Another Romanian Corps, part of 4th Army, moved into place on the southern flank and was joined by another one in November to support the German 4th Panzer Army. Major General von Mellenthin recalled:

It became known that Hungarian, Italian and Romanian armies had occupied positions on the Don from Voronezh southwards; this certainly did not serve to encourage the German troops. The fighting value of our allies was never overestimated, nor was their poor equipment calculated to enhance their reputation... In November a new panzer corps, consisting of a German and a Romanian armoured division, moved into the Don bend. This was the 48th Panzer Corps, and at the end of November I was appointed its chief of staff.[12]

Soviet intelligence on enemy tank strength was reasonably good. Marshal Zhukov noted:

The main forces of Army Group B were in the Middle Don area, at Stalingrad, and also southwards in the vicinity of Sarpinskiye Lakes. They comprised the 8th Italian Army, the 3rd and 4th Romanian Armies and the German 6th and 4th Panzer Armies. Each division held from nine to twelve miles. The effective strength of this group totalled over one million officers and men, 675 tanks and assault weapons, over 10,000 guns and mortars. Numerically the confronting forces were nearly equal, with the exception of a slight superiority in tanks on the Soviet side.[13]

The main attack of the Soviets' Operation Uranus was to be launched over 100 miles west of Stalingrad, cutting a swathe south-east. Lieutenant General N.F. Vatutin's South-Western Front, spearheaded by the 1st Guards Army and 5th Tank Army, was to fall on the Romanian 3rd Army, pierce its defences and race south-east to reach the Don at Kalach. This would cut off the Germans' lines of retreat from Stalingrad. To the south of the city the Romanian 4th Army was to receive similar treatment at the hands of the Soviets' 51st, 57th and 64th Armies.

Unfortunately the Romanian 3rd Army did not have the strength to occupy a forty-mile long area south of the Don. Mellenthin complained bitterly: 'Nobody could understand why Romanian formations had given up part of the huge Don bend, allegedly to save troops for other purposes, but actually yielding an area which it would have been easy to defend, and thus handing over a most valuable bridgehead to the Russians.'[14] Antonescu even approached Hitler about the dangers facing his troops but to no avail. Hitler's allies' complete lack of adequate tanks and anti-tank guns was to be their undoing.

When the Red Army attacked the Romanian 3rd Army on 19 November they broke through in two places and the defenders took fright and fled. The diary of a Romanian artillery officer from the 6th Division recalls the sense of terror and helplessness: 'Gun-fire so heavy the ground shudders and the windows shatter ... Enemy tanks appear ... raced through our positions ...our guns having no effect.' The following day he noted with despair: 'Currently we are encircled by enemy troops. In pocket are the 5th, 6th and 15th Divisions and remnants of the 13th Division.'[15] The 1st Romanian Tank Division and 7th Romanian Cavalry Division were thrown into the fight to halt the 5th Tank Army, but they were brushed aside. Some ran, but many simply threw away their weapons and surrendered where they stood. The Romanians lost all their Skoda LT-35 tanks which were later replaced by ex-German PzKpfw 38(t)s and Panzer IVs.

Bereft of its tanks just two days after the assault started, the writing was on the wall for the beleaguered Romanian 3rd Army. Marshall Zhukov recalled:

> The enemy buckled and, panic-stricken, fled or surrendered. German units holding positions behind the Romanian forces, mounted a powerful counterattack in an attempt to check our advance but were crushed by the 1st and 26th Tank Corps. The tactical breakthrough on the South-Western Front was now an accomplished fact.[16]

The 26th Tank Corps' advance guard seized a bridge over the Don on 26 November. By the end of the month the remnants of the Romanian 3rd Army had been driven back between Chernyshevskaya to the north and Oblivskaya to the south.

Far to the south-east the Romanian 4th Army suffered a similar fate.

Just twenty-four hours after the South-Western and Don Fronts had opened their offensive, the 51st, 57th and 64th Armies of the Stalingrad Front joined the attack. At 10.00 on 20 November Soviet artillery opened their bombardment. Within a few hours 10,000 Romanian troops had been taken prisoner. The 1st, 2nd, 18th and 20th Romanian Divisions were barged out of the way as was the 29th German Motorised Division. In an attempt to stem the 57th Army's advance on Kalach, the 16th and 24th Panzer Divisions foolishly got in the way. By 16.00 on 23 November the Russians were in the vicinity of Sovietsky to the east of Kalach. It was only a matter of time before a link up was effected, trapping the Germans deployed between the Don and the Volga.

Approximately 270,000 men were trapped in the *Kessel* or 'Cauldron' as the Stalingrad pocket became known, including up to 13,000 Romanian troops from the 1st Cavalry and 20th Infantry Divisions. Those in the pocket proved just as unreliable as those deployed on the flanks. The German 297th Infantry Division, under attack from the Soviet 64th Army, soon found it had half a mile gap in its flank after the 82nd Romanian Regiment fled. Operation Winter Storm, Field Marshal von Manstein's attempt to get through to the *Kessel*, spearheaded by 6th Panzer Division, involved two Romanian cavalry divisions. When it commenced on 12 December, tantalisingly, those trapped in Stalingrad could hear the guns.

Operation Saturn followed the encirclement of Stalingrad, designed to smash the Italian 8th Army, which at the time had just fifty-five L6/40 light tanks.[17] The latter's light armour and inadequate 47mm meant it was totally incapable of fending off the masses of Soviet T-34/76 that stormed across the frozen Don. On 16 December General Italo Gariboldi's 8th Army rapidly collapsed into a state of chaos. The 2nd and 35th Corps disintegrated almost immediately, leaving the Alpine Corps on its own and a massive hole in the front line. The Italian 3rd Mobile Division was destroyed during the retreat. The dazed survivors were regrouped in Ukraine, but Hitler had such little faith in their fighting ability that he had them packed off back to Italy.

The Russians unleashed a third major offensive on 15 January 1943 south of Voronezh, against the 2nd Hungarian Army. The Hungarian 1st Armoured Division, under German tactical control, was held back and not permitted to counter-attack in time to help restore the situation. Major General von Mellenthin recalls in his memoirs: 'The Hungarian troops were of a better quality than the Romanians or Italians, but they could not withstand the flood. The Russian columns poured through a gap 175 miles wide, and by the end of January had captured Kursk, and were over the Donets to the southeast of Kharkov.[18]

The Hungarians lost 80,000 men and all their tanks and heavy equipment. It was the worst military disaster ever experienced by the Hungarian Army, who were quick to blame the Germans for abandoning them to their fate. Horthy ordered the remains of 2nd Army home, leaving behind two weak Corps for security duties. 'I never want to see another soldier of our Eastern Allies on the Eastern Front,' ranted Hitler after these disasters.[19] Field Marshal Friedrich Paulus with the German 6th Army surrendered at Stalingrad on 31 January 1943, with the loss of up to 200,000 troops. Shortly after Hitler's panzers received a deathblow at the Battle of Kursk.[20]

The Hungarians reconstituted their 1st Armoured Division in mid-1943 and created a second. These were organised along German lines, but equipped with a mixture of Turan and Turan II medium tanks. In addition eight assault artillery (6th, 7th, 10th, 13th, 16th, 20th, 24th and 25th) battalions were created, which were to have been equipped with the Zrinyi assault gun.[21] However, there were only enough of these to arm two battalions so the others used German StuG IIIs. The Hungarians also raised the 1st Cavalry Division, which was later renamed the 1st Hussar Division. The Slovak Mobile Division, having lost all its heavy equipment, was reorganised as an infantry division, used for coastal defence duties. Between 1942-1944 Hitler was obliged to supply Hungary and Romania over 700 tanks to try and prop up their flagging armies.

Hitler's allies, having seen their armies badly mauled, sought to abandon him. Romania changed sides in August 1944 and, after the Red Army crossed into Bulgaria on 8 September, it placed its 450,000 troops under Soviet command.[22] The Germans moved swiftly to deal with their former allies in Serbia and Macedonia disarming the Bulgarian 1st Army; only the 5th Army offered short-lived resistance. The Germans confiscated all the Bulgarians' weapons stocks, reissuing them to local security forces.

The Germans had planned to disable the Bulgarian 1st Armoured Brigade. *Panzertruppen* instructors from the combat school at Nis in Serbia were put on alert to move to the German training camp at Plovdiv in Bulgaria from where they would act. Instead the 1st Armoured moved to block the Sofia-Nis road outside the Bulgarian capital and local German forces were disarmed.

The 1st Armoured went into action against its former allies on 8 October; sixty tanks were thrown into the attack two days later, destroying much of the 7th SS Mountain Division's vehicles. It then went on to fight with the Russians in Hungary. Romania's defection exposed Hungary's southern frontier and, desperately trying to stem the Soviet and Romanian forces pushing from the east, the Hungarians succeeded in briefly giving the Soviets a bloody nose at Arad on the River Lipova.

Although Finland opened negotiations in February 1944 the unforgiving Soviets threw half a million men, 800 tanks, 10,000 artillery pieces and 2,000 combat aircraft at the Finnish Army four months later. The Finns mustered 268,000 men, supported by just 110 tanks, 1,900 guns and 248 combat aircraft.[23] Their armoured division was outnumbered and the T-26s were no match for the battle hardened T-34/85s. The Finns requested six German divisions and, although Hitler sent the 122nd Infantry Division, an assault gun brigade and anti-tank weapons, the Finns were driven back with the loss of 36,000 troops. Finland finally made piece with Moscow in August and, monitored by Finnish armour, the Germans withdrew into northern Norway to continue the war.

By October it was obvious Horthy was intent on joining Romania and Bulgaria in defecting to the Soviet camp. The Germans temporarily stabilised the situation by installing a puppet government, but the Russians were soon hammering at the gates of Budapest. The mixed German-Hungarian garrison included the Hungarian 1st Armoured, 10th Mixed and 12th Reserve Divisions as well as a number of armoured cars and assault artillery battalions.[24] The city capitulated on 12 February. Hitler decided to counter-attack between Lakes Balaton and Velencze using the 6th SS Panzer Army and 6th Army, supported by the Hungarian 3rd Army under Operation Spring Awakening on 6 March 1945.

The 3rd Hungarian Army consisted of one tank division, two infantry and a cavalry division,[25] but the Hungarian 2nd Armoured, armed with the Turan II, was considered inadequate for offensive operations and, in the event, only a single Hungarian infantry division was actually committed to the attack.[26] By 15 March over 500 panzers were flaming wrecks and 40,000 men had been lost. The following day the Soviets launched their own counter-stroke and the skeletal Hungarian 3rd Army withdrew west, losing the 1st Hussar Division. Its remaining divisions, including the 2nd Armoured, eventually surrendered to the American forces in Austria. Horthy and Antonescu had proved truly unreliable allies, their paucity of heavy equipment contributing fundamentally to

Hitler's defeat on the Eastern Front.

Hitler's similar attempts to utilise Spain and Vichy France's meagre armoured forces also had unforeseen results. In late October 1940 Hitler was like a petulant child. His meeting at Hendaye on the 23rd with General Franco came to nothing, even though Franco owed his triumph in the Spanish Civil War to the considerable array of hardware provided by Hitler and Mussolini. Hitler wanted Franco to attack Gibraltar but the Spanish dictator would not agree to anything. Hitler later told Mussolini he would rather have his teeth pulled out than go through the meeting again. The following day Hitler met Marshal Petain, ruler of Vichy France, at Montoire. Despite paying lip service to the Führer's demands the old Marshal also avoided France's active participation in the war against Britain. Hitler was further infuriated when he arrived in Florence on the 28th to confer with Mussolini only to discover the Italians had committed themselves to a futile campaign against the Greeks.

Four months earlier Franco had informed Hitler that in return for French colonies, including Morocco and western Algeria, and German weapons, he would support Germany in the war. Now that the Nazis were triumphant across the Europe, the last thing Franco wanted to do was help Hitler and Mussolini carve up the Mediterranean between them. He might like the idea of acquiring France's African possessions, but not at the expense of tying his armed forces to Hitler's war effort against the British or indeed the forthcoming war against the Soviet Union.

Franco had a record of fighting shoulder to shoulder with the French in Morocco. France may have tacitly supported the Republic against him during the civil war but had not directly intervened as Stalin had done. France had allowed 200 tanks, 4,000 trucks and 9,579 other vehicles to cross the frontier to reach the Republicans. These supplies had come from Russia, Czechoslovakia and America, although some had come directly from the French government, which sent 200 aircraft direct to the Republic.[27] According to German intelligence, between September 1936 and March 1938 the Soviets supplied the Republicans with 731 tanks, 730 guns, 247 aircraft and 1,386 trucks, many of which ultimately fell into Franco's hands.[28] The German Military Attaché in Ankara monitored Soviet weapon shipments through the Bosporus.

By early 1939, having won the civil war, General Franco had a million men under arms and Hitler wanted to get his hands on these veteran troops. The year before, the exhausted Republican Army had just forty-nine tanks left; Franco by contrast could muster 300 Panzer Is, T-26s and FT-17s, organised into two battalions to form the *Agrupacion de Carros de Combate de la Legion*. On 3 January 1939 Franco's Nationalist forces crossed the Ebro and the Republican front collapsed. At the end of March Franco marched triumphantly into Madrid marking the end of the war. Hitler, meanwhile, was busy annexing the remains of Czechoslovakia.

At Hendaye Hitler announced he wanted Spanish assistance to seize Britain's vital naval base at Gibraltar. Under the codename of Operation Felix two panzer divisions, three infantry divisions and a mountain corps were to strike the landward defences, while two German regiments and a Spanish division would seize the Rock of Gibraltar on 10 January 1941. While Franco successfully avoided committing himself, he was forced to reconsider his position when Hitler finally invaded Russia eight months later. He knew he would have to make some token gesture to placate Hitler, repay the military assistance and avenge himself against Stalin.

Franco had no intention of wasting his meagre mechanised forces in Hitler's invasion of the Soviet Union. In any case Spain's few hundred tanks would have been of little value on the Eastern Front. The Spanish armed forces did have the German-supplied 8.8cm anti-aircraft gun, whose greatest successes had been against ground targets during the civil war, as well as batteries of German 15cm and 10.5cm field howitzers and 10.5cm field guns. Colonel Walther Model had been sent to Spain in 1937 to assess the tactics and weapons used by both sides.[29] He was probably briefed by Lieutenant Colonel Ernst Hertzer, who commanded the German Imker-Horch signals intelligence company, also known as Walther Gruppe Wolm, one of the main intelligence gathering units sent to Spain.[30]

General Nehring also had first hand knowledge of the equipment that reached Franco's Army. During the second half of 1936 while serving as a lieutenant colonel on the General Staff with Guderian, he had been seconded for four months to oversee the flow of equipment and volunteers to Spain. Hitler provided Franco's forces with a total of 122 Panzer Is[31] and Mussolini sent 149 L.3s.[32] In fact the Nationalists' use of the German 37mm Pak35/36 anti-tank gun did the *Panzertruppen* a disservice. While Thoma's *Panzergruppe Drohne* warned about the inadequacies of the Panzer I, the success of the 37mm anti-tank gun in Spain meant it became the standard weapon of the Panzer III until mid-1940.

Elated by Hitler's sweeping success against Stalin in June 1941 and Spanish Foreign Minister Ramon Serrano Suner's call to arms, tens of thousands of Spaniards answered the call for a volunteer infantry division. The Spanish were not to take any supporting tanks and at most they were only ever to enjoy the assistance of a handful of German panzers. General Agustine Munoz Grandes, former commandant of the garrison opposite Gibraltar and an old Franco comrade from the Moroccan campaigns, flew to Berlin on 14 July 1941.

The Spanish mustered 18,693 officers and men, consisting of three infantry regiments supported by an artillery regiment, which included an anti-tank group equipped with thirty-six 3.7cm anti-tank guns. Once they joined the *Wehrmacht* they were issued with German uniforms and equipment and designated the 250th Infantry Division. Hitler, furious over Franco's lack of cooperation with Gibraltar, ensured that the Spaniards were not equipped with German armoured vehicles or motor transport.

It was intended the division should join Army Group Centre near Smolensk, but in the event found itself supporting Field Marshal von Leeb's Army Group North near Leningrad where they fought with distinction. By mid-1943 the Allies were in a strong enough position to pressure Franco to declare strict neutrality and withdraw his 'volunteers'. On 5 October the 250th repulsed a Russian attack in what turned out to be its last major action and by the end of the month it was back in Spain.

Following the defeat of France, Hitler gained an unlikely ally in the guise of Petain's Vichy government. While Hitler confiscated wholesale the French Army's tanks in mainland France, he also gained several hundred more in France's colonial possessions controlled by Vichy with which to indirectly resist the Allies. Metropolitan France's heavy armoured and mechanised divisions disappeared during the disastrous attempts to stave off the German blitzkrieg. Under the Armistice, the Vichy regime was permitted to maintain in the Free Zone a force of 100,000 with no armour or heavy artillery. In fact Petain's Armistice Army had just forty-five Panhard armoured cars, all that remained of France's once mighty armoured formations.[33] Whilst there had never been a real need for medium or heavy tanks in the colonies, Marshal Petain had a considerable number of light tanks, principally FT-17s and R-35s deployed throughout France's overseas possessions.

Vichy's first real major clash with the Allies was over the Levant when General de Gaulle, commanding the Free French, suggested his forces in Palestine invade Vichy controlled Syria and Lebanon. The Vichy Army in the Levant was extremely strong, consisting of 51,000 men, with a sizeable armoured force of ninety tanks, including R-35/39s and 150 armoured cars as well as 120 guns.[34] The fear was that with the *Luftwaffe* operating from the Greek Islands, the Germans might be tempted to occupy Syria and from there could threaten Britain's position in Egypt and the vital oilfields in Iraq.

When Iraq sought German assistance against the British presence, Hitler sought Vichy Syria's cooperation. Admiral François Darlan, commander of the French Navy and one of Petain's key supporters, agreed to permit 75 per cent of the weapons gathered in Syria under the control of the Italian Armistice Committee, to be transferred to Iraq to assist the revolt and granted the *Luftwaffe* landing rights. Under orders General Henri Dentz, Vichy High Commissioner and Commander-in-Chief in Syria made no attempt to impede the Germans.

By the end of May alarm bells began to ring in London that a German takeover was imminent, especially in light of their airborne landings on Crete on 21 May. Wavell, trying to cope with the invasion of Crete, responded to Churchill with gloomy news: 'This Syrian business is disquieting, since the German Air Force established itself in Syria they are closer to the Canal and Suez than they would be at Mersa Matruh. The [Vichy] French seem now wholly committed to the Germans. I am moving reinforcements to Palestine ...'[35]

The defence of Egypt and Crete had to take priority, which greatly restricted the resources available for the Syrian operation. Wavell's invasion force under General Wilson consisted of the 7th Australian Division, part of the 1st Cavalry Division, the 5th Indian Infantry Brigade and the Free French Forces under General Le Gentilhomme, consisting of six battalions, an artillery battery and a company of tanks. Initial air support consisted of seventy aircraft. The plan was to secure Damascus, Rayak and Beirut as quickly as possible.

Operation Exporter commenced on 8 June 1941 and met practically no opposition. However, the Free French Forces were held up ten miles from Damascus and the Australians on the coast road made slow progress. British and Free French Forces then found themselves under attack by Petain's panzers. Vichy troops launched a counter-attack with two battalions of tanks at Kuneitra and overwhelmed a British battalion. British artillery fire then succeeded in destroying a large concentration of Vichy tanks outside Sidon on 13-15 June and the port quickly fell.

British troops also invaded from Iraq and by 21 June, after three days of heavy fighting, the Australians had captured Damascus. After the fall of Beirut, Vichy regional headquarters, it was all over and the Free French took control. General Dentz, although he still had 24,000 men under arms, knew continued resistance was pointless. Churchill recalls: 'At 8.30 on 12 July Vichy envoys arrived to sue for an armistice. This was granted, a convention was signed and Syria passed into Allied Occupation.' He adds: 'Our casualties in killed and wounded were over 4,600; those of the enemy about 6,500.'[36] Dentz lost about half his tank force, the rest were taken over by the Free French.

The Allies' plans to trap Rommel in North Africa, by landing troops in his rear, required the cooperation of French Northwest Africa. General Eisenhower hoped that Vichy would not resist the arrival of the Allies but noted: 'However, there was nothing in the political history of the years 1940–42 to indicate that this would occur; it was a hope rather than an expectation. Consequently we had to be prepared to fight against forces which in all, numbered 200,000.'[37]

It was not clear how the fourteen French divisions would react; there were approximately 55,000 ground troops in Morocco, 50,000 in Algeria and 15,000 in Tunisia, equipped with 250 tanks and up to 500 aircraft.[38] The armoured forces included the *Legere Mecanique* Brigade commanded by Colonel Vigier. Whilst most of the French armour was obsolescent it was, nonetheless, serviceable and posed a threat until American tanks could be dry-landed. Throughout Operation Torch Vichy tanks were to prove a headache for the Allies, largely because they could not get their own armour ashore quickly enough.

To try and avoid antagonising the French, it was decided Operation Torch would largely be an American affair. However, there were insufficient American forces for the attack on Algiers so they were supported by British troops. Unknown to the Allies, when they launched their invasion, Admiral Darlan was in Algiers visiting his sick son. This completely compromised General Juin, Algiers' French Military Commander, who had planned to act for the Allies. The eastern advance on Algiers was brought to a temporary halt by the threat of attack by just three French tanks. Similarly with the landings at Casablanca, French tank and infantry columns approaching from Rabat had to be driven off by aircraft from the American battleship USS *Texas*.

General Truscott, at Port-Lyautey, was warned that a French armoured column was on its way from Rabat. Fortunately for Truscott seven M5 light tanks under Lieutenant Colonel Harry H. Semmes from the 2nd Armored Division arrived just in time to block the Rabat-Port

Lyautey road. On 9 November Semmes came under attack from two battalions of French infantry and up to eighteen Renault tanks. The latter were completely outclassed with their inadequate 37mm guns and attacked in groups of two or three in a vain effort to overwhelm the Americans. Within ten minutes Semmes' tanks also armed with 37mm guns had knocked out four Renaults and their machine guns had mown down the French infantry. The French tanks, whose armour-piercing rounds largely bounced off the M5s, also found themselves under naval gunfire when the destroyer USS Savannah came to Semmes' assistance. The French withdrew down the Rabat road and when Semmes inspected the battlefield he discovered two armour-piercing shells imbedded in his tank's armour.[39] American reinforcements helped drive off another attack forcing the French to abandon twenty-four tanks, with just eight escaping to fight another day.

Near the vital Tafaraoui airfield, twelve miles south of Oran, another tank battle erupted on the 9th between French and American armour. The day before elements of the 1st Armored Division, under Colonel John Waters (General George S. Patton's son-in-law) had pushed inland to help the US 509th Parachute Infantry Battalion secure the Tafaraoui and La Senia airports. After taking 300 POWs at Tafaraoui, Waters was heading for La Senia when he received a message to turn back as a French armoured column was just seven miles east of Tafaraoui. A reconnaissance platoon of M3 light tanks led by Lieutenant William Beckett was despatched to hold up the French attack. Joined by Captain William R. Tuck's light tanks and tank destroyers, they knocked out fourteen French tanks for the loss of one tank and a halftrack.[40] At Bou Thelis the Americans came up against French armoured cars armed with 37mm guns, while at Bredeah they encountered French 75mm field guns.

It was only when Sherman tanks were finally put ashore at Safi and Oran that the Allies were able to field quantities of medium armour and by then the French had called for a ceasefire. Admiral Darlan instigated this on 10 November, only to have it overruled by Petain. Continued resistance was futile and Darlan reached a settlement with the Allies three days later, in which the French colonies would be treated as friendly, not occupied, territory. Darlan was assassinated in Algiers on 24 December 1942.

Fortunately losses were not as great as in Syria, but Vichy's intransigence still cost the Americans 1,404 casualties, including 556 killed, 837 wounded and forty-one missing in a needless four-day war. The British sustained 300 casualties and the French 700 dead, 1,400 wounded and 400 missing.[41] American planners, fearing the worst, had anticipated up to 18,000 casualties. While Vichy had not thwarted Allied ambitions in North Africa, it had fought a needless proxy war on Hitler's behalf. Petain's panzers had served their purpose and unwittingly helped give the Germans a much-needed breathing space that resulted in the war spilling over into Tunisia and dragging on for another six months.

Colonel Vigier's *Legere Mecanique* subsequently fought against the Axis in Tunisia and became the French 1st Armoured Division at the end of the campaign. A squadron of S-35 tanks sent to Senegal from mainland France, following the British attacks on the French Fleet at Dakar and Mers-el-Kebir, also took part in the last phase of fighting in Tunisia as the *12e Regiment de Chasseurs d'Afrique*. From the remains of the Vichy armoured formations in the region the French eventually formed the 3rd and 5th Armoured Divisions, though these were equipped with American supplied armour.

Hitler's response to the landings was swift and predictable, the *Wehrmacht* and SS occupied the Free Zone. Hitler issued the occupation order on the evening of 10 November and Operation Atilla was carried out the next day without meeting any resistance, except for futile protests from Petain. The Armistice Army was disarmed and disbanded and the Germans seized Vichy's remaining armoured forces.[42] From the disbanded Armistice Army the Germans raised a regiment and various railway flak units.

Vichy security forces subsequently employed light tanks and armoured cars against their fellow countrymen throughout metropolitan France. Joseph Darnand supplied Hitler with a small private army with which to fight the burgeoning Resistance and he sought to turn it into a French *Waffen-SS*. Following the complete occupation of France the Vichy government approved Darnand's creation of the *Milice Francaise*, whose main arm the *Franc Garde* consisted of 13,000 paramilitary police. They, along with the French Police's 10,000 strong *Groupes Mobiles de Reserve* (GMR), supported *Wehrmacht* security operations.[43] In reward for his efforts against his own countrymen in January 1944 Vichy appointed Darnand to the post of General Secretary for the Maintenance of Order. He became one of the most hated men in France. The last of Vichy's FT-17s was abandoned on the streets of Paris in August 1944 in the face of the Free French 2nd Armoured Division.

Chapter Ten

Losing the Tank Production War

Albert Speer, in his role as Minister of Armament and War Production, presented his situation report to Hitler at the end of June 1944 and it was not good news. If Germany's synthetic oil production plants and the Hungarian and Romanian oilfields were not adequately protected from the Allies unrelenting bombing, then by September everything would grind to a halt with tragic results. In response Hitler ordered the flak and smoke defences to be increased, but the real problem was the *Luftwaffe*'s inability to prevent the Allied bombers pressing home their attacks. Even though Speer had ensured German fighter production was up, it could not keep pace with the heavy losses that, in part, were due to the Allies bombing the aircraft factories and oil refineries.

On 5 September Speer reported again and things had not got any better. Germany's weapons factories were running out of energy supplies and raw materials. Based on the assumption that Hitler was prepared to abandon the occupied territories in northern and southern Europe, Speer's industries could continue production for about a year before they reached crisis point. Hitler refused to accept the situation and refused to make any withdrawals; he knew to do so would mean an increase in air attacks on Germany's heartland. Speer, realising that the Third Reich was doomed, began secretly to make what preparations he could to save Germany's industries from the Allies and Hitler.

In the late 1930s Hitler failed to grasp the urgency of the looming tank race. By early 1940 the Germans were producing fewer than 200 armoured fighting vehicles of all types a month. To make matters worse the switch to production of the Panzer III and IV caused a major drop in the number of operational tanks, from 2,980 in September 1939 to 2,574 in May 1940 and at this stage a significant proportion were still the Czech LT-35s and LT-38s.[1] Similarly the Army had 120,000 motor vehicles, but production stood at just 1,000 a month, insufficient to replace regular wear and tear, let alone combat losses.[2] In addition military deliveries were being made to Russia (until March 1940), Italy, Yugoslavia, Finland and Romania causing a further drain on available equipment. Germany became increasingly reliant on certain captured factories for armoured vehicle and motor transport production.

Italy was even slower to grasp the nettle in expanding its tank fleet. The Italian Army opened the war with limited numbers of the M11/39 medium tank and L6/40 light tank; its main strength lay with some 2,000 largely useless L3 tankettes. Subsequently the Italians built less than 2,000 M13/40s and just eighty-two M15/42. In terms of self-propelled guns, numbers were just as small with less than 1,000 75/18 and 75/34 being built. Without German help in North Africa the Italians would have simply been overwhelmed.

The Allies were not ignorant of the important role being played by armament factories in the occupied territories. Initially Britain attempted to disrupt France's motor transport production for the *Wehrmacht*, in particular the Renault factory at Billancourt that was producing 14,000 trucks a year. The Royal Air Force (RAF) raided the site on 3–4 March 1942 with 235 bombers. The RAF was still perfecting its techniques and used target illumination flares, followed by incendiary and high-explosive bombs. In total 470 tons of bombs were dropped on Billancourt and the raid appeared a resounding success.[3]

Air Marshal Sir Arthur Harris, Commander-in-Chief Bomber Command, who had selected Billancourt as his very first target takes up the story:

> It is somewhat ironic that the first completely successful operation carried out after I took command should have been not only a diversion from the main offensive against Germany but also a precision attack on a key factory. This was the attack on the Renault works, near Paris, one of the French factories most actively engaged in producing war equipment for the enemy. This was a very short range target and it was almost undefended, which meant that we could attack it in clear weather and brilliant moonlight and that aircraft could come down very low to identify the factory... . The Renault factory was high in the list of collaborating French factories which had been given to me and this extremely destructive raid not only deprived the enemy of a considerable quantity of equipment, but was also of some value in discouraging the production of war material for the enemy elsewhere in France.[4]

Harris painted a rather overly optimistic picture of the attack, especially as all but twelve aircraft claimed to have bombed the target. Although a sizeable tonnage of bombs was dropped and the initial assessment was that their concentration around the aiming point was exceptional, the final judgement was a little different. Subsequent bomb damage assessment conducted by the RAF indicated that not only had French civilian casualties been high, but that the plant suffered a loss of less than two months' production capacity.[5] Harris attempted to 'discourage' other French factories with a series of bomber raids. The Gnome et Rhone works at Gennevilliers, and the Ford factory at Poissy, as well as the Dutch Philips works at Eindhoven were all bombed that year with limited results.

Billancourt was clearly of considerable value to the Germans who, using slave labour, took nine months to repair the damage. German efficiency was such that they even managed to increase production from 1,000 vehicles a month to 1,500. The United States Army Air Force (USAAF) also had a go at shutting down the factory on 4 April 1943, when eighty-five bombers dropped 251 tons of bombs. The leading formation of eighteen aircraft placed eighty-one tons of explosives square on the target.[6] Unfortunately the follow-on force was not so accurate and again civilian casualties were incurred. Although the Germans failed to intercept the bombers en route their fighters harassed them all the way back to Rouen. When the RAF Spitfire escort appeared, it was also attacked and lost five aircraft for the loss of no *Luftwaffe* aircraft.

The attack seems to have been a success. Afterwards when the French Resistance smuggled photographs of the Renault works back to Britain they showed that the Americans had inflicted severe damage on the factory. The USAAF returned in June to attack the Triqueville airfield and aircraft factory at Villacoublay, also in the Paris area. Again the *Luftwaffe* vigorously defended these targets and the Americans lost five aircraft.

Mussolini's armament industries felt the wrath of the RAF's bombers in the autumn of 1942. To support the efforts to drive the Axis forces out of North Africa, Bomber Command pounded the industrial cities of northern Italy. Genoa suffered six nights of attacks, Turin endured seven nights and Milan was subjected to one daylight attack. The latter showed just how weak Italy's air defences were. A shaken Mussolini declared there would be a nightly evacuation of the industrial cities of the north. The RAF had tried to attack Milan as early in June 1940 from Marseilles, but despite Italian troops attacking French soil, France had almost given up the fight. When the bombers tried to take off, French trucks were deliberately driven onto the runway to obstruct them and the attack had to be aborted.

The seizure of Czechoslovakia's tank factories was to prove a major long term blessing for the Nazi war effort. They represented a 1,200 mile round trip for RAF Bomber Command and the USAAF. Such distances meant that the bombers were exposed to German fighters for much longer. In the RAF raid on Pilsen on 17 April 1943 over 28 per cent of the attacking force was put out of action.[7] Air Marshal Harris recalled:

> In April and May 1943, my Command made two attempts to destroy the Skoda Armament Works at Pilsen, which had become of much greater importance to the enemy now that Krupps at Essen had been so heavily damaged. Unfortunately both attacks were unsuccessful; the bombing concentrations were remarkably good for so distant a target, but the main force had aimed with great accuracy at markers placed a mile or two away from the aiming point.[8]

In fact, in these attacks on Skoda, the RAF missed the target by some considerable distance. 'I remember particularly a raid on the Skoda Works at Pilsen, duly announced by the BBC, ' grumbled RV Jones, head of Britain's wartime scientific intelligence. 'A friendly Czech indignantly told us that everyone in Pilsen knew that there had been no raid, and that the nearest bomb that had fallen was fifty miles away.'[9] During the raid in April the RAF's pathfinders had mistaken a lunatic asylum for the Skoda works, resulting in the main force bombing the open countryside around it.

In Bohemia and Moravia, von Neurath's administration was characterised by student demonstrations, though the factories remained unscathed. SS-Gruppenführer Frank did more to undermine Neurath's authority than the subjugated Czechs. In September 1941 SS-Obergruppenführer (Lieutenant General) Reinhard Heydrich, Head of the Reich Central Security Department, became Deputy Protector and by the following February the threat to German security had been overcome largely through guile and an uncharacteristic policy of being firm but fair. Three months later he was mortally wounded in a bomb attack conducted by two Czech resistance fighters flown in from Britain. German retribution was harsh, executing 199 men from the village of Lidice near Kladno and Frank became Protector until the end of the war.

The first real threat to the vital Czech tank plants did not occur until August 1944. Despite being loyal allies on the Eastern Front, the Slovaks under Defence Minister, General Catlos and part of the Slovak Army under General Golian rose up against Premier Tiso's government and the Germans at Neusohl in the Carpathians. For Hitler this was a potential disaster as it was not only a threat to the Skoda and BMM's tank plants in neighbouring Bohemia and Moravia, but also could impede the retreat of the defeated German 8th Army from Galicia. Troops were scraped together and the rebellion swiftly put down.

The Allies' strategic bomber campaign really began to take its toll on Italy's factories and infrastructure after the German occupation. Continuous Allied air attack made it almost impossible for the Germans to receive new motor vehicles and adequate supplies of fuel from Germany. In addition the production of motor vehicles by Italian factories was seriously reduced. Prisoners captured by the Allies in Italy in 1944 reported: 'that German trucks were habitually overloaded, and when they broke down could with difficulty be repaired because of the shortage of spare parts created by our strategic bombing of the factories in Milan and Turin.'[10]

Intense Allied bombing of the Italian rail network forced the Germans to rely increasingly on trucks to move their supplies from the Florence area. In the first three weeks of April 1944 an American fighter-group claimed to have destroyed or damaged over 400 German trucks caught on Italy's open roads.[11] The Official British History of the campaign records: 'The destruction of motor-vehicles was so enormous and the shortage of petrol so severe, the German Armies were compelled to rely increasingly on horses and oxen to move their transport, and to commandeer farm wagons, urban buses, and civilian cars of every description.'[12]

Hitler became convinced he needed to centralise his *Panzertruppen* and appointed General Guderian as Inspector General of Armoured Troops in early 1943. Guderian was made responsible for the development, organisation and training of all armoured forces with the Army, *Waffen-SS* and *Luftwaffe*, answerable directly to Hitler. He had an uphill struggle in the face of vested interest, particularly from the artillery who were not going to give up their towed anti-tank guns, assault guns and self-propelled guns. To assess the condition of German tank production, Guderian made a point of visiting Daimler-Benz at Berlin and the Alkett Company at Spandau. Their vulnerability to air attack soon became apparent.

Once in office, one of Guderian's first moves was to request that Germany's tank factories be moved before they attracted the attention of the Allies bombers. At a conference in Munich on 4 May 1943 the Assistant Minister for Armament and War Production, Herr Sauer, opposed this claiming the enemy was currently concentrating on destroying the *Luftwaffe*'s aircraft factories. Oddly Sauer did not consider the tank factories at risk, even in the event of the Allied bombers succeeding in destroying the aircraft plants.

Instead Guderian had to make do with bolstering the air defences around Cassel, Friedrichshafen and Schweinfurt, Germany's principal tank manufacturing centres. His fears soon came to fruition on 22 October 1943 when the Henschel works at Cassel was severely bombed and all production came to a temporary halt. The General travelled to Cassel to offer his condolences to the workers and their families. The following month the bombers again turned their attentions on Germany's tank factories, attacking the Berlin works of Alkett, Rheinmetall-Borsig, Wimag and the Deutsche Waffen-und Munitionsfabriken on 26 November.

Guderian indeed had cause for concern about the future safety of Germany's tank plants. In the autumn of 1941 the British Target Committee had called for intelligence on the German ball bearing industry, which was vital for the production of not only aircraft but also tanks. The following year British intelligence assessed that a Swedish company, Svenska Kugellager Fabrik (SKF), through its German subsidiary Vereinigte Kugellager Fabrik (VKF), with two main factories in Schweinfurt provided the bulk of Germany's needs. Helpfully VKF's principal rival, Kugelfischer, was also located at Schweinfurt.[13]

British intelligence identified two other major plants at Steyr in Austria and at Carstadt-Stuttgart, Berlin. Along with thirty-five other plants they supplied 75 per cent of German industrial needs; the rest came from Sweden, France and Italy. Schweinfurt though was the key chokepoint and its two ball-bearing manufacturers were attacked on 17 August 1943. The air defences were ferocious, the USAAF's bombers, lacking long-range escort fighters, suffered very heavy casualties and only managed to halt production for just four weeks. The bombers returned on 14 October with only slightly better results, dislocating production for six weeks and inconveniencing it for six months.

In the run up to the Second World War, despite German rearmament, the *Wehrmacht* had just 5,420 armoured fighting vehicles, of which only 530 were Panzer Mk III and IV. To resist the German invasion, British and French forces were able to pit 4,000 tanks against 2,800 German ones. They still lost. When Germany then turned on Russia, the Red

Army had 17,000 armoured vehicles on its inventory; they were also crushed within weeks. In light of these figures the blitzkrieg tactics of the German Army look even more awesome.

Prior to the invasion of the Soviet Union, the German *Panzerwaffe* saw a switch of emphasis, in terms of being a tank striking force. The increase in *Sturmgeschütze* or assault guns, essentially a tank without a turret, would provide anti-tank support rather than the panzers themselves in the infantry battle. These assault guns should not be confused with self-propelled anti-tank guns (*Panzerjäger* and *Jagdpanzer*) and self-propelled artillery, of which the latter was not designed to fight enemy tanks. However, within the German Army they all came under the jurisdiction of the Artillery and not the *Panzertruppen*.

The nature and success of Hitler's initial blitzkrieg in Russia lulled him into a false sense of security. The fluid fighting meant, apart from the panzers that bore the brunt of the fighting, losses had been comparatively light. Hitler signed a memorandum on 14 July 1941 restricting the manufacture of all equipment except tanks; this was not reversed until January 1942 and caused severe ammunition shortages. By the autumn of 1941 Hitler was so sure of victory against Stalin that he diverted production from the Army to the *Luftwaffe* and *Kriegsmarine*. German efforts at rationalising tank production came to nothing. The German Army wanted to switch all production onto the Panther and Tiger tank in 1942, but as the Panzer IV formed the backbone of the panzer arm, to cut it would have caused a drastic shortfall in tank production while the factories changed over.

Hitler was slow to gear up for total war and by 1942 90 per cent of the German armament industry was still working a single shift and much of it was still producing consumer goods. Gradually armoured vehicle production began to be stepped up; 2,875 medium tanks and assault guns were produced in 1941, as well as 2,200 light armoured vehicles. The following year saw 4,300 tanks and assault guns come off the factory floor as well as 1,200 self-propelled guns. While phasing out the Panzer III and introducing the Panther and Tiger caused problems in 1943, medium tank and assault gun production still amounted to 6,700, in addition to 2,500 heavy tanks and 2,600 self-propelled guns. In 1944 German industry managed an incredible 17,800 medium/heavy tanks and assault guns.[14] This though was achieved by exhausting available raw materials.

Despite these ongoing efforts, by December 1943 Field Marshal Rommel had lost faith in Germany's weapons industries. Lieutenant

General Fritz Bayerlein recalled: 'In France also - and in the East - he believed that Victory could no longer be gained by mobile warfare - not merely because of the British and American air superiority, but also because the German armaments industry was no longer capable of keeping pace with the Western Allies in the production of tanks, guns anti-tank guns and vehicles.'[15]

Unfortunately for Guderian his role as overseer of Hitler's panzers soon fell victim to inter-service rivalry, which was to greatly and needlessly hamper tank production. His level of authority and direct access to the Führer caused deep resentment within certain elements of the German High Command. His terms of reference signed by Hitler on 28 February 1943 stated:

> The Inspector-General of Armoured Troops is responsible to me for the future development of armoured troops along lines that will make that arm of Service into a decisive weapon for winning the war.
>
> The Inspector-General of Armoured Troops is directly subordinate to myself. He has the command powers of an army commander and is the senior officer of armoured troops.[16]

The latter was defined as tank troops, Panzergrenadiers, motorised infantry, armoured reconnaissance troops, anti-tank troops and heavy assault units. Guderian had deliberately included the artillery's assault guns because they were taking up such a high proportion of the tank production. In Guderian's view the calibre of the guns on these vehicles and the towed anti-tank guns was insufficient. He wanted to provide the infantry divisions with assault guns, in place of the towed guns, and provide the panzer divisions with assault guns until tank production was sufficient to meet the panzer divisions requirements. In some quarters this was seen as heresy.

However, the word 'heavy' was inserted into the terms of reference which meant Guderian only had authority over the latest *Jagdtiger* and *Jagdpanther*, the thousands of *Sturmgeschütze* remained beyond his jurisdiction. At his first conference with Hitler on 9 March 1943 he tried to rectify the situation, but the assembled staff refused to relinquish command of the assault guns and Hitler refused to acquiesce. Guderian recalled with some bitterness: 'The results of this decision were far-reaching: the assault artillery remained an independent weapon; the anti-tank battalions continued to be equipped with ineffective, tractor-drawn guns, and the infantry divisions remained without adequate ant-tank defence.'[17]

At the end of 1943 Guderian finally got his way and Hitler's Czech tanks were once again to play a key role in his war effort by helping with the increasingly defensive war being fought on the Eastern Front. Guderian recalls:

On 7 December it was decided that the full production capacity of the old Czech 38-ton tank be switched to tank destroyers, these, to be built on Czech tank chassis, and protected by sloping armour plate, were to mount a recoilless gun and a machine gun with a curved barrel. They passed their tests very satisfactorily. This tank destroyer was intended to be the basic weapon for the anti-tank battalions of the infantry divisions, and thus the belated answer to my proposals made on March the 9th.[18]

The production of Germany's weapons was placed in the very capable hands of Albert Speer, an architect by profession who, in February 1942 at the age of thirty-six, was appointed Minister of Armament and War Production. Speer proved to be exactly the man Hitler needed. Within a year the Reich's supply of steel, coal, oil and other raw materials reached its highest level ever. To Speer's credit the production of weapons and munitions reached remarkable levels. By making use of existing civilian industrial capacity he was able to double monthly output during 1943. General Guderian greatly respected Speer's abilities.

Despite constant and intense Allied bombing throughout the second half of 1944 Speer managed to keep weapons' production on an even keel. The only decline was in tanks. During June, July and August his factories constructed 2,430 Panzer IV, Tiger and Panther tanks; over the next three months this slipped to 1,764 and almost 400 of these were not delivered due to the disruption of Europe's rail networks.[19] The USAAF's attacks on the Henschel works at Cassel deprived the Germans of at least 200 Tiger tanks.

This decline in tank production was partly offset by the increase in assault gun output. The factories were mainly located in Czechoslovakia where they remained largely immune to bomber attack and assault gun production rose from 766 in August 1944 to 1,199 in November.[20] The only drawback with this, as Guderian had already foreseen, was that this represented an increase in defensive power not strike power.

Although Guderian had prevailed with his ideas and triumphed over Hitler, he goes on to say:

The defensive weakness of the infantry against the ever-growing masses of Russian tanks had resulted in increased casualty figures. One evening during his briefing Hitler burst out in a long and violent diatribe against the senselessness of sending infantry divisions into action with insufficient anti-tank weapons. I happened to be present at the time. I was standing opposite Hitler while he let himself go on this subject, and doubtless noticed the somewhat sarcastic expression on my face, for he suddenly broke off, gazed at me in silence for a moment or two then said: 'You were right. You told me all this nine months ago. Unfortunately I didn't listen to you.' I was now at last in a position to carry out my ideas on this score, but it was too late. Only one third of our anti-tank companies could be equipped with the new weapon by the time the Russians launched their 1945 winter offensive.[21]

To make matters worse Hitler insisted that the bulk of these new weapons go, not to the front line divisions, but to the twenty-five *Volksgrenadier* Divisions being raised in Germany. Massive German manpower losses in France and on the Eastern Front during the summer of 1944 had to be made good. Total mobilisation was finally announced on 24 August 1944. This was followed on 18 October by a call-up of every able-bodied man between sixteen and sixty to form the *Volkstrum*, Germany's answer to Britain's Home Guard. By September Hitler had 10 million men under arms, of whom 7.5 million were in the army and the *Waffen-SS*. Fortunately for the Allies he insisted on keeping them scattered across Europe.

In 1940, prior to Hitler's titanic struggle with Stalin, his factories produced just over 1,500 tanks. By 1944 they were turning out almost 8,000, but by then it was too few too late. Total German tank production amounted to about 25,000 plus another 12,000 assault guns and assault artillery. The upshot was that the panzers could not sustain their momentum on the Eastern Front and the initiative passed over to the Red Army. Additionally the Germans seemed unable to stick to one tank type, instead producing a vast variety of platforms for different roles.

The German Army suffered terrible standardisation problems, made worse by the use of motor vehicles taken from its allies and the occupied territories. This included motor transport from Austria, Czechoslovakia, France, Hungary, Italy and Romania. During Germany's re-armament, designers had been given free reign and it was not until the Schell programme that 113 truck types were reduced to thirty, fifty-two car types cut to nineteen and 150 motorcycles to thirty; load classes were standardised and the various types produced by different firms in Germany and Austria.[22]

In the case of the famous Opel Blitz 3-ton S type both Opel and Daimler-Benz manufactured it. They produced it in 4x2 and 4x4 versions and over 70,000 chassis were supplied to the *Wehrmacht* from 1937-44. Other principal German truck types included those produced by Bussing-NAG, Mercedes-Benz and Saurer, as well as Czech Tatra. The Germans suffered raw material shortages and from 1944-45 steel truck cabs were substituted with pressed cardboard panels on timber framing. In Russia the appalling roads forced the Germans to convert conventional wheeled trucks into half-tracks or semi-tracks known as Maultier.

Once Stalin recovered from the shock of the German invasion, he re-evaluated his production strategy and made reconstructing his tank fleet a national priority. Stalin's answer was Tankograd at Chelyabinsk, which produced a staggering 18,000 tanks and self-propelled guns. In one year alone, 1942, Russian factories produced 24,670 tanks, of which almost 60 per cent were T-34s.

In the 1930s Guderian and Nehring tried to warn Hitler of the dangers posed by Soviet tractor production. Nehring became aware that Soviet tractor output was very high and that if the factories were ever converted to tank production the Soviets would have the capacity to produce over 1,000 armoured vehicles a month. At the time Hitler dismissed the figures. After the outbreak of war for a while Soviet tank production not only included the T-34 and KV, but also the discredited T-60 and T-70 light tanks. This was a case of expediency as they were faster to produce and at least ensured the infantry had some armour. Eventually their production ceased as the Russian went over to self-propelled guns.

The largest motor vehicle manufacturers in the Soviet Union were AMO (Avtomobilnoe Moskovskoe Obshchestvo, later ZIS – Zavod Imeni Stalina) in Moscow and GAZ (Gorkovsky Avtomobilny Zavod) in Gorky. They were churning out copies of American Autocar and Ford designs and these formed the bulk of the Red Army's motor vehicles when the Germans invaded. Production was vast; for example 104,200 ZIS-5 trucks were built between 1933 and June 1941, although this included civilian vehicles.

In May 1942 the Russians had about 5,000 tanks. Despite combat losses this had doubled by the same time the following year. According to Soviet figures, by early November 1942 German strength on the

Eastern Front totalled about 6.2 million men, organised into 266 divisions equipped with 5,080 tanks and assault guns, 51,700 pieces of artillery and mortars, and 3,500 combat aircraft. Soviet drafting and industrial muscle ensured that, by this stage, the Red Army's massive losses of 1941 had been made good. Stalin was already beginning to tip the balance in his favour with about 6.6 million men under arms, equipped with 7,350 tanks, 77,800 guns and mortars, and 4,500 combat aircraft. On top of this the Soviet high command had considerable reserves.

By early 1944 Stalin's tank strength had fallen to 5,350, but by early 1945 had risen to almost 13,000 despite the massive battles fought with the retreating *Wehrmacht*. For the German forces on the Western and Eastern Fronts it became a matter of mathematical attrition; they simply could not knock out the Shermans and T-34s fast enough. Military might lies in industrial muscle which, by 1944, the Germans did not have regardless of the contribution of the factories in the occupied territories.

Events in France in May 1940 were a disaster for Britain's armoured forces with over 700 tanks left behind. Between 1940–45 Britain churned out 24,800 tanks, a figure comparable with Germany's, but nowhere near the massive numbers achieved by America and Russia. Britain's initial star was the Matilda II, of which 3,000 were built before production ended in 1943. The tank's armour proved its greatest asset in North Africa against the Italians, but it was ultimately let down by its poor armament.

The British Commonwealth also did its bit for the tank effort. Between 1939–45 Canada produced 1,420 Valentine tanks, most of which went to Russia, and 2,000 Ram tanks and 250 Grizzlys (based on the American M3 and M4 respectively). Most of the former were converted to armoured personnel carriers for use in Europe. The Canadians also built 2,150 Sexton self-propelled guns using the Ram chassis.

The number of tanks produced by Britain's factories was never sufficient to meet the requirements of the British and Commonwealth armies. There can be no hiding the fact that British designed tanks were not up to the job and the British Army would not have overcome the *Wehrmacht* but for the supply of American tanks. In particular the Sherman was supplied in such volume that it outnumbered all the other British-built types combined.

Motor transport was a different matter. In North Africa, having defeated the Italians in 1941, Britain was able to out produce the Germans. In August 1942 British Commonwealth forces received 7,000 motor vehicles; Rommel needed 1,500 trucks not to mention more panzers but received none. Many British vehicles were shipped to Egypt in kit form, where four assembly plants turned out 180 a day, totalling 45,000 by October 1942. The biggest supplier of military vehicles to the British Commonwealth was Canada. In July 1940 in the wake of Dunkirk, Britain asked Canada to supply 7,000 desperately needed replacement motor vehicles. The Canadians successfully combined British War Office designs with American mass-production techniques. Within a year Canada was the main supplier to the whole British Empire, producing 189,178 military MT vehicles during 1941 alone. Between 1939-45 the Canadians manufactured a total of 815,729 transport vehicles as well as 10,054 wheeled armoured fighting vehicles.

America, of course, beat everyone hands down in the mass production stakes, producing 88,410 tanks, as well as 18,620 other armoured fighting vehicles based on tank chassis. All this was achieved from a standing start. American tank building went from just 330 in 1940 to 29,500 at its peak in 1943. The Detroit Tank Arsenal, which was constructed from scratch, between 1940-45 accounted for 25 per cent of all America's tanks - producing over 25,000 vehicles.

The best known was the universally famous M4 medium Sherman, which succeeded the M3 series Lee/Grant in early 1942, and first saw action with the British Army in North Africa. In total the M4 made up about 50 per cent of all American tank construction. Although the lighter tanks such as the M3 and M5 series were built in considerable numbers in the opening stages of the war, the Americans, like the British and Russians, dropped light tanks in favour of medium armour.

America's factories also churned out 3.2 million transport vehicles, 41,170 half-tracks and well over 82,000 tractors. The bulk of the trucks fell into the light (up to 0.75 ton) class of which 988,167 were built, followed by 812,262 light-heavy (2.5 ton) class. Medium and heavy accounted for almost another 582,000 vehicles. Peak procurement occurred in June 1942 when the US Army received 62,258 trucks of all types. Under the Lend-Lease programme America's Allies were provided with thousands of military vehicles. Prior to that thousands had been supplied on a commercial basis. Many destined for France ended up in German hands or were diverted to Great Britain.

After the German invasion of the USSR, America supplied the Red Army with over 430,000 military vehicles. About 25 per cent of the trucks were 2.5-ton 6x4 and 6x6 Studebakers, the rest comprised Jeeps, Dodge Weapons Carriers, Chevrolet and Dodge 4x4 1.5-tonners. Many Lend-Lease trucks were assembled in Iran and then driven northward. Canada also supplied GM trucks and Britain sent Albion, Austin, Bedford and Ford trucks. This greatly overshadowed Soviet domestic production amounting to 343,600 motor vehicles. After the war Stalin failed conspicuously to acknowledge the debt.

In this war of output Germany's industries were compelled to rely on forced labour. This policy was one of many abhorrent aspects of the Nazi regime. By mid-1943 there were 2.25 million Frenchmen working for Hitler, 1.1 million as prisoners of war, the rest either in French factories producing war material for Germany, or in forced labour drafts in Germany. The following year the Germans were so desperate for additional manpower that they assigned all French men from sixteen to sixty and all women eighteen to forty-five to the labour service.[23] Italy sent 170,000 volunteer labourers to Germany, but when the *Wehrmacht* occupied northern Italy they were enslaved and treated like the rest of the forced labour.[24] The Germans also conducted labour round ups in northern Italy until October 1944.

Total slave labour working in Nazi Germany amounted to some 7.5 million people by the end of September 1944. This had been achieved by brutal forced deportation and wholesale kidnap. The senior Nazi official in charge of labour allocation later admitted that not even 200,000 workers had come willingly.[25] On the Eastern Front, under Operation Haystack in 1944, Army Group Centre and Army Group Ukraine North were involved in kidnapping Russian juveniles. While this was intended to help replenish Germany's apprentices it was also seen as a good method of denying Soviet partisans vital manpower.

The Germans added to this a further 2 million prisoners of war. In defiance of the Hague and Geneva Conventions over 500,000 were put to work in German weapons factories. According to Albert Speer 40 per cent of all POWs were employed in the production of weapons and munitions and in subsidiary industries in 1944.[26] In addition hundreds of thousands of prisoners were forced to move ammunition to the front-lines, build fortifications and even man the Reich's anti-aircraft defences.

The Russians lost 3.8 million prisoners of war during the opening stage of the war; they could have served the Nazi war effort, especially as a rival force to Stalin's regime. Instead Hitler's treatment of them was despicable; most were left to starve or freeze to death during the winter of 1941-42. Only several hundred thousand were fit for work by February 1942, the 3 million Russians, enslaved to work in the factories, were civilians.[27]

Germany's war industries had to function under constant air attack by the Allies strategic bomber campaign, which saw the RAF striking by night and the USAAF by day. RAF Bomber Command, from October 1944 until the German surrender, concentrated on the destruction of Germany's industrial cities, individual factories and vital lines of communication. The strategic bomber campaign's greatest contribution to the defeat of Hitler was the destruction of his fuel stocks that fed his armies and factories.

Germany was heavily reliant on the oilfields of its allies, notably the Romanian oil fields at Ploesti and Hungarian oilfields at Nagykaniza. American raids ensured output from Ploesti fell and mining of the Danube hampered what was produced being transported to Germany. Early raids on Ploesti did not go well. The Americans first attempted to bomb the oilfields in the spring of 1942, but attacking at night in poor visibility the bombers failed to locate the target. The following year USAAF conducted Operation Statesman on 1 August 1943 with the intention of bombing Ploesti and the Steaua Rimana refinery at Campina. One of the bomb groups got lost and attacked from the wrong direction, the flak was heavy and the bombers were set upon by German, Italian and Romanian fighters suffering major losses.[28] This disaster halted USAAF's deep-penetration daylight missions over southern Europe until long range escort fighters became available in 1944.

In mid-April 1944 Ploesti came under sustained attack and within six weeks had been raided twenty times. By the middle of the year Germany was receiving just 10 per cent of the 2.5 million tons it had been getting the year before from Romania and Hungary. Imports plummeted from 200,00 tons in February 1944 to just 11,000 tons by the summer.[29] When Marshal Malinovsky's troops swept into Ploesti in late August 1944, the Germans failed to destroy the oilfields. Their loss mattered little as by this stage they were contributing little to Germany's industries and the *Wehrmacht*.

The crumbling German war effort on the Eastern Front also threatened the loss of the vital Hungarian oilfields at Nagykaniza once the Red Army was less than fifty miles away. These and the Austrian oil fields were providing 80 per cent of Germany's oil supplies and Hitler convinced himself that they could be saved by a massive counter-offensive that would throw the Soviets back over the Danube and secure Vienna. The Führer's Hungarian adventure, Operation Spring Awakening, launched in early March 1945, was an effort the exhausted *Wehrmacht* could ill afford. Its outcome was defeat for his elite *Waffen-SS*.

The Allies also conducted a concerted air campaign to smash German synthetic oil production. The aim was to keep the *Luftwaffe* from the skies and cripple the *Wehrmacht* and *Waffen-SS*'s panzers. On 12 May 1944 the Allies attacked the synthetic oil plants at Brux, Bohlen, Leuna, Lutzendorf and Zwickau.[30] After two years of a largely indifferent strategic bombing effort, the results were immediate and spectacular. The production of gasoline for road vehicles plummeted from 134,000 tons in March 1944 to 39,000 tons in March 1945.[31]   This systematic and concerted destruction of the synthetic oil plants meant that by September 1944 German petrol stocks, which had stood at 1 million tons in April, had fallen to 327,000 tons.[32] Similarly the production of diesel oil fell from 100,000 tons to 39,000 tons over the same period.[33]

The panzers, always short of fuel, now began to feel the pinch more than ever. In the case of Hitler's Ardennes offensive in December 1944, fuel was critically short. Each German tank had just 150 gallons, enough for two to three days of combat and for them to cover about 150 miles. After that they were on their own. The offensive ended in defeat.

In the case of aviation fuel for the *Luftwaffe* production was brought to a complete standstill. The Germans had produced 156,000 tons of aviation fuel in May 1944; in June it had dropped by two thirds to 52,000 tons. The RAF and USAAF kept up the relentless pressure and in July production had fallen to 35,000 tons and in August to 17,000. By January 1945 the figure stood at 11,000 tons and had ceased by March.[34] By September 1944 the *Luftwaffe* was left with just five weeks of fuel and Germany's arms' industries had soaked up the last of the raw materials that could not be replaced. The Third Reich was haemorrhaging to death and there was nothing Speer could do about it.

Had the Allies attacked Germany's oil supplies earlier it would undoubtedly have helped to shorten the war. Speer supported this after Germany's capitulation, stating:

The Allied air attacks remained without decisive success until early 1944. This failure, which is reflected in the armament output figures for 1943 and 1944, is to be attributed principally to the tenacious efforts of the German workers and factory managers and also to the haphazard and too scattered form of attacks of the enemy who, until the attacks on the synthetic oil plants, based his raids on no clearly recognisable economic planning ... The Americans' attacks, which followed a definite system of assault on industrial targets, were by far the most dangerous. It was in fact these attacks which caused the breakdown of the German armaments industry.[35]

When the time came Field Marshal Model, commanding Army Group B and charged with defending the industrial heartland of the Ruhr, with the support of Albert Speer, refused to destroy Germany's battered industries. By that stage the factories in Czechoslovakia and France had long been liberated by the Allies.

Chapter Eleven

Impact of Hitler's Great Panzer Heist

During 1940–41 it was German military leadership and doctrine as much as equipment that gave Hitler his dramatic victories across the length and breadth of Europe. Daring and audacity were the hallmarks of the *Wehrmacht*'s blitzkrieg that so successfully unhinged the defences of country after country, which were completely unprepared for this new style of mechanised warfare. Hitler's generals defeated opponents who were more numerous and generally had the qualitative edge in armour, but simply did not know how to use it.

By 1942 the over-engineered excellence of the panzers reigned supreme. The Allies had one simple solution to this – overwhelm the panzers, assault guns and self-propelled guns with a few designs that were easy to mass-produce. Ultimately Germany could not win an industrial war of attrition against America and the Soviet Union.

In Belgium, Czechoslovakia, France and the Netherlands the Germans had seized military supplies and factories that helped transform their war fighting capabilities. Although German war production was cut back, France's motor vehicle industry, plus the vehicles abandoned by the British and other European armies, greatly alleviated the Germans' motor transport shortages on the eve of the invasion of the Soviet Union. Similarly Germany's replenished oil stocks and other raw materials gave Hitler a two year war-fighting potential.

In the chaos of the Second World War it is impossible to be definitive, but Hitler's great panzer heist across Europe netted him a conservative estimate of 95,182 military vehicles, consisting of 16,651 much needed armoured fighting vehicles, 5,776 tracked weapons carriers and tractors, and in excess of 72, 755 motor vehicles. In contrast he supplied his allies with a meagre 1,250 tanks. Total German armoured fighting vehicle production was just over 72,000, including 25,897 tanks.

From France Hitler captured some 2,400 tanks that were in a re-useable condition. The Italians built well over 5,300 tanks, the vast majority of which ended up indirectly serving Hitler's cause, while he gained another 1,500 Italian armoured vehicles through confiscation and continued manufacture, following the occupation of northern Italy. The Hungarian contribution to the Nazi war effort on the Eastern Front was a modest 850 – 1,250 armoured vehicles, while the Finns provided about 150 tanks. Thousands of motor vehicles were seized, but the Austrians specifically manufactured over 24,000 motor vehicles and the French over 48,000 for the *Wehrmacht*. This was a considerable haul by anyone's standards.

The Protectorate of Bohemia and Moravia proved to be the greatest asset, by far. Czech industries contributed nearly 8 per cent of all military vehicles delivered to the German armed forces. Hitler kept the Czech LT-38 tank in production, right up until the end of the war. Overall the Czech contribution was the most numerous, providing over 6,500 armoured fighting vehicles including 1,400 tanks, 2,000 self-propelled guns and 2,500 tanks destroyers. Similarly after the occupation of Italy in September 1943, the Germans continued to build Italian M15/42 and P40 tanks as well as 75/18, 105/25 and 75/46 self-propelled guns for their own use. These though, amounted to little more than 1,000 vehicles. The Germans also converted captured French tank chassis into self-propelled guns of varying calibre; again numbers were insignificant, amounting to about 560 vehicles.

Hitler's foreign panzers saw action on all the major fronts, although they clearly made the most impact in France and Poland. The Germans used 100 Czech tanks during the invasion of Poland and over 300 during the invasion of France. In North Africa, in response to the British Matilda tank, the Germans despatched Czech Marder III tank destroyers as well as French self-propelled guns to help restore the situation. Captured equipment helped Rommel's small panzer force keep almost half of Britain's operational strength, the equivalent of over twenty divisions, tied up. While his refurbished British tanks were too few in number to have any noticeable impact on the fighting, the large number of captured British lorries enabled him to keep his operations fluid and maintain the pressure on the British Army.

It was only when the British amassed a six to one superiority in tanks and aircraft that the tide turned against Rommel, and his *Afrika Korps* was finally ground down. In the case of the veteran 21st Panzer Division, which was badly mauled in North Africa, it found itself largely re-equipped with French armour when it came to resisting the D-Day landings.

Most of France's confiscated armour served as little more than a stopgap, providing the German Army with a few thousand extra tanks and self-propelled guns. Tellingly, in his memoirs as Inspector General of the German Armoured Troops, General Guderian mentions the valued contribution of the Czech LT-38 on a number of occasions, but makes only one reference to re-use of French tanks. Despite discussing German tank and self-propelled gun hybrid merits at length, he makes no comment on the French panzers' role on the Eastern Front or elsewhere. Ultimately French tanks made no significant strategic contribution to the German war effort. Indeed neither Guderian nor Rommel was very impressed by French armour; the former referred to it as 'inferior'.

The role of France's armour fighting alongside the *Wehrmacht* tended to be short-lived. In June 1941 18th Panzer Division had been equipped with French tanks and by the end of the year nearly all of them had been lost on the Russian Steppe. The 6th Panzer Division, after being badly mauled on the Eastern Front, was pulled out of the line and sent to France in April 1942. There it was issued with French tanks to provide an anti-invasion defence force. However, when the division returned to the bloodletting in Russia the following November it was equipped with German tanks.

Guderian, in his new role as inspector of Hitler's armoured forces, flew to Paris in April 1943 to meet the Commander-in-Chief West, Field Marshal von Rundstedt, and to visit armoured units in the area. At Yvetot he visited Panzer Regiment 100, which was equipped with French tanks. Later in the year he was displeased when the reconstituted 21st Panzer Division in France and the newly raised 25th Panzer Division in Norway had to be equipped with poor quality captured equipment.

Initially 25th Panzer was re-equipped with German armour when it arrived in France. Then, in October 1943, it was obliged to hand over its 600 new vehicles to the reconstituted 14th Panzer Division; another new unit that was destined for the Eastern Front. Disastrously 25th Panzer was told to make do with French vehicles and then ordered east. Guderian interceded and after inspecting the division informed Hitler it needed a month for the issuing of new equipment and training. It did no good and the ill-equipped and ill-fated men of the 25th Panzer Division were sent to their doom.

Field Marshal Rommel inspected the reformed 21st Panzer Division at the end of May 1944, a week before D-Day. The unit he reviewed was not the battle-hardened formation that had fought with such tenacity and determination in North Africa. He was photographed reviewing

French Hotchkiss self-propelled guns armed with 7.5cm and 10.5cm guns[1] as well as French Chenillette tracked carriers converted to makeshift rocket launchers[2] and did not look the least bit impressed. Rommel met Colonel von Opplen-Bronikowski who may have taken the opportunity to grumble. He had firsthand experience of the inadequacies of recycled foreign armour with the 22nd and 21st Panzer Divisions.

The *Panzertruppen* of 21st Panzer 'cursed' their French tanks, which had to be equipped with radios, while the artillery troop had to make do with Russian anti-tank guns and the mortar troop was armed with French mortars.[3] This multitude of weapons caused no end of problems with ammunition supply. 'Our best weapons are our old corporals, sergeants and NCOs,' joked Second Lieutenant Holler, a veteran of the original 21st Panzer Division, lost in Tunisia.[4] The division also contained survivors from Crete and the Eastern Front; all appreciated that courage alone was not enough to stem the anticipated Allied assault.

By 3 June, just three days before D-Day, Rommel was acutely aware of the manpower and material inferiority his troops would have in fending off an Allied invasion. His assessment was that the garrison forces in Normandy were too weak, their equipment inadequate for modern warfare and ammunition stocks were too low. The prognosis was not good.

Following his successful invasion of France, Hitler had set about expanding his Army. This meant halving the tank strength of the old panzer divisions to make the tanks go round the new formations. General Guderian observed:

> The simultaneous doubling of the motorised infantry divisions placed such a terrific burden on the motor vehicle industry, that Hitler's orders could only be carried out by making full use of available supplies, including the material captured in countries of Western Europe. These captured vehicles were markedly inferior in quality to the German ones and were particularly ill-suited for any employment that might be foreseen in the Eastern or African theatre.[5]

When preparing for the invasion of the Soviet Union, Guderian repeated his complaints about European equipment, in particular that confiscated from France:

> Unfortunately most of the vehicles of the new divisions which

Hitler had ordered to be set up were, as already stated, French. This equipment was in no way capable of meeting the demands of warfare in Eastern Europe. German vehicle production was insufficient to meet our greatly increased requirements; we could not therefore replace the palpably inferior captured vehicles with German ones.[6]

Guderian was proved right. Austrian and French built trucks did not assist greatly in their efforts to conquer the Soviet Union. The reliance on wheeled motor transport ultimately cost the Germans dearly on the Eastern Front. They had mechanised with wheels rather than tracks and wheeled vehicles constituted the bulk of their motor transport. Their armoured cars and trucks soon came to grief in the mud and once the tanks ran out of fuel they too became stranded. The Germans developed numerous half-tracks that could cope with the mud, but they were really needed in the opening stages of the war.

German lorry production could not keep up with the losses on the Eastern Front. By the winter of 1941-42 the transport available was insufficient for the fighting troops and the supply units. No replacements were received and the troops had to make use of whatever they could find, in particular sleds and sledges. Hitler's less than helpful solution was to reduce the number of supply troops.

France's remaining armour, in the Vichy controlled territories, similarly proved to be no more than a nuisance in the overall scheme of things. Vichy's armour gave the Allies a few scares during the initial stages of the invasion of French North-West Africa, in part because of the delay in getting their own armour ashore. In total a division's worth of French tanks had opposed the Allies. Privately the Americans were quite pleased that the French had chosen to fight, it gave them the opportunity to blood their inexperienced army, especially the tank crews, before it had to contend with the battle hardened panzers. The invasion also provided a vital testing ground for the subsequent amphibious assaults against Axis forces in Sicily and France. In that respect it highlighted a whole range of deficiencies that would have to be ironed out for future operations.

Mussolini's tanks proved to be more of a liability than an asset to Hitler. At the outbreak of the Second World War Italy's military strength and economy had already been sapped by the costly invasion of Ethiopia and considerable commitment to the Spanish Civil War. For Hitler, Italy was a useful fascist distraction in the Mediterranean that kept Britain and France preoccupied. However, after the Italian Army failed to deal with the British in North Africa and the Greeks in the Balkans, Hitler was forced to commit his panzers to secondary campaigns that interfered with his timetable for the Soviet Union and stretched resources. Only when the Germans took over northern Italy were the Italian's newer assault guns a welcome addition, helping to stiffen the German's strained defences. Kesselring and Vietinghoff were particularly grateful for the confiscated Italian armour, as the Eastern Front always took priority over whatever requirements they might have in Italy and the Balkans.

In late November 1941 an investigative team from the Army Ordnance Office, Armaments Ministry and leading tank designers, arrived in Russia at Guderian's urging. He had reported the superiority of the Soviet T-34 over their Panzer IV and called for the rapid production of a heavy anti-tank gun, capable of penetrating the T-34's armour. Guderian argued that only by examining Soviet tanks on the battlefield and drawing on the experiences of the *Panzertruppen* could adequate new tank designs be developed. Significant numbers of self-propelled anti-tanks guns were not available until 1941-42 and this is when obsolescent Czech, French and German tank chassis came to the rescue.

On the Eastern Front re-used Russian tanks were too few in number to ever have anything more than a local impact on the fighting. Numerically, the Germans greatest gain, in terms of vehicles, was several thousand Russian tracked tractors, which proved useful overcoming the mud. Countering the T-34 and KV-1 tanks required a quick fix and ironically the Russians provided it themselves. One of the most useful pieces of equipment that the Germans took from the Red Army in the summer of 1941 was the 76.2mm M1936 field gun. They captured so many of these guns that they were re-bored to take German anti-tank rounds and entered service in 1942 as the 7.62cm Pak 36(r).

Lieutenant Heinz Schmidt recalled receiving some of these guns in North Africa in September 1942: 'We had recently received new anti-tank guns. They included captured Russian 76.2mm guns. I trained the legionaries [former German French Foreign Legion] and sailors specially in the use of this weapon.'[7] His unit was tasked with covering Rommel's retreat from El Alamein. Mounted on a 38(t) chassis, this gun provided a timely and valuable self-propelled anti-tank gun; a stop-gap for the Eastern Front and North Africa.

It had soon become apparent that the 38(t) tank was obsolete and too slow for a reconnaissance role, on the other hand its workhorse chassis was too good to waste. A prototype, mounting the Pak 36(r) was built in December 1941 and went into production in March 1942 with BMM of

Prague. Known as the Marder just over 360 were produced by October 1942 and served with the *Panzerjäger* units fighting in the Soviet Union. Almost seventy were sent to North Africa to assist Rommel during July–November 1942 and served with the 15th Panzer Division. Subsequent improved versions were armed with a German 7.5cm Pak 40.

The Marder III self-propelled anti-tank gun, based on the 38(t) and Panzer II, was used extensively by the Army and *Waffen-SS*. The Czech built Marder IIIs of the 1st SS Panzer Division *Leibstandarte Adolf Hitler*'s Tank Hunter Battalion, helped recapture Kharkov in March 1943 and subsequently triumphantly paraded through the streets in a show of strength. In Italy at the Battle of Monte Cassino the 3rd Panzergrenadier Division deployed both the Czech Marder, and the Grille self-propelled guns, against the Allies.

SS Kampfgruppen, equipped with Marder IIIs, also helped inflict a major setback on the British Army. When General Montgomery launched Operation Market Garden on 17 September 1944, it was intended to take the Allies over the Rhine and into the Ruhr, the Nazi industrial heartland. Although potentially a masterstroke, Market Garden was flawed, especially as the British airborne spearhead came up against recuperating elements of 9th SS and 10th SS Panzer Divisions at Arnhem. The SS were extremely under strength but the outcome of pitting lightly armed paratroops against Marders, StuG III and Tiger tanks was inevitable.

As well as providing welcome mobile anti-tank gun support to the *Wehrmacht*, the 38(t) chassis was also used for mobile artillery. Another self-propelled gun that was built in some numbers was the Grille or Bison armed with a 15cm field gun. These were used to equip the Panzergrenadier regiments within the panzer divisions and provided valuable support in Russia, Tunisia, Italy and Normandy. The self-propelled gun company of the 2nd SS Panzergrenadier Regiment, serving with *Kampfgruppe Peiper* during the Battle of Bulge, included six Grille. They got as far as La Gleize where their crews abandoned them. In 1944 Skoda had even started producing new artillery in the shape of an improved 10.5cm field gun.[8]

The impact of the little Skoda 38(t) and its subsequent German designed variants on the *Wehrmacht* was considerable, and the crews developed a healthy respect for its capabilities. In fact Guderian became very concerned over Hitler's reliance on the Czechoslovak tanks. By 1942 the preoccupation had become the production of self-propelled guns rather than tanks. To make matters worse the self-propelled guns, mainly the *Panzerjäger* 38(t) and *Jagdpanzer* 38(t), were being armoured with unhardened steel.

Guderian recalled: '...the troops were already beginning to complain that a self-propelled gun on a Panzer II or Czech LT-38 chassis was not a sufficiently effective weapon.'⁹ Hitler would not be swayed and the following year instructed that the production of the Czech tank and Panzer II be devoted solely to making chassis for self-propelled guns. General von Thoma, who was captured in North Africa, was also dismissive of the early hybrids. In criticising the *Wehrmacht*'s conduct of the war on the Eastern Front he noted: 'Another handicap was the defectiveness of our self-propelled artillery. This weapon is invaluable. But those we used were only makeshift, and the chassis was overloaded.'¹⁰

The vehicle that had the greatest impact on Hitler's war effort was undoubtedly the *Jagdpanzer* 38(t) Hetzer tank destroyer. This served on the Eastern Front and in the West, particularly during the Ardennes offensive. The early self-propelled variants of the 38(t) had failed to provide adequate overhead protection for the crew and by March 1943 Guderian, in his role as Inspector General of the Armoured Troops, was calling for an enclosed low silhouette light tank destroyer. Development was completed by December 1943 and the production facilities for the 38(t) was switched to the new *Jagdpanzer* 38(t). Production commenced at BMM in April 1944 followed by Skoda in September.

The *Jagdpanzer* 38(t) was not used to equip the panzer battalions, but instead was deployed with the infantry divisions' *Sturmgeschütze* companies that had not been equipped with the ubiquitous StuG assault gun. The first combat units to operate the Hetzer were the 731st and 743rd Tank Hunter Battalions and the 15th and 76th Infantry Divisions. It first entered service in the *Waffen-SS* with the assault gun battalion of the 8th SS *Kavallerie Division Florian Geyer*, though the issue of this compact armoured fighting vehicle did little to save the division. It was annihilated in Budapest in February 1945 by the Red Army, along with sister division 22nd *Freiwilligen Kavallerie Division der SS Maria Theresa*.

The Czech chassis was deemed so successful that the Germans were planning to continue using it once they had won the war. Plans had been afoot for a new design 10.5-ton light reconnaissance tank dubbed the T-15, and a 22-ton medium tank known as the T-25. Both were to use a lengthened and widened version of the Skoda 38(t) chassis with sloping armour, thought to have been the influence of the T-34. In light of

Germany's crumbling defences neither tank got much beyond the design stage. In late 1944 or early 1945 the *Wehrmacht* was also planning a tracked troop carrier using a stretched 38(t) chassis, but this project was abandoned as well.

In February 1945, just three months before the end of the war, plans were drawn up for the *Panzerjäger* 38(d) series. This was to have provided a short-term light tank replacement until the E-10 was ready with tank destroyer, anti-aircraft, reconnaissance, armoured personnel and armoured weapons carrier variants. Development of a 7.5cm armed self-propelled version was given priority in 1944-45, presumably as a replacement for the Hetzer. It seems the Germans were planning their final heist from the Czechs by turning production of the PzJg 38(d) over to the German factories that had produced the Panzer III and IV. They were planning to produce 2,000 a month but, with the end of the war, the project was abandoned.[11]

One new successor Czech vehicle that almost got off the ground was the *Waffenträger* self-propelled gun that was to use 38(t) components. Development of this gun carriage with two variants began in 1943 with armament ranging from a 88mm to a 15cm howitzer. The drawings for both were ready by March 1945 and moves toward production were being made. It was intended that this would commence in the spring of 1945 with an output of up to 350 vehicles a month. Components were to come from both the 38(t) and 38(d) programmes and once again production would have been turned over to a German firm, Ardelt, in Eberswalde, in this instance.

Epilogue

Tanker Gustav and vehicle mechanic, Stuhlmacher, from *Panzer Abteilung 213* revved up their French Char B tank and put it into gear. Under the watchful eyes of members of the 135th Field Ordnance Unit of the Royal Army Ordnance Corps they lurched forward, belching oily smoke and began to mangle the line of derelict *Wehrmacht* vehicles. Gustav and Stuhlmacher were probably the last *Panzertruppen* to drive one of Hitler's captured tanks, not in anger but as a steamroller.[1]

Ultimately the process that had started with Austria and Czechoslovakia ended there. Inspired by the news that Paris had been liberated and that Romania had changed sides, the Slovaks were premature in trying to throw off the Nazi yoke on 23 August 1944. Hitler had no troops available to fight this unwelcome rebellion and an improvised armoured regiment had to be raised from the various SS training schools in Bohemia and Moravia. The Slovaks had no tanks with which to resist the panzers, as their remaining armour had been lost with the Slovak Mobile Division on the Eastern Front.

The *Wehrmacht* moved quickly to disarm the Slovak Army's two regular army infantry divisions and many of the soldiers fled to central Slovakia to join the partisans. Czechoslovak airborne forces flown in by Stalin also joined them. Unfortunately Neusohl, the centre of the rising, could not be held without heavy weapons and fell by the end of the month to the German armour. The arrival of elements of the 14th SS Grenadier and 18th SS Panzergrenadier Divisions sealed the fate of the remaining rebels. The Slovak people would have to wait until the spring for the arrival of the Red Army before they would taste freedom and see the Nazis finally pack their bags.

Despite repeated counter-attacks, the Russians cleared the Germans from the Hungarian capital, Budapest, by 13 February 1945, capturing 138,000 prisoners. In the face of fierce German resistance the country was liberated by early April. Hungary's vehicle factories, that had singularly failed to keep pace with even the Hungarian Army's requirements, were overrun. The turncoat workers at the Manfred Weiss armoured fighting vehicle plant were quick to pledge their allegiance when the Russians turned up, declaring: 'On this historic day we solemnly vow to be worthy of the men of the Red Army, mobilise all our strength and knowledge in order to meet the orders of the Red Army ahead of time and thereby make our contribution to the last battles.'[2]

The Russians pushed toward Czechoslovakia with their 4th and 2nd Ukrainian Fronts, the latter included 21,000 men of the 1st Czechoslovak Corps and 81,500 men of the 1st and 4th Romanian Armies. The plan was to encircle the Germans' Army Group Centre, east of Prague. Upon the approach of the Red Army the Slovaks rose up once more, this time in the industrial town and railway junction of Banska Bystrica. The Slovak capital of Bratislava was liberated on 4 April and the Red Army rolled into the Vienna plain and reached the Czechoslovak-Austrian border. The factories of Austro–Daimler and Steyr ground to a halt. German resistance in Vienna was overcome by 13 April and the Soviets shifted their attention to capturing Brno, the main industrial centre in Czechoslovakia. When the Russians stormed Wiener Neustadt, the cadets from the Austrian War Academy, Erwin Rommel's old command, put up a considerable fight and the castle was reduced to a heap of rubble.

During the spring of 1945 Czech partisan brigades stepped up their activities wrecking factories and bringing many of them to a standstill. Mid-April saw heavy fighting in the Czechoslovakian towns of Istebna, Vrutky and Hodonin and by the end of the month Russian troops had attacked the industrial centres of Moravska-Ostrava and Brno. For the last time the Germans made use of Czech military resources; the old fortifications that they had modernised held up the Russians, but only for a while.

The *Wehrmacht* put up a stubborn defence at Brno, which came under attack on 23 April. The Russians, crossing the famous Napoleonic battlefield of Austerlitz, reached the eastern suburbs the following day only to lose over thirty tanks to a vigorous German counter-attack. Bringing up reinforcements to cut off the Germans' retreat the Soviets secured Brno on 26 April, liberating the Zbrojovka armaments factory. It had been six long years since Guderian visited Brno, precipitating Hitler's first major panzer heist. Now a shattered battlefield, this was its reward for fuelling Hitler's war machine. On 29 April Russians troops entered Moravska-Ostrava's western suburbs under strict instructions to avoid damaging the factories and other industrial installations. The exhausted German defenders withdrew, leaving the town which had also been occupied in March 1939, to its fate.

In the meantime the Red Army overwhelmed Berlin's defences by 2 May. Despite all Albert Speer's efforts Hitler only managed to muster 650 panzers with which to resist the Russian onslaught on his capital, involving 6,250 tanks, assault guns and self-propelled guns. On 1 May twenty remaining panzers attempted to break out. The Russians, suspecting they might be bearing senior Nazis, destroyed all of them ten miles north-west of Berlin the next day.

After Hitler's suicide Admiral Dönitz, whilst prepared to end hostilities with the Western Allies, had no intention of giving up the fight in the east. The *Wehrmacht* surrendered in northern Italy on 2 May and in the rest of Western Europe on 4 May. At this point, largely encouraged by the approach of the Americans from the west, the Czechs in Bohemia and Moravia decided to rise up and thrown off the Nazi yoke. Fighting first broke out in Prague on 1 May followed by a general rising in the city four days later. All the key installations were seized, including the Skoda, Avia and Walther factories. The workers in Kladno, one of the largest industrial centres, rose up on 4-5 May followed by those in Pilsen.

The last few Hetzer 38(t) tank destroyers to come off Skoda's production line for the *Wehrmacht* were destroyed in the fighting on the streets of Prague. Ironically the renegade Russian Liberation Army's 600th Division, numbering 18,000 men with a few tanks, under Generals Vlasov and Bunichenko, ended up fighting against the SS alongside the desperate Czech insurgents.[3] Ultimately though they found themselves disowned by both sides and fought their way out of the city alongside the SS.[4]

A battle group from the 2nd SS Panzer Division was despatched to crush the revolt in Prague, but in the event ended up covering the evacuation of German troops and fleeing administrators. Soviet tanks, supported by the Czechoslovak 1st Tank Brigade, rolled into the city early on 9 May, overwhelming the remaining defenders. Work at BMM, Tatra and Skoda had long since stopped. Breaking Hitler's once firm grip on Czechoslovakia cost Stalin 140,000 dead. In a final act of poetic justice on 10 May the German garrison trapped in Dunkirk surrendered to a Czechoslovak armoured brigade. The latter paraded triumphantly through Prague the following month.

Major General Sir Edward Spears summed up Czechoslovakia's plight: 'Our troops no doubt, when plastered with shells made of Witkovitz steel and fired from a Skoda gun, thought a mistake had been made, but what of the Czechs before the war, during the war and after the war?'5 They had truly paid a terrible price for Hitler's great panzer heist. Those responsible for cooperating with Hitler's war effort were swiftly punished.

Czech President Hacha was arrested on 14 May 1945, but died before he could be tried. Slovak Premier Jospeh Tiso was executed in 1947. Bohemia and Moravia's Reich Protector, Karl Frank, was sentenced to death and publicly hanged near Prague on 22 May 1946. Civil Administrator Konrad Henlein, after being captured by Czech resistance forces, committed suicide in 1945. Hungarian ruler Miklós Horthy, after being ousted by the Germans, lasted out the war under house arrest. Although Yugoslavia demanded he be tried as a war criminal, he died in exile in Portugal in 1957. The deposed Antonescu was put on trial in May 1946 in Romania and found guilty of a host of crimes. He was executed the following month.

The last remnants of Hitler's great panzer heist were finally captured on British sovereign territory in the spring of 1945. After the Allies landed in Normandy on 6 June 1944 and with the capture of St Malo on 15 August, the German garrison on the Channel Islands found itself besieged. By this stage Panzer Battalion 213 was commanded by Major Kopp, his predecessor Major Lecht having been posted to the Eastern Front in March 1944, and Lieutenant Ulricht, who had replaced Graf Hoyos. Starved of fuel, Hitler's French panzers remained idle, their engines being started only occasionally to make sure they were still in running order.

The 27,000 strong German garrison showed no inclination to surrender and the Allies had no wish to attack the islands considerable concrete fortifications. They were the most heavily defended sector of Hitler's much-vaunted Atlantic Wall. Vice Admiral Huffmeier had succeeded von Schmettow as Commander-in-Chief of the Channel Islands in February 1945 and his deputy Brigadier General Heine was also commander on Guernsey.

Task Force 135 finally arrived on 9 May 1945 to accept the garrison's capitulation. Heine signed the surrender on the quarterdeck of HMS *Bulldog* at 07.14, followed by Brigadier General Wulf, commander on Jersey, some time after 10.00. *Panzer Abteilung 213* is probably the only German armoured unit never to have fired a shot in anger. The German tank crews and infantry were shipped off to England, though some 3,200 troops were kept on the islands to help clear up the anti-invasion defences.6 The Panzer Workshop Kompanie remained behind to help the Royal Engineers clear up and the French panzers were assembled on Jersey at Circus Field Millbrook, where they remained for eleven months.

First there was the massive task of removing over 1,000 guns, and 50,000 tons of ammunition, as well asthousands of rifles and machine guns. Amongst the huge concrete casements built to repel sea borne invasion, the British troops discovered French 10.5cm K331(f) field guns and Czech 4.7cm Pak 36(t) anti-tank guns. They also had to remove *Panzerstellung* or tank positions dotted throughout the islands, which consisted of French H-35, R-35 and FT-17 tank turrets, mounted on concrete bunkers.

The British Army was presented with a major clearance problem at Jersey's Springfield Football Ground, which the Germans had used as an Army Vehicle Park. The place was clogged with broken down vehicles and other military debris. It was decided to crush most of it in order to make it more manageable. Behind the RAOC's HQ in the town arsenal, in Rouge Bouillon, they discovered an old steamroller. German POW Gustav claimed he knew how to operate such equipment and was soon clanking around Springfield. Unfortunately when he attempted to crush the scrap the steamroller slipped on the soft ground. Instead the Char B tank was enlisted and used to crush the derelict vehicles.

It was not until 17 May 1946 that the last of Hitler's French panzers were loaded onto a former tank landing craft at La Haule Slip, St Aubin's Bay, Jersey and shipped back to their original owners.[7] Only one Char B was kept, No. 114 which is preserved at the UK's Bovington Tank Museum, restored in French colours. The Renault FT-17 light tanks on Guernsey and Jersey were cut up, while those on Alderney were rumoured to have been dumped in a quarry near Braye Harbour. The remaining two mobile FT-17s were found in a shed at St Peter's Barracks on Jersey and were sold for scrap in July 1946. On Guernsey the French self-propelled artillery, armed with Czech guns, were sealed up in a German tunnel, but were later removed for scrap. Hitler's panzer heist was finally at an end.

In France the name of Louis Renault was tainted by Hitler's French panzers. Although he had refused to cooperate with the tank programme, he had built thousands of transport vehicles for the German Army and allowed his factories to repair French tanks and assist German technicians. He was arrested for treason after the liberation on 23 September 1944 and died under suspicious circumstances in Fresnes prison near Paris on 24 October. Pierre Lefaucheux subsequently took over Renault and ironically the company went on to become one of the world's leading automobile manufacturers.

Marshal Petain and the rest of his Vichy government were moved to Sigmaringen in Germany in early September 1944. Petain returned to Paris in April 1945, was convicted of treason and sentenced to death. Charles de Gaulle subsequently commuted this to life imprisonment. The old Marshal was incarcerated on the Ile d'Yeu, an island off France's Atlantic coast, where he died in 1951. Prime Minister Pierre Laval fled but was handed over to the new French government on 30 July 1945. He was sentenced to death and shot by firing squad at Fresnes.

General Henri Dentz, whose tanks caused the British so much grief in the Levant, also received a death sentence on 20 April 1945. Although this was communed to a life sentence he died in Fresnes prison on 13 December 1945. SS-Sturmbannführer Joseph Darnand, founder of the hated *Milice Française*, was executed in France on 10 October 1945.

In Germany the SS requisitioned the last samples of Hitler's great panzer heist. At the end of April 1945 Marshal Rokossovsky's 2nd Belorussian Front clashed with *SS-Standartenführer* (Colonel) Walter Harzer's 4th SS Polizei Panzergrenadier Division in the Stettin area. He came under the command of SS General Felix Steiner's 3rd SS Panzer Corps, part of General Hasso von Manteuffel's 3rd Panzer Army, defending the Stettin and Schwedt region. Steiner had gathered the remnants of the once proud *Waffen-SS* around him for the last battle. His command, as well as the 4th SS, included the remains of the 5th SS Panzer Division, 11th SS Panzergrenadier Division and the 3rd Navy Division totalling just 15,000 men.

The captured vehicles that had been so painstaking gathered at the Army Weapons Office at Kummersdorf and Stettin-Altdamm fell victim to the collapse of the Third Reich. The defenders of 'fortress' Stettin had nothing with which to stop the Soviets; the 3rd Panzer Army desperately short of artillery had stripped the Stettin area of 600 anti-aircraft guns. On 9 March 1945 Army Group Vistula authorised the removal of the armour stored at the tank museum at Stettin-Altdamm for deployment in the defence of Stettin. The very last units to be created using foreign tanks were Panzer Company Kummersdorf, its strength included two Shermans, and Panzer Company Berka, which included three Shermans and three *Jagdpanzer* 38(t) Hetzers, formed at the end of March.

Steiner was ordered to move north-east of Berlin to hold Manteuffel's southern sector in the forests of Eberswalde. The 11th SS Panzergrenadier Division, through lack of petrol, failed to get into line or counter-attack at the Seelow Heights, twenty-eight miles from Berlin and withdrew on the city. General Steiner in the meantime at the headquarters of the 25th Panzergrenadier Division at Nassenheide, was ordered to attack across the line of the 1st Belorussian Front's assault. Steiner refused; he had hardly any artillery and only a few anti-tank guns and panzers - in his own words - 'a completely mixed up heap that will never reach Spandau from Germendorf.'[8] He avoided Berlin, retreating through Brandenburg to prudently surrender to the Americans. The tanks from the museum and Panzer Companies Kummersdorf and Berka were lost in the chaos.

Colonel General Heinz Guderian, who had been appointed Chief of the General Staff in July 1944, was dismissed the following March for standing up to Hitler once too often. Joining his old command, the staff of the Inspectorate General of Armoured Troops in Tyrol, he surrendered to the Americans in May 1945. Field Marshal Rommel was implicated in the July 1944 bomb plot to kill Hitler and forced to commit suicide three months later. General von Thoma arrived in North Africa in September 1942 to relieve Rommel, who was due to receive medical treatment in Austria. Just after Rommel returned, Thoma was captured by the British.

The man initially charged with the intelligence exploitation of foreign armour, Walther Model, rose to the rank of field marshal. Commanding Hitler's forces on the Western Front he failed to stop the Allies capturing the Ruhr and shot himself on 21 April 1945. Field Marshal Kesselring was badly injured in a car crash in late 1944 and did not return to the war in Italy until February the following year. Hitler appointed him Supreme Commander West in March 1945 and he subsequently surrendered to the Americans with the cessation of hostilities.

General Nehring ended the war in Czechoslovakia commanding the 1st Panzer Army. He had hoped to withdraw to Germany but, when the surrender came, was at Deutsch Brod. He and his troops managed to reach Tabor where they capitulated to the Americans. Hermann von Oppeln-Bronikowski, after fighting with the 21st Panzer Division in Normandy, was promoted to brigadier general and took command of the 20th Panzer Division on the Eastern Front. The Americans captured him on 18 May 1945 near Plauen. The daring Otto Skorzeny ended the war fighting in Prussia and Pomerania. For his efforts to pass off Panzer Brigade 150 as an American armoured unit he was tried as a war criminal by an American tribunal at Dachau in 1947 but acquitted. He escaped from prison in July 1948 and fled to Spain where he died of cancer in 1975. Brigadier General Franz Bake survived his early experiences with his Skoda tanks in France and Russia and ended the war commanding the remnants of the 13th Panzer Division, which surrendered in Austria.

The victorious Red Army showed little interest in the military vehicles that had come out of the factories in Czechoslovakia and Hungary, which were to remain within the Soviet zone of occupation. In contrast the Czechs turned the tables on the *Wehrmacht*, by modifying the German Sd Kfz 251 half-track and putting it into production in the late 1940s as the OT 810 Tatra for the Czechoslovak Army. The Hetzer design lived on after the war and about 150 were exported to Switzerland between 1946-52, where they were designated the G13. Nonetheless, it would not be very long before the very facilities that had supported Hitler's war effort were put to work producing Soviet designed tanks and armoured fighting vehicles for the armies of the Warsaw Pact, helping to fuel the Cold War.[9]

In an act of supreme post-war irony Germany eventually got its hands on Skoda's factories again, but this time by much more peaceful means. Following the collapse of the Warsaw Pact and the Soviet Union in April 1991 Skoda became part of Europe's largest carmaker, the Volkswagen group. The first joint automobile project, the Felicia, was launched three years later and in the late 1990s was followed by the successful Octavia and Fabia. Volkswagen Slovakia also has a plant in Bratislava producing off-road vehicles. Today Skoda is a major automobile manufacturer with assembly plants in India, Ukraine and Bosnia-Herzegovina; its wartime legacy long forgotten.

Appendix I

Military Vehicles acquired by the *Wehrmacht* 1938-45

Armoured Fighting Vehicles	No.
Austria	126
Czechoslovakia	6,571
France	2,410
Hungary	851
Italy	5,326
Italy (German Italian build)	932
Poland	115
Russia	300
Yugoslavia	20
Total:	**16,651**

Tracked Carriers/Tractors	No.
Belgium	300
France	3,276
Poland	200
Russia	2,000
Total:	**5,776**

Motor Vehicles	No.
Austria	24,241
France	48,514
Total:	**72,755**

Overall Total:	**95,182**

Appendix II

Foreign Armour Technical Specifications

American Armour

Type:	Medium Tank
Designation:	Sherman M4/PzKpfw M4 748(a)
Weight:	29.6 tons
Speed:	42 km/hr
Frontal Armour:	75mm
Armament:	1x75mm, 2xmg
Crew:	5
Range:	160km

British Armour

Type:	Cruiser Tank
Designation:	Cruiser Mk VI Crusader I/II/ Kreuzer PzKpfw Mk VI 746(e)
Weight:	19 tons
Speed:	43 km/hr
Frontal Armour:	40mm/49mm
Armament:	1x2 pdr, 2xmg
Crew:	5
Range:	160km

Type:	Infantry Tank
Designation:	Matilda Mk II/Infanterie PzKpfw Mk II 748(e)
Weight:	26.5 tons
Speed:	24 km/hr
Frontal Armour:	78mm
Armament:	1x2 pdr, 1xmg
Crew:	4
Range:	256km

Type:	Infantry Tank
Designation:	Valentine Mk III/Infanterie PzKpfw Mk III 749(e)
Weight:	16 tons
Speed:	24 km/hr
Frontal Armour:	65mm
Armament:	1x2pdr, 1xmg
Crew:	3
Range:	144km

Czech Armour

Type:	Light Tank
Designation:	PzKpfw 35(t)
Weight:	10.5 tons
Speed:	35km/hr
Frontal	Armour: 25mm
Armament:	1x37mm, 2xmg
Crew:	4
Range:	190 km

Type:	Light Tank
Designation:	PzKpfw 38(t)
Weight:	8.5 tons
Speed:	35km/hr
Frontal Armour:	25mm
Armament:	1x37mm, 2xmg
Crew:	4
Range:	250 km

Type:	Self-Propelled Gun
Designation:	Marder III
Weight:	10.5 tons
Speed:	42km/hr
Frontal	Armour: 20mm
Armament:	1x7.5cm, 1xmg
Crew:	4
Range:	190 km

Type:	Tank Destroyer
Designation:	*Jagdpanzer* 38(t) Hetzer
Weight:	15.75 tons
Speed:	42km/hr
Frontal Armour:	60mm
Armament:	1x7.5cm, 1xmg
Crew:	4
Range:	177km

French Armour

Type:	Light Tank
Designation:	FT-17/18/PzKpfw FT-17/18 730(f)
Weight:	6.7 tons
Speed:	7.7 km/hr
Frontal Armour:	22mm
Armament:	1x8mm or 37mm
Crew:	2
Range:	35km

Type:	Light Tank
Designation:	Renault R-35/ PzKpfw 35-R 731(f)
Weight:	10 tons
Speed:	20km/hr
Frontal Armour:	32mm

Armament:	1x3.7cm, 1xmg
Crew:	2
Range:	140km
Type:	Light Tank
Designation:	Hotchkiss H-38/PzKpfw 38H 735(f)
Weight:	12 tons
Speed:	36 km/hr
Frontal Armour:	34mm
Armament:	1x3.7cm, 1xmg
Crew:	2
Range:	150km
Type:	Medium Tank
Designation:	Renault Char B1 Bis/ PzKpfw B-1/B-2 740(f)
Weight:	32 tons
Speed:	28 km/hr
Frontal Armour:	60mm
Armament:	1x7cm, 1x4.7cm, 1xmg
Crew:	4
Range:	150km
Type:	Self-Propelled Anti-Tank Gun
Designation:	Marder I 7.5cm Pak40/1 auf Geschutzwagen (GW) Lorraine Schlepper (f) (Sd Kfz 135)
Weight:	8 tons
Speed:	34 km/hr
Frontal Armour:	12mm
Armament:	1x7.5cm, 1xmg
Crew:	5
Range:	135km
Type:	Self-Propelled Anti-Tank Gun
Designation:	4.7cm PaK(t) auf Panzerkampfwagen 35R(f) ohne Turm
Weight:	10.5 tons
Speed:	19 km/hr
Frontal Armour:	32mm
Armament:	1x4.7cm
Crew:	3
Range:	140km

Hungarian Armour

Type:	Light Tank
Designation:	38M Toldi I/II
Weight:	8.5 tons/9.3 tons
Speed:	50 km/hr/47 km/hr
Frontal Armour:	20mm/35mm
Armament:	1x20mm/1x40mm
Crew:	3
Range:	200km

Type:	Self-Propelled Anti-Aircraft/Anti-Tank Gun
Designation:	40M Nimrod
Weight:	8 tons
Speed:	35-50 km/hr
Frontal Armour:	13mm
Armament:	1x40mm
Crew:	5
Range:	200km

Type:	Medium Tank
Designation:	40M Turan I/II
Weight:	18.2 tons
Speed:	47 km/hr
Frontal Armour:	60mm
Armament:	1x40mm/1x75mm, 2xmg
Crew:	5
Range:	165km

Type:	Self-Propelled Howitzer
Designation:	42M Zrinyi II
Weight:	21.5 tons
Speed:	40 km/hr
Frontal Armour:	75mm
Armament:	1x105mm
Crew:	4
Range:	220km

Italian Armour

Type:	Light Tank
Designation:	L3/35/ PzKpfw L3/35 731(i)
Weight:	3.2 tons
Speed:	26mph
Frontal Armour:	13.5mm
Armament:	2xmg
Crew:	2
Range:	75 miles

Type:	Light Tank
Designation:	L6/40/ PzKpfw L6/40 733(i)
Weight:	6.9 tons
Speed:	42 km/hr
Frontal Armour:	30mm
Armament:	1x20mm, 1xmg
Crew:	2
Range:	200km

Type:	Medium Tank
Designation:	M11/39/PzKpfw M11/39 734(i)
Weight:	11 tons
Speed:	32 km/hr
Frontal Armour:	30mm
Armament:	1x37mm, 2xmg

Crew: 3
Range: 200km

Type: Medium Tank
Designation: M13/40/PzKpfw M13/40 735(i)
Weight: 14.3 tons
Speed: 32 km/hr
Frontal Armour: 30mm
Armament: 1x4.7cm, 1xmg
Crew: 4
Range: 200km

Type: Medium Tank
Designation: P26/40/ PzKpfw P40 737(i)
Weight: 26 tons
Speed: 42 km/hr
Frontal Armour: 50mm
Armament: 1x7.5cm, 1xmg
Crew: 4
Range: 275km

Type: Assault Gun
Designation: DA 75/34 Sturmgeschütz M42
                         mit 75/18 850(i)/75/34 851(i)
Weight: 15 tons
Speed: 38 km/hr
Frontal Armour: 30mm
Armament: 1x7.5cm, 1xmg
Crew: 3
Range: 230 km

Polish Armour

Type: Light Tank
Designation: 7TP/PzKpfw 7TP 731(p)
Weight: 11 tons
Speed: 32 km/hr
Frontal Armour: 40mm
Armament: 1x37mm, 1xmg
Crew: 3
Range: 160km

Russian Armour

Type: Light Tank
Designation: T-26B/PzKpfw T-26B 738(r)
Weight: 9 tons
Speed: 32 km/hr
Frontal Armour: 25mm
Armament: 1x45mm
Crew: 3
Range: 225km

Type:	Medium Tank
Designation:	BT-7/PzKpfw BT 742(r)
Weight:	14 tons
Speed:	53 km/hr
Frontal Armour:	22mm
Armament:	1x45mm, 1xmg
Crew:	3
Range:	430km
Type:	Medium Tank
Designation:	T-34/PzKpfw T-34 747(r)
Weight:	26-30 tons
Speed:	50 km/hr
Frontal Armour:	40-45mm
Armament:	1x76.2mm, 2xmg
Crew:	5
Range:	300km

Appendix III

Foreign Armoured Fighting Vehicle Designations

Wehrmacht **Country Codes:**
(a) Amerikanisch/American
(b) Belgisch/Belgium
(e) Englisch/British
(f) Französisch/French
(h) Hollandisch/Dutch
(i) Italienisch/Italian
(o) Österreichisch/Austrian
(p) Polnisch/Polish
(r) Russisch/Russian
(t) Tschechisch/Czechoslovakian

Wehrmacht **Group Codes:**
200 armoured cars
300 half-track vehicles
400 armoured half-track vehicles
600 tracked artillery tractors
630 armoured artillery tractors
700 tanks (including British armoured cars)
800 self-propelled guns

Abbreviations:
PzKpfw: Panzerkampfwagen (Tank/Armoured Fighting Vehicle)
Pz Sp Wg: Panzerspahwagen (Armoured Scout Car)
Gep Mannschaft Tr Wg: Gepanzeter Mannschaftstransportwagen (Armoured Personnel Carrier)

American Light Tanks
M2A2 PzKpfw M2A2 740(a)
M3/PzKpfw M3 747(a)

American Medium Tanks
M4/PzKpfw M4 748(a)

American Look-alikes
PzKpfw Mk V/M10

Austrian Armoured Cars
Austro-Daimler ADGZ/Polizei-Panzerkampfwagen ADGZ

Belgian Artillery Tractor

Familleureux Utility B tracked light artillery tractor/Art Schl VA 601(b)

British Light Tanks
Mk II/leichter PzKpfw Mk II 733(a)
Mk IV/leichter PzKpfw Mk IV 734(a)
Mk VIB/leichter PzKpfw Mk VIB 735(a)
Mk VIC/leichter PzKpfw Mk VIC 736(a)
Mk VII/leichter PzKpfw Mk VII 737(a)

British Cruiser Tanks
Mk I/Kreuzer PzKpfw Mk I 741(e)
Mk II/Kreuzer PzKpfw Mk II 742(e)
Mk III/Kreuzer PzKpfw Mk III 743(e)
Mk IV/Kreuzer PzKpfw Mk IV 744(e)
Mk V/Kreuzer PzKpfw Mk V 745(e)
Mk VI/Kreuzer PzKpfw Mk VI 746(e)

British Infantry Tanks
Matilda Mk I/Infanterie PzKpfw Mk I 747(e)
Matilda Mk II/Infanterie PzKpfw Mk II 748(e)
Valentine Mk III/Infanterie PzKpfw Mk III 749(e)

British Armoured Cars
Scout Mk I Dingo/leichter Pz Sp Wg Mk I 202(e)
Armoured Reconnaissance Car Ironside/ leichter Pz Sp Wg Ir 204(e)
Armoured Reconnaissance Car Morris/ Pz Sp Wg Mo 205(e)
Armoured Reconnaissance Car Ford/SPz Sp Wg F 208(e)

British Carriers
Bren-gun/Universal Carrier/ Gepanzerter Maschinengewehr Träger Bren 731(e)

German built British Self-Propelled Guns
10.5cm leFH16 auf Geschutzwagen MarkVI(e)

German built British Munitions Carriers
Munitionspanzer auf Fahrgestell Mk IV(e)

Czech Tanks
LT-35/Panzerkampfwagen 35(t)
LT-38/Panzerkampfwagen 38(t)

German built Czech Self-Propelled Guns
Marder III/Panzerjäger 38(t)
75mm & 150mm Panzerkampfwagen 38(t)
Flakpanzer 38(t)

German built Czech Tank Destroyer
Jagdpanzer 38(t) Hetzer

Dutch Light Tanks
Renault FT/PzKpfw FT 731(h)

Dutch Armoured Cars
Pantserwagen M39 Van Doorne/Pz Sp Wg DAF 201(h)
Landsverk M36/38/Pz Sp Wg L/P 202 (h)

French Light Tanks
Renault AMR 33VM/PzSpWg VM 701(f)
Renault AMR 35ZT/PzSpWg ZTI 702(f)
FT-17/18/PzKpfw FT-17/18 730(f)
Renault R-35/PzKpfw 35-R 731(f)

French Tanks
Char D-1/PzKpfw D-1 732(f)
Char d'Assault D-2/PzKpfw D2 733(f)
Hotchkiss H-35/PzKpfw 35H 734(f)
Hotchkiss H-38/PzKpfw 38H 735(f)
Char ZM/PzKpfw 736(f)
Char de combat FCM/PzKpfw FCM 737(f)
AMC 1935 R/PzKpfw AMC 738(f)
Somua S-35/PzKpfw 35-S 739(f)
Renault Char B1 Bis/ PzKpfw B-1/B-2 740(f)
Char 3-C/PzKpfw 3-C 741(f)

French Armoured Cars
AMD White-Laffy/Pz Sp Wg Wh 201(f)
AMD Laffy/Pz Sp Wg Laf 202(f)
AMD Panhard TOE/Pz Sp Wg 203(f)
AMD Panhard P-178/Panhard Pz Sp Wg 178-P.204(f)

French Tracked Infantry Carrier
Chenillette d'infanterie Renault/AMX UE/Infanterie Schlepper UE 630(f)

German built French Self-Propelled Guns
4.7cm PaK(t) auf Panzerkampfwagen 35R(f) ohne Turm
Marder I 7.5cm Pak40/1 auf Geschutzwagen (GW) Lorraine Schlepper (f) (Sd Kfz 135)
15cm sFH13/1 (Sf) auf Geschutzwagen Lorraine Schlepper (f) (Sd Kfz 135/1)
10.5cm leFH18(Sf) auf Geschutzwagen Lorraine Schlepper (f)
10.5cm leFH18/3 (Sf) auf Geschutzwagen
7.5cm PaK40(Sf) auf Geschutzwagen 39H(f)
10.5cm leFH18(Sf) auf Geschutzwagen 39H(f)
10.5cm leFH16(sf) auf Geschutzwagen FCM(f) & 7.5cm Pak40(Sf) auf Geschutzwagen FCM(f)

Italian Light Tanks
L3/35/PzKpfw L3/35 731(i)
L3/33/PzKpfw L3/33 Flammenwerfer 732(i)
L6/40/PzKpfw L6/40 733(i)

Italian Medium Tanks
M11/39/PzKpfw M11/39 734(i)
M13/40/PzKpfw M13/40 735(i)
M14.41/PzKpfw M14/41 736(i)
P26/40/PzKpfw P40 737(i)
M15/42/PzKpfw M15/42 738(i)

Italian Assault Guns
L/40 DA47/32/Sturmgeschutz L6 mit 47/32 770(i)

DA 75/18/Sturmgeschutz M42 mit 75/18 850(i)
DA 75/34/Sturmgeschutz M42 mit 75/34 851(i)
Sturmgeschutz M43 mit 75/46 852(i)
DA 105/25/Sturmgeschutz M43 mit 105/25 853(i)

Italian Armoured Cars
AB40 & 41/Pz Sp Wg AB40 und 41 201(i)
AB Lince/Pz Sp Wg 202(i)
AB 43/Pz Sp Wg AB43 203(i)
Autoprotetto S 37/Gep Mannschaft Tr Wg S 37 250(i)

Polish Light Tanks
7TP/PzKpfw 7TP 731(p)
TK3/TKS/leichte Panzerkampfwagen TK-3/TKS(p)

Russian Light Tanks
T-37/Schwimm-PzKpfw T-37 731(r)
T-38/Schwimm-PzKpfw T-38 732(r)
T-40/Schwimm-PzKpfw T-40 733(r)
T-27A/PzKpfw T-27A 734(r)

Russian Tanks
T-26A/PzKpfw T-26A 737(r)
T-26B/PzKpfw T-26B 738(r)
Flammenwerfer PzKpfw 739(r)
T-26C/PzKpfw T-26C 740(r)
BT-7/PzKpfw BT-742(r)
T-60/PzPkfw 743(r)
T-28/PzKpfw 746(r)
T-34/PzKpfw T-34 747(r)
T-28 V/PzKpfw V 748(r)
T-35A/PzKpfw T-35A 751(r)
T-35C/PzKpfw T-35C 752(r)
T-70/PzKpfw T-70(r)
KVIa/PzKpfw KVIa 753(r)
KVII/PzKpfw KVII 754(r)
KVIb/PzKpfw KVIb 755(r)

Russian Assault Guns
SU 85/Jgd Pz SU 85(r)
SU 122/StuG SU 122(r)

Russian Armoured Cars
BA-20/PzSp Wg BA 202(r)
BA-10/Pz Sp Wg BAF 203(r)

Russian Tracked Artillery Tractors
STZ-5-2TB/CT3-601(r)
KhPZ Voroshilovets/Stalin 607(r)
STZ Komsomolets/Gepanzerter Artillerie Schlepper 630(r)

Yugoslavian Light Tanks
T-32/Skoda 36

Appendix IV

Breakdown of Foreign Armoured Fighting Vehicle and Motor Vehicle Numbers

Austrian Tanks Seized in March 1938

Model	No. Built/In-service	No. re-used by Germany
M35/L3/35 tankette	74	74
M35 ADGZ armoured car	27	52 (including additional batch)
Total:	**101**	**126**

Czech Tank, Self-Propelled Gun and Assault Gun Production 1935-44

Model	No.	Manufactured
Panzerkampfwagen 35(t) light tank	424 *(219 confiscated March 1939)*	1935-38
Panzerkampfwagen 38(t) light tank	150xAusf A	May-November 1939
	325xAusf B,C & D	January-November 1940
	525xAusf E & F	Nov 1940-October 1941
	90xAusf S	May-December 1941
	321xAusf G	October 41-June 1942
38(t) Light Tank Subtotal:	**1,411**	**1939-42**
Marder III Panzerjäger 38(t) fur 7.62cm PaK36(r) (Sd Kfz 139) self-propelled gun	344 *(+19 conversions)*	April-October 1942
Marder III 7.5cm Pak40/3 auf Panzerkampfwagen38(t) Ausf H (Sd Kfz 138) self-propelled gun	242 *(+ 175 conversions)*	November 1942-April 1943
Marder III Panzerjäger 38(t) mit 7.5cm PaK40/3 Ausf M (Sd Kfz 138) self-propelled gun	975	April 1943-May 1944
Grille 15cm Schweres Infanteriegeschutz 33 (Sf) auf Panzerkampfwagen 38(t) Ausf H (Sd Kfz 138/1) self-propelled heavy gun	90	February-April 1943
Grille 15cm Schweres Infanteriegeschutz 33/1	282	April-June 1943 & October 1943-September 1944

auf Selbstfahrlafette 38(t)
(Sf) Ausf K (Sd Kfz 138/1)
self-propelled heavy gun

Flakpanzer 38(t) auf Selbstfahrlafette 38(t) Ausf L (Sd Kfz 140) self-propelled anti-anti-aircraft gun	140 *(+1 conversion)*	November 1943-February 1944
15cm Schweres Infanteriegeschutz 33/2 (Sf) a uf Jagdpanzer 38(t) Hezter self-propelled heavy gun	24 *(+ 6 conversions)*	From December 1944

38(t) Self-Propelled Gun Subtotal:	**2,097**	**1942-44**
Munitionspanzer 38(t) (Sf) Ausf K (Sd Kfz 138) ammunition carrier	102	January-May 1944
Aufklarer auf Fahrgestell Panzerkampfwagen 38(t) mit 2cm KwK38 oder 7.5cm KwK38 L/24 armoured reconnaissance vehicle	52 (50+2)	February-March 1944
Jagdpanzer 38(t) Hetzer Panzerjäger 38(t) fur 7.5cm PaK39 tank destroyer*	2,584	April 1944-May 1945
Bergepanzer 38(t) Hetzer armoured recovery vehicle	106 *(+64 conversions)*	October 1944-May 1945
Total:	**6,571**	**1939-45**

* The 20 Flammpanzer 38(t) Hetzer are not listed as they were converted from existing stocks. Similarly other variants converted from existing holdings have not been counted toward the overall manufacture total.

German Self-Propelled Gun conversions using Czech anti-tank guns 1940

Model	No.	Conversion date
4.7cm PaK(t) (Sf) auf Panzerkampfwagen I Ausf B	202	March 1940-February 1941

Polish Tanks Captured in September 1939

Model	No. Built	No. re-used by Germany
7TP/Vickers light tank	219	60
TK/TKS tankette	700	55
Total:	**919**	**115**

French Tanks Captured in May 1940

Model	No. built	Operational	No. re-used by Germany
FCM 2C	?	6	0
FCM 36	100	90	50

Hotchkiss H 35/39	1000	820	600
Renault FT 17	3000	534	500
Renault B1	380	313	160
Renault D2	100	75	0
Renault R 35/40	1600	1035	800
Somua S-35	450	243	300
Total:	**6,630**	**3,116**	**2,410**

German Self-Propelled Gun conversions based on French Tanks 1941-43

Model	No.	Conversion date
4.7cm (PaK(t) auf Panzerkampfwagen 35R(f) ohne Turm	174	May-October 1941
Marder I 7.5cm Pak40/1 auf Geschutzwagen (GW) Lorraine Schlepper (f) (Sd Kfz 135)	170	July-August 1942
15cm sFH13/1 (Sf) auf Geschutzwagen Lorraine Schellepr (f)(Sd Kfz 135/1) & 10.5cm leFH18(Sf) auf Geschutzwagen Lorraine Schellepr (f)	106 (94+12)	July 1942
10.5cm leFH18/3 (Sf) auf Geschutzwagen	16	1942
7.5cm PaK40(Sf) auf Geschutzwagen 39H(f) & 10.5cm leFH18(Sf) auf Geschutzwagen 39H(f)	72 (24+48)	1942
10.5cm leFH16(sf) auf Geschutzwagen FCM(f) & 7.5cm Pak40(Sf) auf Geschutzwagen FCM(f)	22 (12+10)	1942 & 1943
Total:	**560**	**1941-43**

French Tanks under Vichy Control 1940-42

Location	No.
Dakar (Senegal)	23
Indo-China	20
Levant (Lebanon & Syria)	90
Madagascar	5
Northwest Africa (Algeria, Morocco & Tunisia)	250
Total:	**388**

Yugoslav Tanks Captured in April 1941

Model	No. In-service	No. re-used by Germany
T-3D/T-32 tankette	8	8
FT-17 light tank	7	12
Total:	**15**	**20**

Italian Tank, Assault Gun & Armoured Car Production 1933-44

Model	Italian build 1933-43	German build 1943-44
L3/33 & 35 tankette	2,000	17 *(+ 148 confiscated)*
L6/40 light tank	283	0 *(unknown number confiscated)*
M11/39 medium tank	100	0
M13/40 medium tank	785	22
M14/41 medium tank	895	01
M15/42 medium tank	92	28 *(+ 92 confiscated)*
P26/40 heavy tank	5 *(200 ordered)*	100
M41/M42 command vehicle	16	41 *(+ 16 confiscated)*
L/40 DA 47/32 light assault gun	300	*(78 confiscated)*
DA 75/18 assault gun	200	55 *(+ 123 confiscated)*
DA 75/34 assault gun	90 *(500 ordered)*	80 *(+ 36 confiscated)*
DA 105/25 assault howitzer	26 *(495 ordered)*	91 *(+ 26 confiscated)*
Rearmed DA 105/25 assault gun with75/34 or 75/46	0	40
AB40 armoured car	24	
AB41 armoured car	500	87 *(+23)*
AB41/43 armoured car	10	120 *(+37 confiscated)*
Lancia Lincie scout car	0	250
Subtotal:		932 *(+ 579)*
Total:	**5,326**	**1,511**

Italian Tank and Assault Gun imports from Germany 1940-43

Model	No.	Delivered
Renault R-35/ PzKpfw 35-R 731(f)	109	1940

Somua S-35/PzKpfw 35-S 739(f)	32	1941
Panzerkampfwagen III	12	1943
Panzerkampfwagen IV	12	1943
Sturmgeschütze III	12	1943
Total:	**177**	**1940-43**

Hungarian Tank, Assault Gun & Armoured Car Production 1939-44

Model	No.	Manufactured
38M Toldi light tank	120 *(up to 200)*	1940-44
40M Turan medium tank	500 *(up to 622)*	1941-44
40M Nimrod anti-aircraft/ anti-tank gun	? *(up to 135)*	1940-?
43M Zrinyi self-propelled assault howitzer	60	1943-44
39M Csaba armoured car	171	1939-44
Total:	**851 (1,188)**	**1939-44**

Hungarian Tank and Assault Gun imports from Germany 1942-44

Model	No.	Delivered
Panzerkampfwagen 38(t)	102	1942
Panzerkampfwagen I	14	1942
Panzerkampfwagen III	10	1942
Panzerkampfwagen IV	32	1942
Hotchkiss H-39/PzKpfw 38H 735(f)	15	1943
Somua S-35/PzKpfw 35-S 739(f)	2	1943
Panzerkampfwagen IV	62	1944
Panzerkampfwagen V Panther	5	1944
Panzerkampfwagen VI Tiger I	3	1944
Sturmgeschütze III	40	1944
Hetzer 38(t)	100	1944
Total:	**385**	**1942-44**

Romanian Tank and Assault Gun imports from Germany 1942-44

Model	No.	Delivered
Panzerkampfwagen 35(t)	26	1942
Panzerkampfwagen III	11	1942
Panzerkampfwagen IV	11	1942
Panzerkampfwagen 38(t)	50	1943
Panzerkampfwagen IV	31	1943
Sturmgeschütze III	4	1943

Panzerkampfwagen IV	100	1944
Sturmgeschütze III	114	1944
Total:	**347**	**1942-44**

Bulgarian Tank and Assault Gun imports from Germany 1940-44

Model	No.	Delivered
Panzerkampfwagen 35(t)	36	1940
Renault R-35/ PzKpfw 35-R 731(f)	40	1941
Panzerkampfwagen 38(t)	10	1943
Panzerkampfwagen III	10	1943
Panzerkampfwagen IV	46	1943
Sturmgeschütze III	25	1943
Panzerkampfwagen IV	42	1944
Sturmgeschütze III	30	1944
Hotchkiss H-39/PzKpfw 38H 735(f)	19	1944
Somua S-35/PzKpfw 35-S 739(f)	6	1944
Total:	**264**	**1940-44**

Finnish Tank and Assault Gun imports from Germany 1943-44

Model	No.	Delivered
Sturmgeschütze III	30	1943
Sturmgeschütze III	29	1944
Panzerkampfwagen IV	15	1944
T-34/PzKpfw T-34 747(r)	3	1944
Total:	**77**	**1943-44**

Captured Tracked Weapons Carriers & Tractors

Nationality	Model	No. built	No. re-used by Germans
Belgian	Familleureux Utility B tracked light artillery tractor/Art Schl VA 601(b)	?	300
Belgian	Ford/Marmon-Herrington 4x4 armoured tractor	68	?
Czech	Praga T6-SS tracked artillery tractor	?	?
French	Chenillette d'infanterie Renault/AMX UE/Infanterie Schlepper UE 630(f)	6,000	3,000
French	Tracteur Blinde 37L tacked prime mover	400	276
Poland	Polski Fiat/PZInz C4P half-track artillery tractor	400	200
Poland	PZInz C2P tracked light tractor	?	?
Poland	PZInz C7P tracked medium tractor	71	?

Russian	STZ Komsomolets/Gepanzerter Artillerie Schlepper 630(r) tracked l ight prime mover	4,400	2,000
Russian	STZ-5-2TB/CT3-601(r) tracked light prime mover	7,000	?
Russian	KhPZ Voroshilovets/Stalin 607(r) tracked medium prime mover	?	?
Total:		**18,339**	**5,776**

Austrian Motor Vehicle Production 1939-44

Model	No.	Manufactured
Austro-Daimler ADGR 6x4 cargo truck	361	1939-40
Steyr 250 4x2 car	1,200	1938-40
Steyr 640 6x4 truck	3,780	1937-41
Steyr 270 1500A/02 4x4 truck	12,500	1941-44
Steyr 470 RSO/01	?	1942-43
Steyr Model 2000A 4x4 truck	6,400	1944
Total:	**24,241**	**1936-44**

Czech Motor Vehicle Production 1939-44

Model	No.	Manufactured
Skoda Popular 1100 OHV 4x2 light car	?	1939-42
Skoda Superb 3000 4x2 medium car	?	1942-43
Skoda 903 6x4 heavy car	?	1941-43
Skoda RSO 4x4 heavy tractor	200	1942-43
Tatra 57K 4x2 light car	?	1941-43
Tatra V809 4x4 medium car	?	1940-42
Tatra 27 4x2 truck	?	1938-41
Tatra T85A 6x4 truck	?	1939-41
Tatra T81	220	1939-42
Wikov MNO 4x2 truck	28	1940
Total:	**448+**	**1939-44**

French Motor Vehicle Production 1939-44

Model	No.	Manufactured
Citroen T23 4x2 truck	3,700	1941-44
Citroen T45/45U 4x2 trucks	15,000	1941-44
Latil TL7-RR 4x4 rail/road tractor	?	1942-43
Matford F917WS 4x2 truck	?	1941-44
Peugeot DK5J/D5A 4x2 truck	14,500	1939-41

Peugeot DMA/DAT 4x2 truck	15,314	1941-44
Renault AHN 4x2 truck	?	1941-44
Renault AHR 4x2 truck	?	1941-44
Renault AHS 4x2 truck	?	1941-44
Unic TU1 half-track tractor	?	1940-43
Total:	**48,514+**	**1940-44**

Appendix V

German Units issued with Foreign Armour

The Germans raised over several hundred divisions, many of which were issued with captured equipment. There were also numerous ad hoc foreign equipped tank battalions and companies. The list below highlights a few of the principal formations that employed foreign armoured fighting vehicles.

Panzer Divisions

1st Panzer Division
TK3/TKS/leichte PzKpfw TK-3/TKS(p), T-34/PzKpfw T-34 747(r) & KVIa/PzKpfw KVIa 753(r)

2nd Panzer Division
15cm PzKpfw 38(t), Flakpanzer 38(t) & T-34/PzKpfw T-34 747(r)

3rd Panzer Division
AMD Panhard P-178/Panhard Pz Sp Wg 178-P.204(f)

6th Panzer Division (1st Light Division)
LT-35/PzKpfw 35(t)

7th Panzer Division (2nd Light Division)
LT-38/PzKpfw 38(t) & AMD Panhard P-178/Panhard Pz Sp Wg 178-P.204(f)

8th Panzer Division (3rd Light Division)
LT-38/PzKpfw 38(t), Jagdpanzer 38(t) Hetzer, Ford/Marmon-Herrington(b) & KVIa/PzKpfw KVIa 753(r)

9th Panzer Division
Flakpanzer 38(t) & T-34/PzKpfw T-34 747(r)

10th Panzer Division
T-34/PzKpfw T-34 747(r) & Valentine Mk III/Infanterie Panzerkampfwagen Mk III 749(e)

12th Panzer Division
LT-38/PzKpfw 38(t)

13th Panzer Division
AB Lince/Pz Sp Wg 202(i)

14th Panzer Division
Renault B1 Bis/PzKpfw B-1/B-2 740 (f)

15th Panzer Division
Panzerjäger 38(t) & Matilda Mk II/Infanterie PzKpfw Mk II 748(e)

16th Panzer Division
Jagdpanzer 38(t) Hetzer

19th Panzer Division
LT-38/PzKpfw 38(t)

20th Panzer Division
LT-38/ PzKpfw 38(t), AMD Panhard P-178/Panhard Pz Sp Wg 178-P.204(f), T-34/PzKpfw T-34 747(r) & SU 85/Jgd Pz SU 85(r) or SU 122/StuG SU 122(r)

21st Panzer Division (5th Light Division)
Matilda Mk II/Infanterie PzKpfw Mk II 748(e), Mk VI/Kreuzer PzKpfw Mk VI 746(e), Marmon-Herrington Mk III, 150mm SFH 13/1 auf GW Lorraine Schlepper(t), S-35/PzKpfw 35-S 739(f) & M4/PzKpfw M4 748(a)

22nd Panzer Division
LT-38/PzKpfw 38(t)

25th Panzer Division
Somua S-35/PzKpfw 35-S 739(f)

26th Panzer Division
DA 105/25/Sturmgeschutz M43 mit 105/25 853(i)

Panzer Division Grossdeutschland
T-34/PzKpfw T-34 747(r)

Panzer Lehr Division
Flakpanzer 38(t)

Panzer Division Kurmark
Jagdpanzer 38(t) Hetzer

Panzergrenadier Divisions

3rd Panzergrenadier Division
150mm PzKpfw 38(t), Bren-gun/Universal Carrier/Gepanzerter Maschinengewehr Trager Bren 731(e) & M4/PzKpfw M4 748(a)

18th Panzergrenadier Division
Jagdpanzer 38(t) Hetzer & T-34/PzKpfw T-34 747(r)

25th Panzergrenadier Division
Jagdpanzer 38(t) Hetzer & M4/PzKpfw M4 748(a)

Assault Gun & Tank Hunter Battalions

197 Assault Gun Battalion
M3/PzKpfw M3 747(a)
561, 731, 741, 743 & 744 Panzerjäger Battalions
Jagdpanzer 38(t) Hetzer

Infantry Divisions

9th Infantry Division
Bren-gun/Universal Carrier/Gepanzerter Maschinengewehr Träger Bren 731(e) &
Renault/AMX UE/Infanterie Schlepper UE 630(f)

14th Infantry Division
Ford/Marmon-Herrington(b)

15th Infantry Division
Panzerjäger 38(t) fur 7.62cm Pak36(r)/Jagdpanzer 38(t) Hetzer (25 infantry divisions
were equipped with the Hetzer by 1945)

18th Infantry Division
Pantserwagen M39 Van Doorne/Pz Sp Wg DAF 201(h)

35th Infantry Division
Ford/Marmon-Herrington(b)

44th Infantry Division
Matilda Mk II/Infanterie PzKpfw Mk II 748(e)

76th Infantry Division
Jagdpanzer 38(t) Hetzer/Panzerjäger 38(t)

82nd Infantry Division
T-70/PzKpfw T-70(r) & T-34/PzKpfw T-34 747(r)

97th Infantry Division
BA 20/PzSp Wg BA 202(r)

98th Infantry Division
T-70/PzKpfw T-70(r)) & T-34/PzKpfw T-34 747(r)

125th Infantry Division
Renault/AMX UE/Infanterie Schlepper UE 630(f)

134th Infantry Division
STZ Komsomolets/Gepanzerter Artillerie Schlepper 630(r)

227th Infantry Division
Landsverk M36/38/Pz Sp Wg L/P 202 (h), Bren-gun/Universal Carrier/
Gepanzerter Maschinengewehr Träger Bren 731(e), 10.5cm leFH16 auf
Geschutzwagen MarkVI(e) & Renault/AMX UE/Infanterie Schlepper UE 630(f)

267th Infantry Division

STZ Komsomolets/Gepanzerter Artillerie Schlepper 630(r)

278th Infantry Division
AB40 & 41/Pz Sp Wg AB40 und 41 201(i)

319th Infantry Division
FT-17/18/PzKpfw FT-17/18 730(f), Renault B1 Bis/PzKpfw B-1/B-2 740(f) &
4.7cm (PaK(t) auf PzKpfw 35R(f) ohne Turm

336th Infantry Division
DA 105/25/Sturmgeschutz M43 mit 105/25 853(i)

352nd Infantry Division
T-34/PzKpfw T-34 747(r)

Airborne Divisions

4th Parachute Division
Humber Mk III

5th Parachute Jäger Division
M4/PzKpfw M4 748(a)

Mountain Divisions

100th Ski Jäger Division
T-34/PzKpfw T-34 747(r)

Security Divisions

444th Security Division
BA 20/PzSp Wg BA 202(r) & BA 10/Pz Sp Wg BAF 203(r)

Waffen-SS Divisions

1st SS Panzer Division Leibstandarte Adolf Hitler
7.5cm Pak40/3 auf PzKpfw 38(t), Panzerjäger 38(t) Marder III, Flakpanzer 38(t) &
AMD Panhard P-178/Panhard Pz Sp Wg 178-P.204(f)

2nd SS Panzer Division Das Reich
Panzerjäger 38(t), *Jagdpanzer 38(t) Hetzer, AMD Panhard P-178/Panhard Pz Sp Wg
178-P.204(f), T-34/PzKpfw T-34 747(r) & BA-64B

3rd SS Panzer Division Totenkopf
AMD Panhard P-178/Panhard Pz Sp Wg 178-P.204(f), T-26B/PzKpfw T-26B 738(r)
& T-34/PzKpfw T-34 747(r)

4th SS Police Division
AB40 & 41/Pz Sp Wg AB40 und 41 201(i)

5th SS Panzer Division Wiking
Panzerjäger 38(t) & T-34/85

7th SS Mountain Division Prinz Eugen
Renault B1 Bis/ PzKpfw B-1/B-2 740 (f), Hotchkiss H-35/H-39/PzKpfw 38-H 735(f) & L3/35/ PzKpfw L3/35 731(i)

8th SS Kavallerie Division Florian Geyer
Jagdpanzer 38(t) Hetzer

10th SS Panzer Division Frundsberg
Jagdpanzer 38(t) Hetzer & M4/PzKpfw M4 748(a)

22nd Freiwilligen Kavallerie Division der SS Maria Theresa.
M15/42/PzKpfw M15/42 738(i)

Allied Armoured and Cavalry Formations

Austria

13th Panzer Division (formerly the 13th Infantry Division part of the German Army included Austrian recruits)

Bulgaria

1st Armoured Brigade
PzKpfw 38(t), Panzer Mk III/IV, StuG III, H-39 & S-35

Finland

1st, 2nd & 3rd Tank Battalions
T-26

1st Independent Tank Platoon
T-26

Armoured Division
(1st & 2nd Tank Brigades, Assault Gun Brigade & Jäger brigade)
T-26, T-34, Panzer Mk IV & StuG III

Hungary

1st & 2nd Cavalry Brigades/1st & 2nd Motorised Brigades
Toldi, Csaba & L.3

1st & 2nd Armoured Divisions
Toldi, Nimrod, PzKpfw 38(t), Panzer Mk III/IV, Turan I/II & Csaba

1st Cavalry Division (1st Hussar Division)
Toldi, Nimrod, PzKpfw 38(t) & Csaba

Assault Battalions
6th & 7th
Zrinyi
10th, 13th, 16th, 20th, 24th & 25th
StuG III

Italy

Babini Armoured Brigade
M11/39 & M13/40

Maletti Group
M11/39 & M13/40

3rd Mobile Division
L.3 & L.6/40

131st Centauro, 132nd Ariete & 133rd Littorio Armoured Divisions
M13/40 & 75/18

Leoncello & San Giusto Groups
M13/40 & M14/41

Romania

1st Tank Division 'Greater Romania'
LT-35, CKD, PzKpfw 38(t) & Panzer Mk IV

1st, 5th, 6th, 7th, 8th & 9th Cavalry Divisions
LT-35, CKD & PzKpfw 38(t)

Slovakia

Mobile Division (11th Tank Company)
LT-35/ PzKpfw 35(t) & LT-38/PzKpfw 38(t)

Security Division
Armoured car platoon (transferred to the Mobile Div)

German Armoured Fighting Vehicle Production 1938-45

Tanks	No.	Manufactured
Panzerkampfwagen I	1,563	1938-42
Panzerkampfwagen II	1,814	1938-42
Panzerkampfwagen III	6,157	1938-43
Panzerkampfwagen IV	8,544	1938-45
Panzerkampfwagen V Panther	5,976	1943-45
Panzerkampfwagen VI Ausf E Tiger I	1,354	1942-44
Panzerkampfwagen VI Ausf B Tiger II	489	1944-45
Total:	**25,897**	**1938-45**

Tank Destroyers		
Pz Jag Ferdinand	90	1943
Jagdpanzer IV	769	1944
Panzer IV/70(V)	930	1944-45
Panzer IV/70(A)	278	1944-45
Jagdpanther	392	1944-45
Jagdtiger	77	1944-45
Total:	**2,536**	**1943-45**

Assault Guns		
Sturmgeschutz III 7.5cm L/24	822	1940-42
Sturmgeschutz III 7.5cm L/43 & L/48	8,587	1942-45
Sturmgeschutz IV	1,108	1943-45
Total:	**10,517**	**1940-45**

Assault Artillery		
Sturminfanteriegeschutze 33B	24	1941-42
10.5cm Sturmhaubitze	1,212	1942-45
Sturmpanzer IV	298	1943-45
Total:	**1,534**	**1941-45**

Self-propelled anti-tank guns

7.5cm Pak40/2(Sf) auf PzKpfw II	476	1942-43
7.5cm PaK40/1(Sf) auf RSO Oak40/2(Sf) auf Pz Kpfw II	60	1943
8.8cm PaK43/1(Sf) auf PzKpfw III/IV	494	1943-45
Total:	**1,030**	**1942-45**

Self-propelled artillery

15cm siG33(Sf) auf Pz Kpfw	12	1941
10.5cm leFH18/2(Sf) auf PzKpfw II	676	1943-44
10.5cm leFH18/1(Sf) auf Pz sf IVb	8	1943
15cm sFH18/1(Sf) auf PzKpfw III/IV	714	1943-45
15cm Pz Wefer 42 auf Maultier	300	1943-44
Total:	**1,710**	**1941-45**

Self-propelled anti-aircraft guns

8.8cm FlaK18 (Sf) auf Zgkw 12t or 18t	25	1938-39
2cm FlaK30 or 38 (Sf) auf Zgkw 1t	610	1943-44
2cm Flakvierling 38 (sf) auf Zgkw 8t3.7cm	319	
Flakvierling 36(Sf) auf Zgkw 5t3.7cm	339	
Flakvierling 36(Sf) auf Zgkw 8t	123	
3.7cm FlaK36 (Sf) auf FlaK PzKpfw IV	240	1944-45
3.7cm FlaK43 (Sf) auf Ostwind I PzKpfw IV	7	1945
Total:	**1,663**	**1938-45**

Ammunition carriers

Mun träger fur Karl (PzKpfw IV)	14	1939-41
Sd Kfz 252	413	1940-41
VK302	28	1941-42
Mun Fahrzeuge Wespe	159	1943-44
Mun Fahrzeuge Hummel	157	1943-44
Mun Kw fu Pz Werfer	289	1943-44
Total:	**1,060**	**1939-44**

Semi-tracked armoured vehicles

Sd Kfz 250	6,628	1939-45
Sd Kfz 251	15,252	1939-45
Total:	**21,880**	**1939-45**

Armoured cars/Reconnaissance vehicles

Kfz13/14 & Sd Kfz 221/222/223/231/233 /234/247/260/263	4,392	1938-45
Total:	**4,392**	**1938-45**

Total:	**72,219**	**1938-45**

Note: The Germans converted numbers of PzKpfw I, II, III and IV to self-propelled guns, artillery and anti-aircraft guns; unless specifically built as self-propelled guns they are counted in the tank production figures. These figures do not include command, flame-thrower, observation, maintenance, bridging and demolition vehicles, which amounted to another 10,290 vehicles.

German Panzer and Panzergrenadier Divisions 1935-45

Panzer Divisions	**(Formed)**
1st Panzer Division	(Weimar 15 October 1935 from 1st Kavallerie Division)
2nd Panzer Division	(Wurzburg 15 October 1935)
3rd Panzer Division	(Wunsdorf, Berlin 15 October 1935)
4th Panzer Division	(Wurzburg 10 November 1938)
5th Panzer Division	(Opplen 24 November 1938)
6th Panzer Division	(Wuppertal 18 October 1939 from 1st Light Division)
7th Panzer Division	(Gera 18 October 1939 from 2nd Light Division)
8th Panzer Division	(Cottbus 16 October 1939 from 3rd Light Division)
9th Panzer Division	(3 January 1940 from 4th Light Division)
10th Panzer Division	(Czechoslovakia April 1939)
11th Panzer Division	(1 August 1940)
12th Panzer Division	(Stettin 5 October 1940 from 2nd Infantry Division)
13th Panzer Division	(Austria 11 October 1940 from 13th Infantry Division)
14th Panzer Division	(15 August 1940 from 4th Infantry Division)
15th Panzer Division	(1 November 1940 from 33rd Infantry Division)
16th Panzer Division	(1 November 1940 from 16th Infantry Division)
17th Panzer Division	(1 November 1940 27th Infantry Division)
18th Panzer Division	(26 October 1940 from 4th & 14th Infantry Divisions)
19th Panzer Division	(1 November 1940 from 19th Infantry Division)
20th Panzer Division	(15 October 1940 from 19th Infantry Division)
21st Panzer Division	(1 August 1941 from 5th Light & 3rd Panzer Divisions)
22nd Panzer Division	(France 25 September 1941)
23rd Panzer Division	(France September 1941)
24th Panzer Division	(Stablack 28 November 1941 from 1st Kavallerie Division)
25th Panzer Division	(Eberswalde 25 February 1942)
26th Panzer Division	(Belgium 14 September 1942 from 23rd Infantry Division)
27th Panzer Division	(France/Russia 1 October 1942 from 22nd Panzer Division)

116th Panzer Division	(France 28 March 1944 from 116th Panzergrenadier Division)
Panzer Lehr Division	(Potsdam November 1943)
Panzer Division Grossdeutschland	(formed as a panzergrenadier division in May 1942)
Führer-Begleit Division	(upgraded from brigade strength January 1945)
Führer Grenadier Division	(upgraded from brigade strength March 1945)

Fallschirm Panzer Division Hermann Goering (*Luftwaffe* unit that came under Army control in 1943)

Reserve Panzer Divisions

155th Reserve Panzer Division	(absorbed by 9th Panzer Division April 1944)
179th Reserve Panzer Division	(absorbed by 116th Panzer Division May 1944)
233rd Reserve Panzer Division	(re-designated 233rd Panzer Division April 1945)
273rd Reserve Panzer Division	(absorbed by 10th Panzergrenadier Division and 11th Panzer Division in March and May 1944 respectively)

Other 'Panzer' Divisions

Various ad hoc panzer formations were scrapped in early 1945 from training and reserve units:

Panzer Division Clausewitz	(elements of Grossdeutschland Panzer Division, Putlos Panzer School & other units)
Panzer Division Courland	(elements of 14th Panzer Division)
Panzer Division Donau	
Panzer Division Feldherrnhalle 2	(elements of 13th Panzer Division & 60th Panzergrenadier Division Feldherrnalle)
Panzer Division Holstein	(elements of 233rd Reserve Panzer Division, used to reform 18th Panzergrenadier Division)
Panzer Division Juterborg	(absorbed by 16th Panzer Division in March 1945)
Panzer Division Kurland	(elements of 14th Panzer Division)
Panzer Division Kurmark	
Panzer Division Munchenberg	(elements of 1st SS Panzer Division)
Panzer Division Nibelungen	(elements of 38th SS Grenadier Division)
Panzer Division Norwegen	(formed August 1943 from elements of 25th Panzer Division, absorbed by parent unit in June 1944)
Panzer Division Schlesien	(absorbed by 18th Panzergrenadier Division in March 1945)
232nd Panzer Division	(formerly Panzer Ausbildungs Division Tatra re-designated 21 February 1945)
Panzer Division Thuringen	
Panzer Division Westfalen	

Panzergrenadier Divisions
Most of these units started life as motorised infantry divisions and were converted in 1943 with the inclusion of an assault gun battalion:

3rd Panzergrenadier Division

10th Panzergrenadier Division

14th Panzergrenadier Division   (re-designated the 14th Infantry Division June 1943)

15th Panzergrenadier Division

16th Panzergrenadier Division   (November 1942, re-designated the 116th Panzer Division March 1944)

18th Panzergrenadier Division

20th Panzergrenadier Division

25th Panzergrenadier Division

29th Panzergrenadier Division

60th Panzergrenadier Division   (re-designated Panzer Division Feldherrnhalle November 1944)

233rd Panzergrenadier Division   (re-designated the 233rd Panzer Division April 1943)

Panzergrenadier Division Brandenburg (September 1944)

Panzergrenadier Division Grossdeutschland (see panzer divisions)

SS Panzer Divisions
These units initially started out as SS Panzergrenadier Divisions but were re-designated Panzer Divisions in October 1943:

1st SS Panzer Division *Leibstandarte Adolf Hitler*

2nd SS Panzer Division *Das Reich*

3rd SS Panzer Division *Totenkopf*

5th SS Panzer Division *Wiking*

9th SS Panzer Division *Hohenstaufen*

10th SS Panzer Division *Frundsberg*

12th SS Panzer Division *Hitlerjugend*

Other SS 'Panzer' Divisions
These SS Panzergrenadier Divisions lacked a second tank battalion so did not qualify for the full title:

4th SS *Polizei* Panzergrenadier Division

7th SS Freiwilligen Gebirgs Division *Prinz Eugen*

11th SS Freiwilligen Panzergrenadier Division *Nordland*

16th SS Panzergrenadier Division *Reichsführer-SS*

17th SS Panzergrenadier Division *Gotz von Berlichingen*

18th SS Freiwilligen Panzergrenadier Division *Horst Wessel*

23rd SS Freiwilligen Panzergrenadier Division *Nederland*

28th SS Panzergrenadier Division *Wallonien*

Appendix IX

Principal Captured Military Vehicle Manufacturers 1935-45

Austria
A. Fross-Bussing KG, Vienna
Graf & Stift Automobilefabriks AG, Vienna-Dobling
Österreichische Automobil-Fabriks-AG, Vienna
Österreichische Saurerwerke, Vienna
Steyr-Daimler-Puch AG, Vienna

Czechoslovakia
Bohmisch-Marische Maschinfabriekn AG, Prague
Ringhoffer-Tatra-Werke AG, Prague
Skoda-Werke, Prague

France
SA Automobiles Peugeot, Sochaux
SA des Automobiles Unic, Puteaux
SA Citroen, Paris
SA Ford, Asnieres
Ets. Laffy, Asnieres
Somua-Werke, Saint-Ouen, Seine
Usines Renault, Billancourt, Seine

Italy
Alfa-Romeo SpA, Milan
Ansaldo-Fossati, Genoa-Sestri
Edoardo Bianchi-Moto Meccanica SpA, Milan
Soc. Ernesto Breda, Milan
SA Giovanni Ceirano, Turin

Fiat SpA, Turin
Fabbrica Automobili Isotta-Fraschini, Milan
Lancia & Co, Fabbrica Automobili-Turin-SpA
OM (Officine Mechaniche) SpA, Milan
Pavesi-Tolotti SA, Milan
Soc. Ligure Piemontese Automobili, Turin

Poland
Polski Fiat, Panstwowy Zaklad Inzynierii (PZinz), Warsaw

References

Chapter One: Guderian's Czech Connection
1. General Heinz Guderian, *Panzer Leader*, (London 1952), p.30.
2. Werner Regenberg, *Captured Tanks in German Service Small Tanks and Armoured Tractors 1939-45*, (Atglen, PA 1998), p.46 & Bart H.. Vanderveen, *The Observer's Fighting Vehicles Directory World War II*, (London 1969), p.305.
3. Guderian, *op. cit.*, p.53.
4. Austria also provided one of Hitler's leading generals. After the *Anschluss* Colonel Lothar Rendulic was enticed out of retirement to become Chief of Staff of the German Army's newly raised 17th Corps. After Poland he was promoted to brigadier general becoming a divisional and then a corps commander on the Eastern Front. He then commanded a Germany Army in the Balkans and Finland and finally Army Group South. See James Lucas, *Hitler's Enforcers, Leaders of the German War Machine 1939-1945*, (London 1996), p.129-145. Another Austrian General SS Obergruppenführer (Lieutenant General) Karl von Pfeffer-Wildrenbruch was charged with the unsuccessful defence of Budapest in 1945.
5. For example 1,200 Steyr 250 4x2 cars were produced for the German Army during 1938-40; 12,500 Steyr 270 1500A/02 4x4 trucks 1941-44; 6,400 Steyr Model 2000A 4x4 trucks 1944; 3,780 Steyr 640 6x4 trucks 1937-41 and 361 Austro-Daimler 6x4 trucks. See Bart Vanderveen, *Historic Military Vehicles Directory*, (London 1989), p.26-33.
6. Len Deighton, *Blitzkrieg From the Rise of Hitler to the fall of Dunkirk*, (London 1979), p.81.
7. H.H.E. Craster (ed), *Speeches on Foreign Policy by Viscount Halifax*, (Oxford 1940), p.234.
8. Marshal of the Soviet Union, G. Zhukov, *Reminiscences and Reflections*, Volume 1, (Moscow 1985), p.209.
9. Winston S. Churchill, *The Second World War*, Volume I, *The Gathering Storm*, (London 1948), p.263. According to Churchill: 'The subjugation of Czechoslovakia robbed the Allies of the Czech Army of twenty-one regular divisions, fifteen or sixteen second-line divisions already mobilised, and also their mountain fortress line which in the days of Munich, had required the deployment of thirty German divisions, or the main strength of the mobile fully- trained German Army.'
10. *Ibid.*, p.271.

11. Halifax, *op. cit.*, p.235.
12. *Ibid.*, p.240.
13. Guderian, *op. cit.*, p.6.
14. Czechoslovakia exported almost 200 LT-34 (export variant) tanks to Afghanistan, Latvia, Peru, Sweden, Switzerland and Yugoslavia.
15. Vanderveen, *Historic Military Vehicles Directory*, p.56-65.
16. Allan Bullock, *Hitler: A Study in Tyranny*, (Harmondsworth 1962), p.479.
17. Richard Overy & Andrew Wheatcroft, *The Road to War*, (London 1989), p.54.
18. Albert Seaton, *The German Army 1939-45*, (London 1982), p.95.
19. The Czech 9mm CZ 38 military pistol became the P 39(t) in German service, but the double-action design and heavy trigger pull compromised accuracy. The Czech 9mm ZK 383 sub-machine gun was a better weapon as were the ZB.vz 30 light and ZB.vz 37 heavy machine guns. See Bruce Quarrie, *Weapons of the Waffen-SS from small arms to tanks*, (London 1988).
20. Major General Sir Edward Spears, *Assignment to Catastrophe*, (London 1956), p.15.
21. *Ibid.*, p.17.
22. Franz Kurowski, *Panzer Aces: German Tank Commanders of WWII*, (New York 2002), p.4-5.
23. *Ibid.*, p.13-14.
24. *Ibid.*, p.14.
25. *Ibid.*, p.15.
26. *Ibid.*, p.456.
27. *Ibid.*, p.459.

Chapter Two: Poland and the Low Countries
1. Guderian, *op. cit.*, p.66.
2. David Miller, *Tanks of the World from World War I to the Present Day*, (London 2004), p.209.
3. Charles Messenger, *The Art of Blitzkrieg*, 2nd Edition, (London 1991), p.129. Soviet sources list Poland having up to 860 light tanks, with two motorised brigades, eleven cavalry brigades and thirty-six infantry divisions. See M.M. Minasyan (Editor-in-Chief), *Great Patriotic War of the Soviet Union 1941-45*, (Moscow 1970), p.22.
4. Cited James Lucas, *Battle Group! German Kampfgruppen Action of World War Two*, (London 1993), p.13-14.
5. Guderian, *op. cit.*, p.72.
6. Messenger, *op. cit.*, p.136.
7. Guderian, *op. cit.*, p.83.
8. Total numbers of indigenous 7TPs manufactured by the Poles varies; Miller cites 169 built between 1934-39 in two variants, one with two turrets each armed with a machinegun and the other with a single Swedish built turret armed with a 37mm. Shortages of the latter meant most were armed with machine guns. B.T. White quotes 170, while Vanderveen states 133 were built between 1936-39 and that only the first sixteen had twin turrets. In addition during the second

half of the 1930s Pzinz had also built 580 TK3 and TKS tankettes armed with machine guns.

9. Regenberg, *op. cit.*, p.5. The Warsaw Light Panzer Company was renamed the Light Panzer Company East in September 1940.

10. Miller, *op. cit.*, p.209.

11. Seaton, *op.cit.*, p.128.

12. The Poles built 4,000 CWS Sokol motorcycles with sidecars during 1933-39; 1,500 Polski Fiat 508/IIIW 4x2 cars 1936-39; over 10,000 Polski Fiat 508/518 4x2 trucks 1935-39 and 12,600 Polski Fiat 621L 4x2 trucks 1935-39. See Vanderveen, op. cit., p. 274-276.

13. Seaton, *op. cit.*, p.166.

14. The Germans response to such sabotage was always brutal, in the case of the railway bombings fifty suspects were hanged. George Bruce, *The Warsaw Uprising*, (London 1972), p.56.

15. Norman Davies, *Rising '44' The Battle for Warsaw*, (London 2003), p.113.

16. SS General von dem Bach-Zelewski, see Nigel Thomas, *Partisan Warfare 1941-45*, (London 1983), p.6.

17. Lieutenant General Reiner Stahel's 12,000 strong German garrison in Warsaw was reinforced by SS Brigadeführer Bratislav Kaminski's Brigade (29th Waffen-SS Grenadier Division), and SS Oberführer Oskar Dirlewanger's anti-partisan brigade (36th SS-Division). These forces were placed under SS General Erich von dem Bach-Zelewski. Their conduct in Warsaw was to horrify even the battle hardened SS. As part of a deliberate plan nearly 40,000 civilians were executed or died in the raging fires.

18. The T15s had been delivered in the mid-1930s so not all of them would have been serviceable in May 1940. See B.T. White, *Tanks and other AFVs of the Blitzkrieg Era 1939-41*, (London 1972), p.96.

19. Werner Regenberg & Horst Scheibert, *Captured French Tanks under the German Flag*, (Atglen, PA 1997), p.30.

20. Lieutenant-General Sir Brian Horrocks, *A Full Life*, (London 1960), p.81.

21. The Belgian Army had several thousand motorcycles with sidecar in service at the time of the German invasion. See Vanderveen, *op. cit.*, p. 34-35.

22. Sixty-eight of these were ordered in 1938/39 for Belgium's cavalry divisions. The armoured body work was constructed by Ragheno of Malines on Dutch assembled Ford chassis with Marmom-Herrington all-wheel dive conversion. *Ibid.*, p.30.

23. British Vickers design licence built in Belgium for the Belgian and Dutch armies in the late 1930s. *Ibid.*, p.38.

24. Peter Chamberlain & Hilary Doyle, *Encyclopedia of German Tanks of World War Two*, (London 2004), p.242.

25. White, *op. cit.*, p.120.

26. Werner Regenberg, *Captured Armoured Cars and other Vehicles in Wehrmacht Service in World War II*, (Atglen, PA 1996), p.9-11.

27. *Ibid.*

28. Such as the Mauser Kar 98K, which was manufactured in 7.65, 7.9 and 7.92mm calibre versions. See Bruce Quarrie, *Hitler's Samurai The Waffen-SS in action*, (London 1985), p.70.
29. William Shirer, *The Rise and Fall of the Third Reich*, (London 1973), p.957.
30. See Carlos Caballero Jurado, *Resistance Warfare 1940-45*, (London 1985)

Chapter Three: Dunkirk and North Africa

1. Horrocks, *op. cit.*, p.85.
2. Roger Parkinson, *Dawn on our Darkness: The Summer of 1940*, (London 1977), p.5.
3. Arthur Bryant, *The Turn of the Tide 1939-1943*, (London 1957), p.154. Figures for abandoned British equipment vary, Parkinson quotes similar numbers for the guns, but also lists 600 tanks, 90,000 rifles, 120,000 vehicles, 8,000 Bren guns, 400 anti-tank rifles and 7,000 tons of ammunition, citing Sir Winston Churchill, *Their Finest Hour*, (London 1949), p.122 & 125 and Basil Collier, *The Defence of the United Kingdom, UK Official history, Military Series*, (London HMSO 1957), p.127. The figure of 120,00 motor vehicles seems high, according to Vanderveen, *The Observer's Fighting Vehicles Directory World War II*, the War Department only had 85,000 motor vehicles in 1939.
4. The quoted number of British tanks lost to the Germans in France also varies. Terry Gander & Peter Chamberlain, *British Tanks of World War 2*, (Cambridge 1976), put the figure at over 700, p.10. Other sources cite over 700 armoured fighting vehicles including 229 tanks (of which 171 were largely useless light tanks) abandoned in France.
5. By 1940 139 Matilda Is had been built and most of them went to France with the 1st Tank Brigade. Following Dunkirk those remaining were only used for training purposes. Matilda IIs equipped a battalion of the 7th Royal Tank regiment in France.
6. Werner Regenberg, *Captured American and British Tanks under the German Flag*, (Atglen, PA 1993), p.26.
7. This figure included 21,500 motorcycles and just under 7,000 trailers. Vanderveen, *op. cit.*, p.120. In 1939 the British Army found itself with a fleet of some 85,000 motor vehicles (26,000 were pressed into service). In fact procurement had been so slow that two private firms supplied MT for manoeuvres. The Army was predominantly equipped with the 15-cwt 4x2, 30-cwt 4x2 and 6x4 and 3-ton 4x2 and 6x4. The term truck, covering vehicles up to 15-cwt, lorry encompassing 3-tonners and over, and light-lorry covering everything in-between defined British MT. The Americans used the term truck for all load carriers.
8. Regenberg, *op. cit.*, p.3.
9. Parkinson, *op. cit.*, p.166.
10. Prime Minister Winston Churchill was furious and wrote to the Secretary of State of War: 'Your minute of 15 July, 1941 [about repair

of tanks at home], states a number of requirements which, if they could all be met, would make life too easy. Everything practicable should be done to meet the various desiderata, but the main contribution must be a genuine effort and good management. I am shocked to see that a month later we still have twenty-five per cent of Infantry tanks out of order... I have no doubt there can be made plenty of explanations for such a failure, but failure it remains none the less.

Pray do not let it be thought that you are satisfied with such a result. If you simply take up the attitude of defending it there will be no hope of improvement.' Winston S. Churchill, *The Second World War*, Volume III, *The Grand Alliance*, (London 1950), p.774-775.

11. In 1933 Fiat-Ansaldo produced the turretless Carro Veloce (Fast Tank) CV.33, but with a crew of two, armed with just machine guns, weighing in at three and a half tons with a top speed of 28mph, it was really only sufficient for police duties. Two years later it was followed by the slightly improved CV.35, with the introduction of standard designations (type, weight, year) they became the L.3/33 and L.3/35 respectively assigned to infantry support and reconnaissance roles. The CTV was initially just equipped with four companies of L.3s and an armoured car company. This grew into a tank group of two CV. L3/35 fast tank battalions supported by armoured cars, such as the Autoblinda 34 and Ansaldo-Lancia IZ.

12. Patrick Turnbull, *The Spanish Civil War 1936-39*, (London 1978), p.16 states the Italians were supported by 250 light tanks. However, according to the Italian Army Staff Historical Branch, Rome, a total of 149 Ansaldos were sent to Spain between 1936-37. By May 1937 there were just eighty-one Ansaldos in Spain, though some had already been lost.

13. Only 100 M11/39s were ever built, it was badly designed, the hull mounted 37mm gun had limited traverse and it was mechanically unreliable. The Italians quickly replaced them with the M13/40. Miller, *op. cit.*, p.171. By the beginning of 1941 the M13/40 started to enter service, mounting a 47mm in a larger turret. The M13 became the standard tank of the Italian armoured divisions, with reinforcement from the M14/41. The first Italian self-propelled gun was based on the M13 and M14 chassis. It also appeared in 1941, designated the Semovente 75/19 mounting an 18-calibre 75mm.

14. Barrie Pitt, *The Crucible of War Western Desert 1941*, (London 1980), p.120.

15. *Ibid.* p.157.

16. Bryan Perret, *Armour in Battle: Wavell's Offensive*, (London 1979), p.66.

17. Pitt, *op. cit.*, p.190 & Perret, *op. cit.*, p.77.

18. Pitt, *op. cit.*, p.190 & Perret, *op. cit.*, p.78.

19. Major General F.W. von Mellenthin, *Panzer Battles*, (London 1955), p.34.

20. In the mid-1930s the Czech firm Skoda built a series of prototype small tanks, resulting in the T-3D. Eight were exported to Yugoslavia

where they were designated the T-32, at least one was used by the Germans on an armoured train in 1941. See Regenberg, *Captured Tanks in German Service Small Tanks and Armoured Tractors 1939-45*, p.40.

21. Anthony Beevor, *Crete: The Battle and the Resistance*, (London 1992) p.54.
22. *Ibid.*, p.345-346. Churchill records the number of British tanks on Crete as nine Infantry tanks (Matildas) and sixteen light tanks, *op. cit.*, p.247.
23. Pitt, *op. cit.*, p.289.
24. *Ibid*, p.334 & Alexander Clifford, *Crusader*, (London 1942), p.60.

Chapter Four: Rommel's Matildas
1. Heinz Werner Schmidt, *With Rommel in the Desert*, (London 1951), p.7.
2. Basil Liddell Hart (ed), *The Rommel Papers*, (London 1953), p.109. There is slight confusion as to when the Armoured Command Vehicles were captured, according to Rommel they were taken near El Agheila at the end March. Lieutenant Schmidt who was on Rommel's staff implies they were taken at Mechili in early April.
3. Schmidt, *op. cit.*, p.27.
4. *Ibid.*
5. Cited Churchill, *op. cit.*, p.192.
6. *Ibid.*, p.220.
7. *Ibid.*, p.223.
8. *Ibid.*, p.775.
9. Pitt, *op. cit.*, p.309 & 333. According to Liddell Hart during Battleaxe the Germans destroyed or captured eighty-seven tanks consisting of fifty-eight 'I' tanks (i.e. Infantry tanks or Matildas) and twenty-nine cruisers, see *Rommel Papers op. cit.*, p.146.
10. Churchill, *op. cit.*, p.307.
11. Major K.J. Macksey, *Afrika Korps*, (London 1972), p.30.
12. Schmidt, *op. cit.*, p.51.
13. Pitt, *op. cit.*, p.333 & Regenberg, *op. cit.*, p.26 & p.33.
14. Although the British Mark VI Crusader cruiser tank was under gunned, Rommel was quite impressed by it, noting: 'Had this tank been equipped with a heavier gun, it could have made things extremely unpleasant for us.' *Rommel Papers, op. cit.*, p.147.
15. Mellenthin, *op. cit.*, p.63.
16. Churchill, *op. cit.*, p.511.
17. Schmidt, *op.cit.*, p.93.
18. *Rommel Papers, op. cit.*, p.170.
19. Pitt, *op. cit.*, p.452.
20. *Rommel Papers, op. cit.*, p.178.
21. Clifford, *op. cit.*, p.175.
22. *Ibid.*, p.117-118.
23. Alan Moorehead, *A Year of Battle*, (London 1943), p.77.
24. Horrocks, *op.cit.*, p.120.
25. Mellenthin, *op. cit.*, p.104-5 & Liddell Hart, *op.cit.*, p.181.

26. *Rommel Papers, op.cit.*, p.182.
27. Moorehead, *op. cit.*, p.202.
28. *Ibid.*, p.208.
29. *Ibid.*, p.209.
30. *Rommel Papers, op. cit.*, p.232.
31. Moorehead, *op. cit.*, p.177.
32. Clifford, *op. cit.*, p.184.
33. *Rommel Papers, op. cit.*, p.250.
34. Regenberg, *Captured American & British Tanks under the German Flag*, p.35.
35. Macksey, *op. cit.*, p.153.
36. Warren Tute, *The North African War*, (London 1976), p. 212-213.

Chapter Five: The French Heist

1. French medium tank holdings in 1939 totalled 2,342, consisting of 311 Char B1 bis, 545 Hotchkiss H-35, 276 Hotchkiss H-39, 950 Renault R-35 and 260 Somua S-35. See Deighton, *op. cit.*, p.196.
2. Spears, *op. cit.*, p.340 & p.352 & Nicholas Harman, *Dunkirk the Necessary Myth*, (London 1990), p.243. The French claimed 300 aircraft were involved in the raid; the British assessed no more than 200.
3. Italy received 109 R-35s and thirty-two S-35s in 1940-41; Bulgaria received forty R-35s in 1941 and nineteen H-39s and six S-35s in 1944; Hungary received fifteen H-39 and two S-35 in 1943.
4. Werner Regenberg & Horst Scheibert, *Captured French Tanks under the German Flag*, (Atglen, PA 1997), p.11.
5. *Ibid.*
6. These vehicles were issued to the *Panzerjäger* (Tank Hunter) and *Panzerartillerie* battalions of the German panzer divisions, whilst other vehicles were used as *Artillerie Schlepper* (artillery tractors) and *Munitionsschlepper* (ammunition carriers). *Panzerartillerie* covered the myriad of equipment not used in an anti-tank role, i.e. *Infanterie Geschutz* (infantry guns), *Sturmhaubitze* (assault howitzers) and *Panzerhaubitze* (armoured howitzers) as opposed to *Sturmgeschütze* (assault guns) and *Panzerjäger*.
7. Richard Overy & Andrew Wheatcroft, *The Road to War*, (London 1989), p.116.
8. Wartime French truck production for the Germans included: 14,500 Peugeot DK5J/D5A 4x2 trucks between September 1939-June 1941; 3,700 Citroen T23 4x2 trucks 1941-44; 15,314 Peugeot DMA/DAT 4x2 trucks 1941-44 and 15,000 Citroen T45/45U 4x2 trucks 1941-44. See Vanderveen, *op. cit.*, p.72-81.
9. Shirer, op. cit., p.943. In total the Germans extracted some $25-40 billion in tribute from the occupied territories.
10. James Lucas, *Hitler's Enforcers, Leaders of the German War Machine 1939-1945*, (London 1996), p.110.
11. Kurowski, *op. cit.*, p.25.
12. Eric Lefevre, *Panzers in Normandy Then and Now*, (London 1983), p.122.

13. 206 Panzer Battalion's strength in May 1944 comprised: fourteen Hotchkiss H-35, H-38 and H-39; four Somua S-35; five Renault B-1 bis some of which were flamethrowers and two Hotchkiss training vehicles; June 1944: sixteen Hotchkiss, two Somua, four Renault B-1 bis and two Renault R-35 tanks. *Ibid.*, p.123.

14. These consisted of two units of eight on Guernsey and Jersey and four on Alderney. See Peter J. Bryans (ed), *German Armour in the Channel Islands 1941-1945*, (Channel Islands Occupation Society, Jersey undated), p.54. According to British Intelligence there may also have been several Czech tanks on Alderney, see Charles Stephenson, *The Channel Islands 1941-45: Hitler's Impregnable Fortress*, (Oxford 2006), p.43.

15. These were organised into the *Schnellabteilung* (Mobile Battalion) 319 and 450, which were stationed on Jersey and Guernsey respectively. At the end of 1942 there were ten French self-propelled guns on Guernsey, nine on Jersey and one on Alderney. Following the Commando raid on Sark two were sent there, where they remained until November 1943. See Stephenson, *op.cit.*, p.40 & Bryans, *op. cit.*, p.54.

16. The First Company was attached to the self-propelled gun Mobile Battalion 319 on Jersey and the Second to the self-propelled gun Mobile Battalion 450 on Guernsey. Bryans, *op.cit.*, p.16.

17. Lefevre, *op. cit.*, p.105.

18. *Ibid.*

Chapter Six: T-34 versus T-34

1. By June 1941 the Soviet Union had a total of five million men under arms, Minasyan, op. cit., p.45. These forces included twenty-nine activated mechanised corps, thirty-one motorised and sixty-one tank divisions, see John Milsom & Steven Zaloga, *Russian Tanks of World War 2*, (Cambridge 1977), p.20.

2. Zhukov, *op. cit.*, p.230.

3. *Ibid.*, p.235.

4. Strobe Talbot (ed), *Khrushchev Remembers*, (London 1971), p.159.

5. Harrison E. Salisbury, *The 900 Days the Siege of Leningrad*, (London 2000), p.100-101.

6. Carlos Caballero Jurado, *The Condor Legion*, (Oxford 2006), p.43.

7. B.H. Liddell Hart, *The Other Side of the Hill*, (London 1983), p.122.

8. *Ibid.*, p.123.

9. *Ibid.*

10. Edgar O'Balance, *The Red Army*, (London 1964), p.159-161.

11. Minasyan, *op. cit.*, p.87.

12. Talbot, *op. cit.*, p.158-159.

13. Between July and November 1941 up to 1,523 factories, including 1,360 large defence plants, were moved to and restarted in the Urals, Siberia, the Volga area and Kazakhstan. In little over five months nearly 1.5 million carloads of freight was moved by rail east. Once in place the tank factories stepped up serial production starting an output war the Germans could not win. Minasyan, *op. cit.*, p.77.

14. Zhukov, *op. cit.*, p.318.
15. Harrison, p.144-145. Marshal Zhukov took an intense dislike to this book and accused it of being anti-Soviet, see Zhukov, p.452-453.
16. Werner Regenberg & Horst Scheibert, *Captured Tanks under the German Flag Russian Battle Tanks*, (West Chester, PA 1990), p.3.
17. *Ibid.*, p.5.
18. Lucas, *op. cit.*, p.81.
19. Will Fey, *Armour Battles of the Waffen-SS 1943-45*, (Mechanicsburg 2003), p.345 & Gordon Williamson, *The SS: Hitler's Instrument of Terror*, (London 1994), p.219
20. Peter Chamberlain and Hilary Doyle, *Encyclopedia of German Tanks of World War Two*, (London 2004), p.238.
20. *Ibid.* The German High Command listed fifty T-34 with its forces on the Eastern Front in May 1943. Also see Fey, *op.cit.*, p.345.
21. Nik Cornish, *Images of Kursk, History's Greatest Tank Battle July 1943*, (Staplehurst 2002), p.186-187.
22. *Ibid.*, p.191 & Fey, *op. cit.*, p.346.
23. Kurowski, *op. cit.*, p.53-54 & Cornish, *op. cit.*, p.177.
24. In particular the Pripet Marshes provided a secure base from which Soviet partisans could sally out to strike German rear area installations. This produced results out of proportion to the numbers of men involved and tied down large numbers of German security forces. The Germans conducted a considerable number of anti-partisan operations which escalated as the war went on: 1942 Greif (Griffon), Grunspecht (Green Woodpecker): 1943 Eisbar (Polar bear), Erntefest (Harvest Home), Freischutz (Marksman), Gizo, Gunther, Hasenjagd (Hare Chase), Hermann, Klette (Burdock), Kormoran (Cormorant), Kottbus, Maigewitter (May Storm), Nachbarhilfe (Neighbourly Help), Schneehase (alpine Hare): 1944 Frulingsfest (spring Feast). See Christopher Chant, *The Encyclopedia of Codenames of World War II*, (London 1986) for further detail on individual operations.
25. Nigel Thomas & Peter Abbott, *Partisan Warfare 1941-45*, (London 1983), p.9-13.
26. O'Balance, *op. cit.*, p.171-172.
27. Paul Adair, *Hitler's Greatest Defeat The Collapse of Army Group Centre June 1944*, (London 1994), p.138.

Chapter Seven: Operation Axis
1. Walter Warlimont, *Inside Hitler's Headquarters 1939-1945*, (New York 1964), p.335.
2. Dwight D. Eisenhower, *Crusade in Europe*, (London 1948), p.180.
3. Major-General Sir Francis De Guingand, *Operation Victory*, (London 1947), p.277.
4. Eric Linklater, *The Campaign in Italy*, (London 1951), p.23.
5. The Carro d'Assalto Fiat 3000 went into production in the late 1920s and although lighter and faster than its French predecessor was obsolete by 1943. Miller, *op. cit.*, p.160.

6. Carlo D'Este, *Bitter Victory The Battle for Sicily July–August 1943*, (London 1988), p.284–285.
7. *Ibid.*, p.296.
8. S.W.C. Pack, *Operation Husky the Allied Invasion of Sicily*, (New York 1977), p.80–81.
9. De Guingand, *op. cit.*, p.294.
10. Shirer, *op. cit.*, p.998–999.
11. D'Este, *op. cit.*, p.514–515 & Pack, *op. cit.*, , p.161.
12. Winston S. Churchill, *The Second World War*: Volume V *Closing the Ring*, (London 1952), p.632.
13. *Ibid.*, p.104.
14. *Rommel Papers, op. cit.*, p.445.
15. Chamberlain and Doyle, *op. cit.*, p.228–233.
16. *Ibid.*, p.231 & 228.
17. Churchill, *op. cit.*, p.166.
18. Jurado, *Resistance Warfare 1940-45*, p.33–35 & Chamberlain & Doyle, *op. cit.*, p.228.
19. John Ellis, *Cassino The Hollow Victory: The Battle for Rome January–June 1944*, (London 1984), p.466.
20. These consisted of sixty-eight M13/40, M14/41 and M15/24 tanks and ninety-three Semovente assault guns. Chamberlain & Doyle, *op. cit.*, p.229 & 231.

Chapter Eight: Recycling Uncle Sam

1. Charles B. MacDonald, *The Battle of the Bulge*, (London 1984), p.69.
2. The initial shipment of eighty-four Stuart light tanks arrived in North Africa in July 1941. The 4th Armoured Brigade first used them against the Germans at Gabr Saleh on 18 November 1941 during the opening of Operation Crusader. George Forty, *United States Tanks of World War Two*, (Poole 1983), p.44.
3. *Rommel Papers, op. cit.*, p.196.
4. *Ibid.* p.207.
5. 318 Shermans had arrived in Egypt by 11 September 1942 ready for the British counter-stroke at El Alamein. Forty, *op.cit.* p.101.
6. *Rommel Papers, op. cit.*, p.309.
7. Forty, *op.cit.*, p.90 & 94.
8. Alan Moorehead, *The End in Africa*, (London 1943), p.129.
9. Schmidt, *op. cit.*, p.160.
10. Warren Tute, *The North African War*, (London 1976), p. 208.
11. *Rommel Papers, op. cit.*, p.398 & 404
12. Lucas, *Battle Group! op. cit.*, p.133.
13. Eisenhower, *op. cit.*, p.164.
14. *Ibid.*
15. This consisted of 21st Panzer with four Sherman tanks, 25th Panzergrenadier four tanks, 10th SS Panzer ten tanks, Panzer Brigade 150 ten tanks, 5th Parachute Jager Division six tanks and Captured Tank Company 281 five tanks. Regenberg, *Captured American & British Tanks ...*, p.13.
16. Paul Carell, *Invasion They're Coming!* (London 1963), p.195.

17. Jean-Paul Pallud, *Ardennes 1944: Peiper and Skorzeny*, (London 1987), p.4.
18. *Ibid.*
19. *Ibid.*, p.5. Skorzeny ended up with six British armoured cars and a dozen American half-tracks according to Charles Whiting, *Ardennes The Secret War*, (London 1984), p.67.
20. MacDonald, *op. cit.*, p.87.
21. Pallud, *op. cit.*, p.5 & p.8.
22. Cited Macdonald, *op. cit.*, p.87-88.
23. Charles Whiting, *Massacre at Malmedy*, (London 1971), p.34. According to Pallud, *op. cit.*, p.22, the column was led by two Panther tanks.
24. Pallud, *op. cit.*, p.23.
25. Lieutenant-General Sir Brian Horrocks, with E. Belfield & Major-General H. Essame, *Corps Commander*, (London 1977), p.77.

Chapter Nine: Unreliable Allies
1. Hungary acceded to the Tripartite Pact on 20 November 1940 having been promised annexations in Yugoslavia and the Soviet Union for agreeing to take part in the war against the USSR. Romania followed suit on 23 November, as the Romanians wanted Soviet Moldavia and the southern part of Ukraine. Bulgaria acceded to the pact on 1 March 1941.
2. Peter Abbott & Nigel Thomas, *Germany's Eastern Front Allies 1941-45*, (London 1982), p.28-29.
3. Vanderveen, *Historic Military Vehicles Directory*, p.210-211.
4. Friction was such with Romania that the Hungarians were forced to keep their best formation, the 9th Corps, in the strategic Carpathian region. In the wake of the First World War Hungary was greatly reduced in size and sought restitution of her lost territories. Southern Slovakia was regained as part of the 1938 Munich settlement, the following year the Hungarian Army occupied Czechoslovakian Ruthenia and in August 1940 Hitler coerced Romania to hand back northern Transylvania. Hungarian forces also occupied disputed Yugoslavian districts in the wake of the German invasion in April 1941.
5. Abbott & Thomas, *op. cit.*, p.14.
6. In 1940 Romania lost Bessarabia and Bukovina to the Soviet Union, followed by half of Transylvania to Hungary and the southern Dobrudja to Bulgaria. That same year the Romanian king abdicated in favour of his son, but pro-Nazi General Antonescu became the power behind the throne.
7. Directive No.21 'Case Barbarossa' 18 December 1940. H.R. Trevor-Roper (ed), *Hitler War Directives 1939-45*, (London 1964), p.95.
8. Abbott & Thomas, *op. cit.*, p.26-28.
9. *Ibid.*, p.15.
10. *Ibid.*, p.22.
11. Liddell Hart, *The Other Side of the Hill*, p.308-309.
12. Mellenthin, *op.cit.*, p.199.

13. Zhukov, *op. cit.*, Volume 2, p.111 .
14. Mellenthin, *op. cit.*, p.199.
15. Zhukov, *op. cit.*, p. 124-126.
16. *Ibid.*, p.122.
17. Cornish, *op. cit.*, p.13.
18. Mellenthin, *op. cit.*, p.250.
19. Abbott & Thomas, *op. cit.*, p.4.
20. According to Soviet sources German losses in the Volga-Don-Stalingrad area amounted to some 1.5 million men, 3,500 tanks, 12,000 guns and 3,000 aircraft.
21. Abbott & Thomas, *op. cit.*, p.16-19.
22. In total Romania lost 350,000 men fighting the Russians and another 170,000 fighting the Germans and the Hungarians.
23. H.P. Willmott, *June 1944*, (Poole 1984), p.120.
24. The 1st Armoured Car and 6th, 8th, 9th and 10th Assault Artillery Battalions formed the grandly titled Billnitzer Assault Artillery Group. Abbott & Thomas, *op. cit.*, p.19.
25. John Erikson, *The Road to Berlin*, (London 1983), p.510. Erikson provides one of the fuller accounts of the Hungarian role in Operation Spring Awakening.
26. Charles Messenger, *Hitler's Gladiator, The Life and Times of Oberstgruppenfuhrer and Panzergeneral-Oberst der Waffen-SS Sepp Dietrich*, (London 1988), p. 166.
27. Hugh Thomas, *The Spanish Civil War,* (London 1961), p.636.
28. *Ibid.*, p.643. These figures came from the German Military Attache, Ankara. How accurate his assessment was is unclear, especially as it does not deal with shipments after March 1938.
29. Lucas, *Hitler's Enforcers*, p.89.
30. Better known as Gruppe Wolm, this unit, some 200 strong, collected signals intelligence from the Republican Army. Hertzer and Colonel von Thoma who commanded Panzergruppe Drohne were the only members of the German Army to receive Spain's second most important military decoration the Individual Military Medal. See Jurado, *The Condor Legion*, p.47-48.
31. *Ibid.*, p.43.
32. According to figures provided by the Italian Army Historical Staff, Rome, October 2004.
33. Regenberg, *Captured Armoured Cars and other Vehicles in Wehrmacht Service in World War II*, p.14.
34. Churchill, *The Grand Alliance*, p.295.
35. *Ibid.*, p.291.
36. *Ibid.*, p.296.
37. Eisenhower, *op. cit.*, p.90.
38. William B. Breuer, *Operation Torch: The Allied Gamble to Invade North Africa,* (New York 1985), p.42. Half the tank force may have been armoured cars.
39. *Ibid.*, p.219.
40. *Ibid.*, p.216.

41. *Ibid.*, p.254.
42. From the forty Panhard armoured cars that had remained with Vichy French forces in the Free Zone, the Germans captured thirty-four that were still serviceable. Regenburg, *op. cit.*, p.14.
43. Carlos Caballero Jurado, *Resistance Warfare 1940-45*, (London 1985), p.22.

Chapter Ten: Losing the Tank Production War

1. Seaton, *op. cit.*, p.128.
2. *Ibid.*, p.129.
3. See Max Hastings, *Bomber Command*, (London 1979), p. 147. Martin W. Bowman & Theo Boiten, *Raiders of the Reich Air Battle Western Europe: 1942-45*, (Shrewsbury 1996), p.13 & Anthony Verrier, *The Bomber Offensive*, (London 1974), p.141.
4. Marshal of the RAF Sir Arthur Harris, *Bomber Offensive*, (London 1947), p.104-105.
5. Hastings, *op. cit.*, p.147.
6. Bowman & Boiten, *op. cit.*, p.62.
7. The bomber force of 327 lost thirty-six aircraft and another fifty-seven were damaged. Cajus Bekker, *The Luftwaffe War Diaries*, (London 1969), p. 394.
8. Harris, *op. cit.*, p.170.
9. R.V. Jones, *Most Secret War British Scientific Intelligence 1949-45*, (London 1978), p.210.
10. Linklater, *op. cit.*, p.215.
11. *Ibid.*, p.215.
12. *Ibid.*, p.420.
13. John Sweetman, *Schweinfurt Disaster in the Skies*, (New York 1971), p.68.
14. 11,000 medium tanks and assault guns, 1,600 tank destroyers and 5,300 heavy tanks. See Seaton, *op. cit.*, p.239.
15. *Rommel Papers*, p.453.
16. Guderian, *op. cit.*, p.290,
17. *Ibid.*, p.298.
18. *Ibid.*, p.314.
19. United States Strategic Bombing Survey, 'Economic Report,' Appendix Table 104 and from the files of the Inspectorate of Panzer Troops OKH, cited Chester Wilmot, *The Struggle for Europe*, (London 1952), p.556.
20. *Ibid.*
21. *Ibid.*, p.314.
22. German load carriers were reduced to four categories; 1½ ton (1,524kg), 3-ton (3,048kg), 4½ ton (4,572kg) and 6½ ton (6,604kg). Within each class there was a Standard Type (S Type) with 4x2 or 6x4 drive and cross-country versions with all-wheel drive dubbed A Type.
23. Willis Thornton, *The Liberation of Paris*, (London 1963), p.59.
24. Gerald Reitlinger, *The SS Albi of a Nation 1922-1945*, (London 1981), p.392.

25. Shirer, *op. cit.*, p.948.
26. *Ibid.*, p. 946.
27. *Ibid.*, p.951-952.
28. Of the 179 B-24 Liberator bombers sent to Ploesti, eleven aborted and two crashed, leaving 166 to press home the attack. Of these fifty-three were lost and most of the others were damaged; 440 aircrew were killed or missing and about 200 captured. Five Medals of Honour were awarded for this raid. See Robert Jackson, *Bomber! Famous Bomber Missions of World War II*, (London 1980), p.135, and Eisenhower, *op. cit.*, p.177-178.
29. USSBS, Economic Report, p.75 cited Wilmot, *op. cit.*, p.440.
30. Brux ceased production entirely and Leuna had 60 per cent of its output affected. On 28 May 1944 Politz was bombed so heavily that synthetic oil production ceased for two months starving the *Luftwaffe* of vital aviation fuel. Bekker, *op.cit.*, p.451.
31. Mark Arnold-Foster, *The World at War*, (London 1974), p.273.
32. Bullock, *op.cit.*, p.758.
33. Arnold Foster, *op cit.*, p.273.
34. *Ibid.*
35. Cited Bekker, *op. cit.*, p.452.

Chapter Eleven: Impact of Hitler's Panzer Heist

1. See Chamberlain and Doyle, *op cit.*, p218 and Lefevre, *op. cit.*, p.57.
2. Regenberg, *Captured Tanks in German Service Small Tanks and Armoured Tractors 1939-45*, p.29.
3. Carell, *op. cit.*, , p.28 & p.112.
4. *Ibid.*, p.28-29.
5. Guderian, *op. cit.*, p.139.
6. *Ibid.*, p.143.
7. Schmidt, *op.cit.*, p.136.
8. This was the leFH 43 designed as an improvement of the German leFH 18 and fired a heavier round at a greater range. See Bruce Quarrie, *Weapons of the Waffen-SS from small arms to tanks*, (London 1988), p.72.
9. Guderian, *op. cit.*, p.279.
10. Cited, Liddell Hart, *The Other Side of the Hill*, p.130.
11. John Milsom, *Panzerkampfwagen 38(t) & 35(t)*, (Windsor 1970), p.8.

Epilogue

1. Bryans, *op. cit.*, p.57-60.
2. Cited Minasyan, *op. cit.*, p.367-366.
3. By 1943 the title Russian Liberation Army (*Russkaia Osvoditelnaina Armiia* - ROA) covered all the Eastern volunteers. It was never really an army and was opposed by the non-Russians who had no desire to support Russian hegemony. Andrei A. Vlasov, a Soviet General captured in 1942, hoped to raise a large national force to fight with the Germans. On 14 November 1944 Vlasov inaugurated the Committee for the Liberation of the Peoples of Russia (*Komitat Osvobozhniia Narodov Rosso* - KONR) in Prague. KONR dreamed of

a Russian Army of twenty-five divisions encompassing the 650,000 Russian troops in German service, but just two were actually formed. Only the 600th Panzergrenadier Division was brought up to strength, while the 605th Panzergrenadier Division ended up containing the remains of the hated Kaminski Brigade. See Reitlinger, *op. cit.*, p.390-391 & Carlos Caballero Jurado, *Foreign Volunteers of the Wehrmacht 1941-45*, p.27-29.

4. General Zverev commanding the 605th Division was captured by the Soviets, though some of his men reached the Americans. Radio Moscow announced on 12 August 1946 the execution of Vlasov, Bunichenko and ten others.

5. Spears, *op. cit.*, p.111.

6. Charles Cruikshank, *The German Occupation of the Channel Islands*, (Guernsey 1975), p.306.

7. Bryans, *op. cit.*, p.62.

8. Cornelius Ryan, *The Last Battle*, (London 1966), p.374.

9. Czechoslovakia produced the T-34/85 MBT and SU-100 self-propelled gun largely for export to the Middle East. In the mid-1950s Egypt arranged a major arms deal with Czechoslovakia, sponsored by the USSR, for 530 armoured fighting vehicles (230 tanks mostly T-34/85s but also some IS-3s, 200 BTR-152 APCs and 100 SU-100 self-propelled guns). These were followed by 120 new T-54s. Some of the armour saw action in the 1956 Suez Crises against the Israeli, British and French armies. The T-55 was then licence built from the mid-1960s for domestic and export purposes, followed by the T-72 in the late 1970s. Czechoslovakia also exported upwards of 3,000 of its OT-64 APC, Iraq being the biggest customer.

Bibliography

Contemporary Sources and Memoirs

Bryant, A., *The Turn of the Tide 1939-1943*, based on the War Dairies of Field Marshal Viscount Alanbrooke, (London 1957)
— *Triumph in the West 1943-46*, based on the War Dairies of Field Marshal Viscount Alanbrooke, (London 1959)
Clifford, A., *Crusader*, (London 1942)
Churchill, W.S., *The Second World War*, Volume I, *The Gathering Storm*, (London 1948)
— *The Second World War*, Volume III, *The Grand Alliance*, (London 1950)
— *The Second World War*, Volume V, *Closing the Ring*, (London 1952)
Craster, H.H.E. (ed), *Speeches on Foreign Policy by Viscount Halifax*, (Oxford 1940)
De Guingand, Major General Sir Francis, *Operation Victory*, (London 1947),
Eisenhower, D., *Crusade in Europe*, (London 1948)
Harris, Marshal of the RAF Sir Arthur, *Bomber Offensive*, (London 1947)
Guderian, General Heinz, *Panzer Leader*, (London 1952)
Horrocks, Lieutenant General Sir Brian, *A Full Life*, (London 1960)
Horrocks, Lieutenant General Sir Brian, with E. Belfield & Major-General H. Essame, *Corps Commander*, (London 1977)
Jones, R.V., *Most Secret War British Scientific Intelligence 1939-45*, (London 1978)
Liddell Hart, B.H. (ed), *The Rommel Papers*, (London 1953)
Liddell Hart B.H., *The Other Side of the Hill*, (London 1951)
Mellenthin, Major General F.W. von, *Panzer Battles*, (London 1955)
Montgomery, Field Marshal Bernard Law, *The Memoirs of Field-Marshal Montgomery*, (London 1958)
Moorehead, A., *Mediterranean Front*, (London 1941)
— *A Year of Battle*, (London 1943)
— *The End in Africa*, (London 1943)
Schmidt, H.W., *With Rommel in the Desert*, (London 1951)
Shirer, W., *The Rise and Fall of the Third Reich*, (London 1960)
Spears, Major General Sir Edward, *Assignment to Catastrophe*, (London 1956)
Talbot, S. (ed), *Khrushchev Remembers*, (London 1971)
Trevor-Roper, H.R. (ed), *Hitler War Directives 1939-45*, (London 1964)
Warlimont, W., *Inside Hitler's Headquarters 1939-1945*, (New York 1964)
Wilmot, C., *The Struggle for Europe*, (London 1952),
Zhukov, Marshal of the Soviet Union G., *Reminiscences and Reflections*, Volume 1 & 2, (Moscow 1985)

Other Published Sources

Abbott, P., & N. Thomas, *Germany's Eastern Front Allies 1941-45*, (London 1982)

Adair, P., *Hitler's Greatest Defeat*, (London 1994)

Arnold-Foster, M., *The World at War*, (London 1974)

Beevor, A., *Stalingrad*, (London 1998)

— *Crete: The Battle and the Resistance*, (London 1992)

Bekker, C., *The Luftwaffe War Diaries*, (London 1969)

Bowman, W,. & T. Boiten, *Raiders of the Reich Air Battle Western Europe: 1942-45*, (Shrewsbury 1996)

Braithwaite, R., *Moscow 1941*, (London 2006)

Brendon, P., *The Dark Valley A Panorama of the 1930s*, (London 2000)

Breuer, W.B., *Operation Torch: The Allied Gamble to Invade North Africa*, (New York 1985)

Bruce, G., *The Warsaw Uprising*, (London 1972)

Bryans, P.J. (ed), *German Armour in the Channel Islands 1941-1945*, (Channel Islands Occupation Society, Jersey undated)

Bullock, A., *Hitler: A Study in Tyranny*, (London 1952)

Carell, P., *Invasion They're Coming!* (London 1963)

Carver, M., *Tobruk*, (London 1964)

Chamberlain, P., & H. Doyle, *Encyclopedia of German Tanks of World War Two*, (London 2004)

P. Chamberlain, P. & C. Ellis, *British and American Tanks of World War Two*, (London 2004)

Chamberlain, P., C. Ellis & J. Batchelor, *German Fighting Vehicles 1939-1945*, (London 1975)

Church, J., *Military Vehicles of World War 2*, (Poole 1982)

Clayton,A.,*Three Marshals of France: Leadership After Trauma*, (London 1992)

Cornish, N., *Images of Kursk, History's Greatest Tank Battle July 1943*, (Staplehurst 2002)

Craig, W., *Enemy at the Gates, The Battle for Stalingrad*, (London 1973)

Crookenden, N., *Battle of the Bulge 1944*, (London 1980)

Cross, R., *The Battle of the Bulge 1944 Hitler's Last Hope*, (Staplehurst 2002)

Davies, N., *Rising '44' The Battle for Warsaw*, (London 2003)

Deighton, L., *Blitzkrieg From the Rise of Hitler to the Fall of Dunkirk*, (London 1979)

D'Este, C., *Bitter Victory The Battle for Sicily July-August 1943*, (London 1988)

Ellis, J., *Cassino The Hollow Victory: The Battle for Rome January-June 1944*, (London 1984)

Engle, E. & L. Paananen, *The Winter War, The Russo-Finnish Conflict 1939-40*, (London 1973)

Erikson, J., *The Road to Berlin*, (London 1983)

Fey, W., *Armour Battles of the Waffen-SS 1943-45*, (Mechanicsburg 2003)

Forty, G., *Tank Action from the Great War to the Gulf*, (Stroud 1995)

— *United States Tanks of World War Two*, (Poole 1983)

— *Fifth Army at War*, (London 1980)

Gander, T., & P. Chamberlain, *American Tanks of World War 2*, (Cambridge 1977)

— *British Tanks of World War 2*, (Cambridge 1976)

Harman, N., *Dunkirk The Necessary Myth*, (London 1990)

Harrison, H.E., *The 900 Day Siege of Leningrad*, (London 2000)
Hastings, M., *Bomber Command*, (London 1979)
Ritgen, Oberst a.D. Helmut, *The 6th Panzer Division 1937-45*, (Oxford 1982)
Jackson, R., *Bomber! Famous Bomber Missions of World War II*, (London 1980)
— *Dunkirk*, (London 1976)
Caballero Jurado, C., *The Condor Legion*, (Oxford 2006)
— *Resistance Warfare 1940-45*, (London 1985)
— *Foreign Volunteers of the Wehrmacht 1941-45*, (London 1983)
Kerr, W., *The Secret of Stalingrad*, (London 1979)
Kershaw, A. & I. Close (ed), *The Desert War*, (London 1975)
Kershaw, A. (ed), *The Tank Story*, (London 1973)
Kurowski, F., *Panzer Aces: German Tank Commanders of WWII*, (New York 2002)
— *Panzer Aces II: Battle Stories of German Tank Commanders of WWII*, (New York 2002)
Lefevre, E., *Panzers in Normandy Then and Now*, (London 1983)
Liddell Hart, B.H., *History of the Second World War*, (London 1970)
Linklater, E., *The Campaign in Italy*, (London 1951)
Lucas, J., *Hitler's Commanders, German Bravery in the Field 1939-1945*, (London 2000)
— *Hitler's Enforcers, Leaders of the German War Machine 1939-1945*, (London 1996)
— *Battle Group! German Kampfgruppen Action of World War Two*, (London 1993)
— *Kommando German Special Forces of World War Two*, (London 1985)
MacDonald, C.B., *The Battle of the Bulge*, (London 1984)
Macksey, K., *Rommel Battles and Campaigns*, (London 1979)
— *Beda Fomm the Classic Victory* (London 1972)
— *Afrika Korps*, (London 1972)
Messenger, C., *The Art of Blitzkrieg, 2nd Edition*, (London 1991)
— *Hitler's Gladiator*, (London 1988)
Miller, D., *Tanks of the World from World War I to the Present Day*, (London 2004)
Milsom, J., *Panzerkampfwagen 38(t) & 35(t)*, (Windsor 1970)
Milsom, J., & S. Zaloga, *Russian Tanks of World War 2*, (Cambridge 1977)
Minasyan, M.M. (Editor-in-Chief), *Great Patriotic War of the Soviet Union 1941-45*, (Moscow 1970)
Morris, E., *Tanks* (London 1975)
O'Balance, E., *The Red Army*, (London 1964)
Overy, R., & A. Wheatcroft, *The Road to War*, (London 1989)
Pack, S.W.C., *Operation Husky the Allied Invasion of Sicily*, (New York 1977)
Pallud, J.P., *Ardennes 1944: Peiper and Skorzeny*, (London 1987)
Parkinson, R., *Dawn on Our Darkness: The Summer of 1940*, (London 1977)
Perret, B., *Armour in Battle: Wavell's Offensive*, (London 1979)
Pitt, B., *The Crucible of War Western Desert 1941*, (London 1980)
Quarrie, B., *Weapons of the Waffen-SS from small arms to tanks*, (London 1988)
— *Hitler's Teutonic Knights SS Panzers in Action*, (London 1986)
— *Hitler's Samurai The Waffen-SS in Action*, (London 1985)
Regenberg, W., *Captured Tanks in German Service Small Tanks and Armoured Tractors 1939-45*, (Atglen, PA 1998)
— *Captured Armoured Cars and other Vehicles in Wehrmacht Service in World War II*, (Atglen, PA 1996)
— *Captured American & British Tanks under the German Flag*, (Atglen, PA 1993)
Regenberg, W., & H. Scheibert, *Captured French Tanks under the German Flag*, (Atglen,

PA 1997)

— *Captured Tanks under the German Flag Russian Battle Tanks*, (West Chester, PA 1990)

Reitlinger, G., *The SS Albi of A Nation 1922-1945*, (London 1956)

Ripley, T., *Steel Storm: Waffen-SS Panzer Battles on the Eastern Front 1943-45*, (Stroud 200)

Ryan, C., *The Last Battle*, (London 1966)

Salisbury, H.E., *The 900 Days the Siege of Leningrad*, (London 2000)

Scurr, J., *Germany's Spanish Volunteers 1941-45*, (London 1980)

— *The Spanish Foreign Legion*, (London 1985)

Seaton, A., *The German Army 1939-45*, (London 1982)

— *The Fall of Fortress Europe 1943-45*, (London 1981)

Stephenson, C., *The Channel Islands 1941-45: Hitler's Impregnable Fortress*, (Oxford 2006)

Strawson, S., *The Battle For North Africa*, (London 1969)

Sweetman, J., *Schweinfurt Disaster in the Skies*, (New York 1971)

Thomas, H., *The Spanish Civil War*, (London 1961)

Thomas, N., *Partisan Warfare 1941-45*, (London 1983)

Thornton, W., *The Liberation of Paris*, (London 1963)

Turnbull, P., *The Spanish Civil War 1936-39*, (London 1978),

Tute, W., *The North African War*, (London 1976)

Tuzin, P., & C. Gurtner, *French Armoured Fighting Vehicles Chars d'Assault Battle Tanks*, (Hemel Hempstead undated)

Vanderveen, B., *Historic Military Vehicles Directory*, (London 1989)

— *The Observer's Fighting Vehicles Directory World War II*, (London 1969)

Verrier, A., *The Bomber Offensive*, (London 1974)

Watkins, H.B.C., & D. Crow, *Panzer Divisions of World War 2*, (Windsor undated)

Wernick, R., *World War II Blitzkrieg*, (New York 1976)

White, B.T., *Tanks and other AFVs of the Blitzkrieg Era 1939-41*, (London 1972)

— *Tanks and other AFVs 1942-45*, (Poole 1975)

Whiting, C., *Ardennes The Secret War*, (London 1984)

— *Massacre at Malmedy*, (London 1971)

Williamson, G., *Waffen-SS Handbook 1933-1945*, (Stroud 2003)

— *The SS: Hitler's Instrument of Terror*, (London 1994)

Willmott, H.P., *June 1944*, (Poole 1984)

Windrow, M., *The Panzer Divisions* (Revised), (London 1982)

— *The Panzer Divisions*, (London 1973)

— *Waffen SS*, (London 1971)

Websites

www.achtungpanzer.com

www.axishistory.com

www.feldgrau.com

www.wwiivehicles.com

Index

For readers' convenience, all armoured and motor vehicles, as well as production figures and losses, are grouped under the main heading for tanks of the nation concerned.